Praise for *Who Killed Health Care?*

*A wonderful Orwellian romp through issues which
carry a deadly irony. The killers of health care are, of course,
the third parties, each of which has an itchy palm and
a commitment to profit or power which exceeds the
commitment to service, with each engaging the others within
a politically shaped box. Rarely has the case for the public
been made with so much force, foresight, and wit,
and a better way forward shown so clearly.*

—JAMES F. FRIES, MD
PROFESSOR OF MEDICINE
STANFORD UNIVERSITY SCHOOL OF MEDICINE

*You can practically hear the war chants as Professor Herzlinger
sets out her view of what's wrong with the health care system
and how to fix it. You'd best read it so you can decide which side
you will be on when the battle is joined.*

—PAUL LEVY
CEO, BETH ISRAEL HOSPITAL,
BOSTON, MA

*Regina Herzlinger, the nation's leading expert on consumer-driven
health care, has given us a brilliant analysis of the flaws in
our health care system and what it will take to get it back on track.
Her latest book is a must read.*

—BILL GEORGE
PROFESSOR OF MANAGEMENT PRACTICE,
HARVARD BUSINESS SCHOOL;
FORMER CEO, MEDTRONIC,
AND AUTHOR OF *AUTHENTIC LEADERSHIP*

Regi Herzlinger has brilliantly articulated a better way—embracing the principles of competition and innovation that cause every other sector of our economy to thrive. Discharging American health care from the ICU can only happen by putting individual Americans—not politicians and bureaucrats—back in charge of their health care decisions.

—U.S. SENATOR TOM COBURN, MD

You don't have to agree with her diagnosis and prescription for the U.S. health care system, but you do have to read her book. Once again, Professor Herzlinger has put together a well researched, well written, and very provocative blueprint for the future of health care.

—PETER L. SLAVIN, MD
PRESIDENT,
MASSACHUSETTS GENERAL HOSPITAL

Following on the heels of her landmark Market-Driven Health Care *and* Consumer-Driven Health Care *publications, Professor Herzlinger lays it on the line with her exposé of what many who work in the health care industry have felt in their gut. Now it is articulated in an entertaining and must-read portrayal of "fat-cat" gridlock, with you and me as the only way out.*

—DENNIS WHITE
EXECUTIVE VICE PRESIDENT
FOR STRATEGIC DEVELOPMENT,
NATIONAL BUSINESS COALITION ON HEALTH

WHO KILLED HEALTH CARE?

AMERICA'S $2 TRILLION MEDICAL PROBLEM— AND THE CONSUMER-DRIVEN CURE

REGINA HERZLINGER

Professor, Harvard Business School

McGraw-Hill

New York Chicago San Francisco Lisbon London
Madrid Mexico City Milan New Delhi
San Juan Seoul Singapore
Sydney Toronto

3 4 5 6 7 8 9 0   DOC/DOC   0 9 8 7

ISBN-13: 978-0-07-148780-1
ISBN-10: 0-07-148780-8

This publication is designed to provide accurate and authoritative information in regard to the subject matter covered. It is sold with the understanding that the publisher is not engaged in rendering legal, accounting, or other professional service. If legal advice or other expert assistance is required, the services of a competent professional person should be sought.

> —*From a declaration of principles jointly adopted by a committee of the American Bar Association and a committee of publishers.*

McGraw-Hill books are available at special quantity discounts to use as premiums and sales promotions, or for use in corporate training programs. For more information, please write to the Director of Special Sales, Professional Publishing, McGraw-Hill, Two Penn Plaza, New York, NY 10121-2298. Or contact your local bookstore.

CONTENTS

ACKNOWLEDGMENTS

I am grateful to the many people who helped me write this book: my editors, Herb Schaffner, Dave Conti, and Mark Reibling, are foremost among them. I am also grateful to Doctors Susan Botein, Eli Friedman, Peter Madras, Bernard Salick, and Thomas Stossel; lawyers Benjamin Falit and my Harvard Business School colleague Professor Constance Bagley; and Professors Amy Finkelstein and Stefan Thernstrom, who helped me by reviewing parts of this manuscript; Jeffrey Cronin and Erika McCaffrey of Harvard Business School's Baker Library for their research assistance; and my literary agent, Bill Leigh, for his steadfast support. The McGraw-Hill production team—Pattie Amoroso and Ruth Mannino—and copyeditor Marci Nugent were exemplary.

But because the status quo fights dirty and fights hard to protect its interests, this book will likely be smeared. So let me be clear that I am solely responsible for its contents.

Let us begin.

INTRODUCTION

The U.S. health care system is in the midst of a ferocious war. The prize is unimaginably huge—$2 trillion, about the size of the economy of China—and the outcome will affect the health and welfare of hundreds of millions of people. Four armies are battling to gain control: the health insurers, hospitals, government, and doctors. Yet you and I, the people who use the health care system and who pay for all of it, are not even combatants. And the doctors, the group whose interests are most closely aligned with our welfare, are losing the war.

The American people must win this battle. A system controlled by the insurance companies or hospitals or government will kill us financially and medically—it will ruin our economy, deny us the health care services we need, and undermine the important genomic research that can fundamentally improve the practice of medicine and control its costs. The current system is well on its way to doing all of these terrible things right now.

There is only one group that can prevent this damage: consumers—you and me—working together with our doctors. I wrote this book to raise the battle cry for American consumers of health care. I want you to know why we must win this war. I also delineate the battle plan that will enable us to turn health care into a system that is responsive to your needs and my needs—a consumer-driven health care system.

This war has been brewing for at least the three decades that I have spent in health care as a researcher and teacher. During that time, I have focused on entrepreneurial health care ventures as a professor at Harvard Business School; a member of the boards of directors of dozens of nonprofit and business health care organizations of all sorts, most of them consumer driven; an advisor to U.S. senators and representatives, as well as congressional staffers; a keynote lecturer at hundreds of large health care meetings; and a consumer of health care for my family and myself. I know the current system from top to bottom. I have seen it from virtually every perspective: from the worm's eye view of young students entering the system to the vantage point of high-level CEOs and elected officials; from personal experiences that include visits to the hospital emergency room and the paneled chambers of corporate boardrooms, the U.S. Congress, and the White House.

In some ways, I have been an insider, attempting to change the system from the inside out, working with those who hold the levers of power, trying to move health care in a direction that would make it more responsive to you and me and, at the same time, cheaper and more efficient.

From a health consumer's perspective, things were never good. Two recent experiences, however, have convinced me that the war is at a fever pitch and that the wrong side is winning. They've convinced me that it's time to go public, to go on the attack, and to let the world at large know what's really going on behind the curtains in the health care industry.

The events I'm referring to took place in the U.S. Congress, in Washington, D.C. Public policy is like sausage: you do not want to see how it is made, and the end product is not good for your health. These two were the straws that broke this camel's back.

Both experiences were meetings in which hospitals, insurers, and researchers argued for important, anticompetitive laws that advanced their interests—and hurt ours. No practicing doctors presented their findings or opinions at either meeting, even though the decisions on the issues involved would profoundly affect them. And there was no consumer representation. In fact, I have never attended a health care public policy meeting that included *any* consumer representation.

The first experience was a hearing in July 2006 before the House Ways and Means Committee Subcommittee on Health.[1] The issue was transparency: should the American people know the *price* of the health care services they use and the *results* doctors and hospitals achieve?[2]

The hearing was triggered by a *Wall Street Journal* article that revealed that U.S. hospitals, most of them nonprofit, charged uninsured patients prices that vastly exceeded those they charged their insured patients.[3] Even though many of the uninsured were poor, some hospitals employed tactics that verged on the criminal in their efforts to collect their inflated bills, driving their uninsured patients into bankruptcy. Ironically, the nonprofit hospitals have been granted immunity from paying taxes as a quid pro quo for their altruism. Where was it?

Transparency would at least help uninsured patients and all consumers of care know what they were going to be charged and the quality of the services they would receive. It was up to the U.S. Congress to force these guys to come clean. But the hospitals and insurers testified at this meeting that transparency would confuse us. They might be willing to post a range of their prices—say, a number between $200 and $3,000—but an exact number? No, too confusing. As for measures of their performance, such as the number of men in their fifties who died after open-heart surgery? No way. Some of the researchers who testified supported these assertions, adding that health care providers, primarily hospitals, would collude on prices once they were clearly known. I had heard these self-serving arguments against transparency many times, but I had never heard them used against the poor uninsured before.

The testimony was completely wrong minded.

One of the key success factors of the U.S. economy is transparency. We know the prices and quality of the goods and services we buy, ranging from our morning cereal to our complex computers to our mutual funds. This transparency has enabled us to be smart shoppers. When we are well informed, we can buy from and reward those who, like Michael Dell, founder of Dell Inc., give us good value for our money. Transparency causes what the economists call *productivity*, meaning that we get fair value in exchange for our money. That is why just about everybody supports transparency in all aspects of our lives—except health care.

So what is going on? Why is it that transparency is not a cure for health care? Why are this massive economic sector's prices shrouded in obscurity? Why are its results totally unknown? Why do I know more about the price and quality of my breakfast cereal than about the prices and quality of the hospitals in which my children were born?

The real issue here is power: the less you and I know about the facts, the greater the power of those in the know—the hospitals, the insurers, and the health policy researchers.

This hearing in 2006 convinced me that some members of the American Congress were not interested in protecting the uninsured by compelling transparency. This got me really worried.

The second experience was also a congressional event, and it proved to be my personal tipping point. It was here that I saw that the U.S. Congress was even willing to suppress competition in order to protect the powerful, entrenched status quo health care institutions.

This epiphany occurred at a meeting set up to inform congressional legislative assistants about a new kind of hospital, a small one that specializes only in certain complex, high-tech procedures, like those for treatment of heart disease.[4] These hospitals were partially owned and managed by doctors. It has long been my view that such specialty hospitals generally provide better, cheaper health care than the everything-for-everybody general hospital. These specialized hospitals can become really expert at the focused services they offer because they are run by knowledgeable and experienced doctors— which is often not the case with nonmedical administrators in the huge general hospitals most of us frequent.

The hospital sector sorely needs innovation. Hospitals account for most of the costs and cost increases in health care, yet they provide such wildly erratic quality that hundreds of thousands of patients die yearly from medical errors that occur in hospitals.[5] Although this innovation of small specialized hospitals was only a gnat relative to the size of the trillion-dollar general hospital sector, it potentially posed a major threat to them, and they knew it. To protect their position, the hospitals did what they always do: they ran to the legislators and tried to kill this potential competitor through politics, urging the Congress to pass the laws that would legislate this form of hospital out of existence.[6]

The key witness at this event was the CEO of a chain of 24 nonprofit hospitals who claimed that the impudent, venal 55-bed specialty hospital in his hospital chain's region would limit the ability of his billion-dollar nonprofit hospital chain to give free care to the poor and subsidize the very sick. He argued that the interloper hospital was hurting his own hospital's ability to help the uninsured because it was siphoning away his best-paying patients, hobbling his ability to help the uninsured as much as he wanted to.[7]

Those in attendance nodded in agreement. They believed him. Most of the legislative assistants were in their twenties—too young to be dubious. How could one argue with the charitable intents of hospitals called "St. Elizabeth's," "Swedish Lutheran," or, in this case, "Sioux Valley Hospitals & Health System" (since renamed Sanford Health)? After all, they've been a cornerstone of our communities for as long as anyone can remember. The other attendees in the room knew better, but they were in their fifties, veterans of Capitol Hill, long pickled and emasculated by Beltway cynicism.

Unfortunately, the U.S. Congress bought the hospital executive's argument too. In a virtually unprecedented move, it shut down his competition with a moratorium on the expansion of specialty hospitals.

Let's peek beneath the veil of the purity and altruism in which this chain of nonprofit hospitals cloaked its argument and look at its financial results. The facts provide staggering repudiation of its expressed point of view. In 2003, while the hospital was supposedly locked in a death struggle with the entrepreneurial specialty hospital, it still managed to earn $26 million in profits after all expenses were paid, and it held another $50 million in cash and liquid investments. This is the money left over after all charitable activities have been completed. These are huge amounts of money for a supposed nonprofit. Then, in 2004, after Congress hamstrung the competitor, profits and liquid assets grew by 15 percent, a rate of growth most

Fortune 500 companies would envy. Indeed, the hospital was fat enough to donate millions to activities like its local high school football league, which received nearly $200,000.

But very little of its money actually went to the uninsured and others who could not pay their full bills. To the contrary: the hospital's charitable care actually diminished by 40 percent as its profits increased. Not that it was ever large—in 2004, it amounted to only $5 million—but by 2005, after its competitor was taken out by the U.S. Congress, the hospital's charitable care fell to $3 million.

As you review these figures, bear in mind that the hospital operates as a nonprofit. We exempted it from paying tens of millions of dollars in taxes, but all we got in return was a piddling amount of free care for the uninsured. And even that paltry amount was puffed up by the kind of accounting gobbledygook that raises this accounting professor's eyebrows. The value of the hospital's charitable care was measured at the hospital's top prices, prices that nobody pays except for the uninsured. The hospital even had the nerve to include the differences between these inflated charges and the amount it received from Medicare and Medicaid in its charitable care calculation.[8] (If these accounting practices were followed by U.S. businesses, they could declare every discount from their list price as charity and claim a tax exemption as a result.)

What most bothered me about these incidents is that both the Democrats and Republicans in Congress lined up behind the attempts to suppress competition and transparency. Some Democrats in Congress really warmed to the task because it would enable them to enlarge the U.S. government's takeover of our health care system, a policy they had long favored. After all, if consumers will only get confused by information, and if providers, like hospitals, will only price fix as a result of transparency, who, other than Uncle Sam, can step into the breach? But some of the Republicans did not object strenuously either. Like the Democrats, they had drunk deeply from the well filled with Beltway Kool-Aid.

In the minds of most of our U.S. senators and representatives, when it comes to health care, the federal government is the savior—not you, not me, not our doctors, not information, not entrepreneurs.

No, the only party that can make health care cheaper and better is Uncle Sam. Indeed, Uncle Sam has recently become Doctor Sam: Congress is actually telling doctors how to practice medicine. And to enforce its cookie-cutter ideas on how to provide care for you and me, the U.S. Congress is using our money so only those doctors who follow the congressional recipes for medical care will be well paid.

The Better Way: Consumer-Driven Health Care

Let us be clear about what we want: a consumer-driven health care system that is simultaneously cheaper and better.

Right now, we pay too much for too little health care. The massive costs of our system of care create major competitiveness issues for our economy and our children. If General Motors spends $1,600 per car on health care and Toyota spends only $110, there is no way that GM cars can compete with Japanese cars on price. The costs of U.S. health care dwarf those of other countries with which we compete—and they do so without readily apparent commensurate improvements in the quality of care. Further, we are leaving our progeny a bitter heritage: they will be holding the bag for our government's health care costs for the elderly and poor, some of which have been funded with borrowed monies they will have to repay. Insurance costs are so high that we have over 46 million people who go without it, which is a shameful scar on the richest country in the world. Indeed, the exclusions the insurers have on what they will pay for are so stringent that some sick people cannot obtain the care they need even when they have insurance.

To add insult to injury, we receive far too little health care for all this money. Sure, we have some great doctors, hospitals, and medical technology; but quality varies wildly among and within providers of health care. And because of the lack of integration of medical care delivery for the chronic diseases and disabilities that account for 80 percent of health care costs, patients fall between the cracks—for example, kidney disease patients don't get the preventive care they desperately need to halt the progression of their deadly disease.

Soaring health care costs that cripple our global competitiveness, uneven quality of care, 46-plus million of uninsured, and Medicare and Medicaid programs whose deficit threatens our children's economic welfare—who can best solve these mind-numbing problems? The government? A technocratic elite? Status quo insurers and hospitals? Or you and me?

There are two broad sets of belief here. One group believes in the transformative powers of big, organized institutions, such as governments and large insurance firms. The other camp believes that small is beautiful. To them, only consumers and the entrepreneurial institutions that serve them can transform health care.

Big-Is-Beautiful Health Care

To those in the big-is-beautiful camp, the government or a health policy, hospital, and insurance elite holds the key to solving health care's problems. The big-is-beautiful camp believes that only the elites, bristling with Ph.D.s in statistics, epidemiology, or health economics, possess the intellectual tools needed to decide how much should be spent, on what, and where. Why?

First, this group believes that as a service industry, the health care sector is incapable of the kind of productivity gains that characterize the rest of an economy. Just as an orchestra's productivity cannot be increased by making it play faster, so too the productivity of health care is fixed. And when it comes to costs, the worst is yet to come with our aging population and marvelous medical technological innovations that will create vastly expensive new drugs and devices. Further, you and I are incapable of the kind of complex decision making that health care requires. To buttress their superiority, the elites regularly publish research in health policy journals that underscores the inability of ordinary Americans to understand critical aspects of health care.

The big-is-beautiful solution? Let the government put a lid on the costs and ration health care through established health insurers and hospitals, with the active advice of the academic policy makers.

The ripest apples on the rationing tree are the sick, the 20 percent who account for 80 percent of health care costs. Once the government manages the sick, it can penalize errant doctors whose inexplicable deviations from centrally prescribed care regimens the health policy world regularly documents. Alternatively, in a nod to competition, this camp would permit large private health insurers to vie for our business. Each insurer would offer identical products so we do not become confused.

Let the Flowers Bloom: Small-Is-Beautiful Health Care

To the small-is-beautiful crowd, consumers who shop in free markets for differentiated products steadily drive down price and increase quality, even for complex goods. For example, the affordability of cars and personal computers has increased along with their quality, although the average consumer likely does not understand how they work. Two characteristics explain these results. The first is the availability of excellent, trustworthy, user-friendly information that focuses on the product characteristics that consumers find important, such as *Consumer Reports'* and J.D. Power's reliability and safety data for cars. This kind of information, available only in consumer-driven industries, enables the average person to buy intelligently. Second, as we all learned in our introductory economics courses, markets are equilibrated by *marginal* consumers, not by *average* ones. The discerning, last-to-buy group consists of the picky, assertive people—like the well-informed parents in the car market who are concerned with safety—who drive down price and improve quality for all the rest of us.

Along with their beliefs in the wisdom of consumer-based free markets, this camp is also much more sanguine about the possibilities for productivity enhancement in service industries. In a 2002 report, McKinsey & Company cited retailing and finance as the top two drivers of the remarkable U.S. increases in productivity in the late 1990s.[9] Entrepreneurial activity, not rationing, offers the best cure for massive health care costs.

Big- versus Small-Is-Beautiful Health Care Systems

These ideological dicta create distinctly differing approaches for reforming our health care system.

Those who distrust markets and consumers prefer a single-payer system, in which the federal government's excellent, centralized management would wring savings from billions of dollars now wasted, in their view, on the hapless, competitive private-sector health insurance firms and wildly inefficient doctors and use the savings to provide coverage for the uninsured. Alternatively, they would restrict insurance choices to a handful of uniform managed care health insurance options. In practice, this idea would work like an automobile market in which every manufacturer offers identical cars designed by a technocratic elite. But this approach, in every situation where it has been tried, stifles new ideas that challenge conventional wisdom, reduces quality, and leads to bureaucratic bloat, fraud, and favoritism for the rich and powerful.

Those who believe in consumers and entrepreneurs opt instead for private-sector solutions. The small-is-beautiful camp would open the health insurance and health care delivery markets to entrepreneurial innovators. For example, the HealthAllies division of the UnitedHealth Group, the country's largest private insurer, already offers insurance products that cost as little as $300 a year. The company gives the little guy access to discounted networks of medical care providers at nearly the same price as the big groups pay. Information entrepreneurs would enable consumers to scrutinize these innovations via excellent, comprehensive information about their quality and price.

And while the big-is-beautiful camp, which believes that productivity increases cannot be attained, would micromanage doctors to standardize their practice patterns and curb "unnecessary" spending on the sick, the other would liberate entrepreneurial health care providers to create new programs that control costs by increasing quality and require the dissemination of information about the prices and quality of care of providers.

Retailing led this country's productivity boom from 1995 through 1999. Health care entrepreneurs could lead the next productivity boom. Just as retailing entrepreneurs redesigned that industry to meet consumers' needs for good prices and convenience—giving us access to Internet shopping, stores such as Staples organized around shoppers' needs, and low prices—so would health care entrepreneurs redesign the health care system from the bottom up. The savings from all this would be used to subsidize the poor uninsured to purchase health insurance.

The fixes are not difficult. We must get back the money our employers and government now take from our salaries and taxes to buy health insurance on our behalf so that we can choose it for ourselves. Our innovative, caring doctors must be empowered to design better, cheaper health care. Our poor should be subsidized by the rest of us, so they can buy health insurance just like everybody else. And our government should help subsidize the poor, provide transparency, and prosecute fraud and abuse. All the other busybodies must get out of the way—the empire-building hospitals, the micromanaging insurers, the self-serving academics. Their role is to support, not to manage, us and our doctors.

These are the choices that confront us—a health care system dominated by established, status quo players or a health care system dominated by consumers. The current system—and the one envisioned by Congress, the hospitals, the academics, and the insurers—is hazardous to our health and our wealth. My hope is that we can change the direction they are trying to drag us in and go in a different direction, one that will deliver high-quality care to everyone cheaply and efficiently.

This book, then, is my attack on the current system and the battle plan for our repairing control of it. Read on and learn, in Parts 1 and 2, who is killing health care and how they are doing it. The villains you'll meet include our hospitals, our insurers, our employers, your representatives in Congress, and the policy-making academic community. You'll also run into a few heroes—including the doctors and medical innovators who are fighting the politics and the odds to bring you better care and a longer life. In Part 3, I lay out the principles as well as the specifics of consumer-driven health care—what it is, why it will work, what it offers all of us—and analyze the lessons from consumer-driven systems like Switzerland's. I describe how it will improve quality and control costs for the sick and the poor. And in Part 4, I close with a comprehensive step-by-step plan of the carrots, the sticks, and the laws that will make this consumer-driven system happen.

WHO KILLED HEALTH CARE?

CHAPTER 1

THE DAY
HEALTH CARE DIED

This book is an attack on our present health care system as well as a presentation of a new, future health care system that differs from everything we have today. I am not conducting a minor skirmish or merely suggesting adjustments to your insurance plan's benefits or adding customer-friendly practices to your hospital. This is a full-blown attack on the structures and the architects of our present system.

Our $2 trillion health care system is as large as the economy of China. And yet, despite all this spending, millions of people cannot get the care they need because it costs too much or because our fragmented health care system cannot efficiently supply integrated, multifaceted treatment for their chronic diseases or disabilities. If they are uninsured, our primarily nonprofit hospitals all too often gouge them with the highest prices they charge and then use criminal-like collection tactics to ensure payment.

You may not realize it, but we all pay for all of this. If we are employed, our boss takes part of our salary and uses it to pay for this system.[1] If we are self-employed, we pay horrendously high premiums for insurance plans. And as taxpayers, we funded the government's 44 percent share of 2004 health care costs.[2]

The system giveth and the system taketh away. It takes your money, time, and health, and it gives generously to Wall Street and fat-cat businesspeople and hospital executives who earn millions of dollars. Dr. William W. McGuire, the former CEO of United-

Healthcare, one of the country's largest health consumers, not only received $1.7 billion worth of stock options during his tenure,[3] but also had a jet at his disposal and a red carpet reportedly rolled out to meet his limo so his tootsies did not have to meet the same ground on which we ordinary mortals step.[4] This money, or at least some of it, could have provided better health care or lower costs for United-Healthcare's enrollees, but instead it wound up in Dr. McGuire's very large bank account and literally fell under his feet.

I am not suggesting that we put more money into our health care system. At close to $2 trillion, or nearly 20 percent of our economy, we put more than enough money into it. Nor do I think that we must set up yet another bureaucracy that will take our money and then ration our health care. All of us can likely have all the care we need with current spending levels. What I am advocating is using the money we currently spend differently and more effectively so that we can get the health care we want and even cover those who are now forced to go without health insurance because they cannot afford it.

The solution I will discuss here goes by the name *consumer-driven health care*. It's a term that I popularized, and it's become a common way to describe this new health care solution. Google it and see for yourself. Consumer-driven health care empowers individuals and brings their force to bear on the offerings of doctors, hospitals, and insurance and pharmaceutical companies. It converts the entire system to one that is responsive to you and me as the ultimate consumers of its goods and services.

As I will show in the course of the book, there are consumer-driven health insurers that give you the health care you need at a price you are willing to pay; there are lower-cost hospitals that do not treat you like a slab of meat; and there are governments that do what they are supposed to—help the poor, provide transparency, and protect against fraud and abuse—rather than telling your doctor how to practice medicine. There is a way to create dynamic markets for health services that are more effective, more efficient, and more responsive to the patient-consumer—and her doctor—than anything we have today. The last chapters are devoted to describing that system, how to make it work, the proper roles of government and business in creating and sustaining it, and the benefits and good health it will bring to you.

Who Killed Health Care?

The day I learned Jack Morgan had died of kidney disease was the day I knew our health care system had died along with him.

Jack needed a kidney transplant, a complex but not uncommon procedure. He found a donor in his loving daughter, who was willing to undergo surgery to have one of her own healthy kidneys removed and given to her dad. Jack's health insurance was paid up and functioning.

What could go wrong? Everything. Jack never got the transplant. Instead, he died of his disease.

The kidney is the body's filtering system. Kidney disease victims are essentially poisoned and drowned. The filters in Jack's kidneys, which were functioning at less than 20 percent of normal, could not effectively remove waste and keep his fluids regulated.

When the disease first struck, the people around Jack, who was normally a lean bundle of energy, noticed that he had become lethargic and puffy. His usually glowing skin was dry and scaly. His HMO doctor thought he was depressed, and he gave Jack a prescription for a generic drug. But, after repeated visits, when his symptoms did not improve, Jack was correctly diagnosed. An artificial kidney, called a *dialysis machine*, replicated the function of his natural kidneys. But after many years of dialysis, it was no longer enough. Jack needed a new kidney, a good one, transplanted into his body.

What could go wrong? Everything. Everything went wrong, and Jack never got the transplant. Instead, he died of his disease.

His death was not painful, at least not for him. He died quickly, poisoned by his own waste, drowned by his own fluids. But it was painful for the many people who loved him because they knew his death was premature. With a new kidney, Jack could have lived another 20 or more years.

What happened?

Jack was killed by an inept, malfunctioning, costly health care system that he thought was protecting him. A system that for all intents and purposes is dead. He was killed . . .

Who exactly killed him? And why?

Remember the book and film *Murder on the Orient Express*, Agatha Christie's story of a man murdered on a train? It turns out that *all* the passengers had a hand in his death.[5]

That's what happened to Jack Morgan—every part of the health care system failed him. Unlike the killers in the Christie mystery, they didn't mean to do it, but they did it anyway. They were so caught up in their self-interest that they forgot what their work was all about—Jack Morgan's health. In the U.S. health care system, and in the United Kingdom, Europe, and Canada, trillions of dollars are spent on health care, but no one gives a voice to its consumers. In these nations, this means that you and I are not being heard. Jack could not speak for himself, and there was no ombudsman to speak for him.

The killers work in insurance and hospital firms that have lost their souls, firms that have become more interested in money and perpetuating themselves than in providing health. Employers, as well as the U.S. Congress and a bevy of health policy academics, are also implicated. They were satisfied with substituting simple, utopian abstractions, like the idea that an insurer or a government can "manage health care" cheaper and better than your doctor, for the thousands of complex interactions that should guide the practice of medicine.

The problem begins with the **hospitals**—the bloated behemoths that account for the largest part of our health care system, nearly a trillion dollars' worth, and represent the major reason for its cost increases. Their costs rise at a pace that generally exceeds the growth of their services. They have managed this through shameless manipulation of their nonprofit image and massive political contributions. The hospitals have convinced the U.S. Congress to suppress potential competitors, such as physician-controlled specialty hospitals, which could provide better and cheaper services, and to grant them valuable tax exemptions. They've also persuaded local judges and juries to strangle competition by allowing mergers of hospitals and other consolidations.

Clearly, the term *nonprofit* when applied to these hospitals is a joke. The reality behind the saintly caregiver image they like to promote is startling. These supposedly altruistic institutions earn hundreds of millions of dollars in profit, keep billions of dollars in cash reserves, and pay their executives millions in salary. They play hardball, screwing the uninsured with inflated charges and collection tactics worthy of criminals.

Outrageous hospital costs have gravely injured the **employers** who buy their employees' health insurance. Since 2000, health insurance premiums have increased by 73 percent compared to cumulative increases in inflation and wages of about 15 percent.[6] Although they themselves are victimized by the system, employers, in their turn, have become killers.

Some employers, especially small ones, no longer can afford to offer health insurance. As for the other larger employers, in an effort to control costs, they have allowed their human resources (HR) staffs to restrict employees' choice of health insurance plans, frequently offering only one—a managed care insurance plan. The HR types believe that by restricting choice and giving the insurance companies a large volume of enrollees, they can achieve meaningful cost control. But they are profoundly wrong in their belief: to the contrary, choice supports competition, competition fuels innovation, and innovation is the only way to make things better and cheaper.

The paternalistic HR staff became convinced that the **managed care insurers** would control costs better than the consumers or the doctors. But they put their faith in the wrong institution; the managed care sector has strayed from its early spiritual roots in the Kaiser organization that originally created the concept of "managed care" as a fundamentally different way of providing better, cheaper health care. As managed care organizations transitioned into an industry, rather than a movement, they lost their souls—all too many were focused on profits at the expense of their enrollees' health care.

Next, the U.S. government's **Congress and executive branch** enabled this series of disastrous events not only by helping hospitals suppress competition but also by passing legislation that forced U.S. employers to offer managed care options whether they wanted to or not. In addition, the Congress has wrung vast, unwitting subsidies out of us to shower on the managed care insurers and drugs they favor. As a final blow, our Congress has begun to practice medicine, through "pay-for-performance" schemes that reward health service providers who follow Uncle Sam's medical cookbook.

Former government executives who sit on the boards of directors of insurance and health services firms keep congressional relationships well oiled. They are well compensated for their work. The person who once ran the U.S. government's massive Medicare program, for example, was a member of the board of directors at United-Healthcare that approved $1.6 billion in payments to Dr. William McGuire, the firm's former CEO and chairman. She did pretty well herself—earning nearly $15 million in stock, in addition to other compensation, for her board services.[7]

The **health policy academics** also enabled Jack's death, motivated by their self-interest and belief in their superior intellects to advocate for a large role in the control of the system. They paved the way, through their intellectual discourse and public policy papers, for technocrats to oversee physicians and usurp their judgments and treatment preferences—the ugly core of managed care and pay-for-performance systems.

The academics succeeded in blaming the failures of health care in this country on the doctors who actually treat patients. They claimed that practicing physicians made mistakes that would be eliminated if they were controlled by academic researchers who, somehow, know how to practice better medicine. Their efforts were all about placing the individual doctor under their control or that of their technocrat surrogates. The last few recent studies of the Institute of Medicine, one of the National Academies and a group of health policy experts set up to advise the U.S. Congress, focus on how terrible the doctors are.[8] Their solution? Just give us more power to tell the clinical docs how to do it right.

But, presently, medicine is more art than science. Unlike the powerful, universal laws of physics that inform the practice of engineering, there are few inviolate rules in the sciences of biology and bio-chemistry to inform the practice of medicine. Scientists are just beginning to understand how our bodies function, as new human genome research decodes the uncertainty of our biology, fate, and health. So where is the science that will enable some bureaucrat to tell your doctor, who knows you so much better than the bureaucrat, how to practice medicine on you? It does not exist.

Some academics accuse the practicing doctors of unbridled greed too, claiming that they give patients medical services they do not need just to jack up their income. Yes, some do, but the majority do not.[9] To the contrary, many doctors lie to insurers only to make sure that their patients can get the medical care they need, and two-thirds donate 11 hours each month of their time to patients for free.[10]

The academics and policy makers had their way. After decades of brainwashing with this kind of academic preaching, the U.S. Congress passed a whole set of laws, twice as long as the King James Bible of 1,377 pages, that constrain doctors who want to go into the health care services business.[11] But in its rush to pass these restrictive laws, Congress was abandoning this nation's passion for innovations and the entrepreneurs who bring them to life. Many of our most important companies were founded by businesspeople who deeply understood their core technologies, in the way that doctors, and only doctors, understand the practice of medicine. Thomas Edison was not only the brilliant businessman who started General Electric; he was also a brilliant inventor. Henry Ford not only founded the Ford Motor Company; he was also a genius mechanical engineer who in only eight years slashed the price of automobiles by more than half with his technological and managerial innovations.[12] Bill Gates was not only the visionary founder of the great business, Microsoft, but also an excellent software writer. But if these guys were doctors, they would likely not be allowed to create the same sort of excellent, effective, efficient businesses in health care.

While the Congress and academics pounded away at the practicing doctors' failures, they did not celebrate their successes. Some of the leaders in the physician community also lost sight of the purpose of health care, having been caught up in the politics. But of all the many participants in the health care system, it is the doctors who have more steadfastly adhered to their ethics as professionals. Through scientific innovations in the practice of medicine, we have witnessed a dramatic increase in life span and decrease in illness. Yet physicians' inflation-adjusted incomes dropped by 7 percent from 1995 to 2003, while those of professional and technical workers increased by 7 percent.[13] And, increasingly, physicians are asked to follow medical care recipes concocted by insurers and government bureaucrats. With their professional autonomy and financial well-being compromised, small wonder that the number of applicants to medical schools decreased by nearly 20 percent between 1996 and 2006.[14] When I ask my MD students why they have enrolled in the Harvard Business School for an MBA, many say, "I cannot practice medicine anymore."

The kind of system that exists now hates innovation. It hates outsiders with good ideas. Yet sometimes, against all odds, the outsiders succeed. Two brilliant scientists who helped Jack to stay alive as long as he did fit into that category. Their genius profoundly altered the pattern of care for kidney disease.

One was the classic academic—a wiry Dutch MD/Ph.D. with a long face, big nose, and Euro-style goatee, clad in the scientific researcher uniform of rumpled chinos, T shirt, and sneakers. Willem Kolff is his name, and he is a raving genius. When I met him, a decade ago, he was a twenty-something in vitality and intellect boxed into an eighty-something body. He invented an artificial kidney that filters the blood of impurities in a lengthy, painful, but life-saving process called *dialysis*. The second was more your idea of a good doctor—grandfatherly, pious, smiling, noble Joe Murray, from Boston's Brigham and Women's Hospital. He introduced kidney transplantation from a living donor.

Mother Nature is the best of engineers: because kidneys are so important, she has given us two of them. But, despite the security blanket, they may both fail, largely because of diabetes (nearly half of new cases) and/or high blood pressure (25 percent).[15]

Transplants are a great solution. Joe Murray performed the first transplant of a kidney taken from a living donor. But as recently as August 15, 2006, there were 67,328 people waiting for a kidney but only 13,268 kidneys available. Sadly, the demand far outstrips the supply.[16]

Dialysis, which rids the body of impurities, is the only alternative to transplants. Roman sweat baths were likely among the first sites for dialysis. Romans who sweated impurities from their bodies were purified but desiccated, trading profound thirst for kidney failure.

The key to an artificial kidney lay in the most mundane of materials—plastics: a membrane so porous that it allowed the impurities in the blood to leach out but sufficiently strong to withstand the pressure created by the flow of blood. During World War II, in Nazi-occupied Holland, Willem Kolff found this membrane in sausage casing made of cellulose acetate. He wound yards and yards of it around a drum, seated it in a vat of liquid, used an engine scavenged from a lawn mower as a power source, and thus created the first artificial kidney.

No good deed goes unpunished in health care. Sure, these two helped people with kidney disease to live good and useful lives, but these doctors also took a lot of abuse along the way. They persevered in the face of unrelenting opposition to their innovations in kidney disease treatment by the status quo medical establishment. You'll hear more about that later.

In the course of my attack, you will meet some other riveting personalities amid the hundreds of thousands of faceless businesspeople, hospital executives, politicians, academics, and bureaucrats who created this destructive system. One was the Prince of Darkness, former President Richard Nixon, who kick-started the managed care insurance movement with legislation that forced employers to offer HMOs as health insurance options to their employees and supported these HMOs with massive federal government subsidies that were funded by the taxpayers and that lowered the prices of the HMOs. They also include the Odd Couple who created Kaiser, a large California HMO—a can-do, huffing, puffing entrepreneur, Henry Kaiser, and Dr. Sidney Garfield, who so admired Kaiser, 24 years his elder, that he married the sister of Kaiser's wife so he could become Kaiser's brother-in-law. Believe it or not, there are some heroes, too, such as doctors Willem Kolff and Joe Murray, whom you've already briefly met, and Richard "Dickie" Scruggs, a Mississippi plaintiff lawyer who, despite his boyish nickname, is as huggable as a shark. Scruggs is bringing the hospitals to their knees in suits about their outrageous overcharges of uninsured patients.

Jack Morgan

Jack Morgan is a pastiche of many patients who have died at the hands of the U.S. health care system. I have given him the average characteristics that shape many of their experiences. I made him a chef who owned a successful French-style restaurant, for example, because self-employed people have a hard time finding health insurance.

Nobody who knew Jack as a kid thought he would succeed. He had been a wild teenager—always ready to party, never ready to study. His initial foray in a community college, to study accounting of all things, was disastrous. He took a job as a dishwasher in a local restaurant just for something to do. But luck was smiling on Jack. The restaurant was an up-and-comer, part of the foodie revolution that started in the United States in the 1980s. Its owner was a renowned chef who sought to merge the best of local, organic ingredients with the best of French cooking techniques. He was as wild as Jack—mercurial, brilliant, demanding; but, unlike Jack, he was successful. The chef stirred Jack's interest in cooking.

Jack's grandmother was French—he was named "Jacques" in honor of his late grandfather. Grandmère was a great home cook and shared her skills with her family. Although Jack thought he knew how to cook, he quickly learned that in a professional restaurant setting, his pride was misplaced. He was promoted from dishwasher to prep chef—one of the army of people who prepared the food that the real chefs cooked. Jack spent his days in the kitchen boning ducks, descaling fish, and dicing thousands of carrots, celeries, and onions into the tiny cubes, all exactly the same size, that would form the mirepoix, the caramelized base of most sauces.

The restaurant's kitchen was small—the smaller the kitchen, the more room for paying customers—and resembled a scene from hell.

Flames from fat fires shot out of the grill; clouds of steam rose from the pasta cooker; and the chefs, mostly men, were packed in tight, under unrelenting pressure to cook and plate the food. But Jack found the environment enthralling. He loved the pace, the creativity, the ribald bonhomie. And most of all he loved the food: its preparation, its presentation, everything about it, except for offal—tripe, liver, sweetbreads—the innards of animals.

To his surprise, he became ambitious. He too wanted to own his own restaurant. Jack knew he needed further training. He applied to a famous French cooking school and was accepted as a student there. In preparation, Jack studied French and created a backpack tour of all the best restaurants in France, using the *Michelin Guide* to plan the voyage.

Jack's first encounter with a kidney occurred in a restaurant in the north of France. It was noted for its lamb. Proud of his mastery of the French language, he ordered the *agneau*. A plate of lamb, beautifully sauced and showered with minced fresh herbs, showed up; but one bite convinced him that this urine-soaked meat was not the *agneau* he had in mind.

Jack had inadvertently ordered lamb kidneys. Their flavor underscored their function: the kidneys produce the urine that removes waste from our bodies. Once the food we eat is digested and used, the body discards both useful and waste products into the blood. The kidney's one million filters separate out about two quarts of excess water. We call the waste *urine*.

Little did Jack know that some 20 years later, long after he had achieved success as a restaurateur, he would have yet another unhappy encounter with a kidney when he developed kidney disease.

This time around, the consequence of the encounter was devastating: Jack Morgan died of his kidney disease. A lot of people mourned for him because he was a great guy: ebullient, charming, demanding. Everybody loved him, including his 29-year-old daughter. She loved him so much she was willing to donate one of her two kidneys to replace his hopelessly diseased ones.

Mother Nature is the world's best bioengineer. She designed us with considerable redundancy, so if, in our careless ways, we destroy one part of our body, another is waiting in the wings to take over the job. She gave us two kidneys, but people can survive with only one, even one transplanted from another person's body.

Mother Nature's engineering miracles include an army that ruthlessly hunts down and destroys any invaders. It is called the *immune system*. But sometimes even the best designers can go awry. If the immune system profiles a donated kidney as foreign, it will destroy it. Kidneys that come from relatives have a greater chance of passing the immune system's inspection. Jack's daughter's kidney was as good a match as one could hope for with Jack's tissues. As brilliant an invention as Willem Kolff's artificial kidney is, there is only so much that it can do. Jack needed Joe Murray's skill.

It was either a kidney transplant or death.

Jack Morgan needed the transplant, but he got death. Badly debilitated by his dialysis, he caught an infection that killed him.

Jack Morgan never had a chance. As a small employer, Jack could afford only one health insurance plan, a managed care one. And it killed him by delaying his transplant through sheer ineptitude, like the California-based insurer Kaiser Permanente, in which more than 100 people died while they waited for kidney transplants. Twenty-five of those waiting had a perfect match.

You and I are all potential Jack Morgans—the victims of the untrammeled vanity, greed, and self-interest of those meant to protect us. The ideas in this book will enable us to wrest the health care system away from those who killed Jack Morgan and put it back where it belongs, under our control in a consumer-driven health care system.

I begin my attack on the health care system by exposing the dysfunctional cultures of the mammoth HMOs and managed care insurers. I'll show how they lost their souls—how their mission became distorted from protection and preservation of their patients' health to self-interest and self-enrichment, and how, in the process, people like Jack Morgan died.

DEATH BY
A THOUSAND CUTS

CHAPTER 2

KILLER NUMBER 1: THE HEALTH INSURERS

Death at the Hands of a Dysfunctional Culture

A group of doctors were in a restaurant on the North Shore of Massachusetts. The Essex River flowed gently outside. The delicious fruits of the Atlantic Ocean—lobster, clams, mussels—filled their plates. The mood was mellow. They had all safely reached middle age: their marriages and health intact and their kids great (so far, so good).

But Paul, a gentle vascular surgeon, was seething. The other doctors knew what was coming: yet another complaint about a managed care insurer. "You won't believe what happened to me this week. I checked an elderly diabetic into my hospital. The guy had a lot of troubles. A great guy, but he just can't manage his diabetes. I had operated on his foot a few weeks ago. And what do you know? As soon as he heals, he goes on a bender. His sugar goes out of control. He was in terrible shape. I checked him into the hospital because I suspected he had an aneurysm (a weakened distention in the wall of a blood vessel). If he tested positive, I knew I had to operate immediately, the next day. That baby could blow any minute and he would bleed to death.

"Well, the PCP (primary care physician) who is my patient's gatekeeper just called me. Because he represents the HMO, the gatekeeper has to approve the bill. He thinks I should not have admitted my patient into the hospital for the tests. He questioned my judgment. He told me I was practicing bad, wasteful medicine. He threatened to throw me out of the insurer's network of doctors if I kept this up. I lost my temper. I told him in no uncertain terms that he just does not understand my kind of medicine. He's out of his league—out of his depth."

Bob, a doctor who moonlighted as a gatekeeper for HMOs, asked: "Did you tell the PCP before you admitted the patient that he was being admitted for a test? That you were going to have to operate immediately if the test was positive? Did you ask for authorization?"

"No," said Paul, his usually quiet voice rising in volume. "Look, this was a life-or-death situation. I had to admit the patient. Immediately. I didn't have time to ask the PCP for permission. Anyway, how can a PCP possibly evaluate my management of this case? He's no vascular surgeon. He does not know my patient."

Jane, another doctor, nodded sympathetically: "He certainly was not very collegial. How could he challenge you like that?"

Paul saved the patient, but he paid a heavy personal price in rancorous, time-consuming interactions with the HMO gatekeeper. Most other doctors have encountered these depressing, negative interactions too—over and over again. Some have retired early, which is a terrible loss for all of us because practice makes perfect, especially in surgery. Meanwhile, lives are needlessly held in the balance as health care providers and HMOs sort out their differences.

The Cultural Imperative

The conversation reminded me of many similar moments in other organizations: "How could he do that? How could she be so stupid, ignorant, assertive?"

I have heard Paul's plaint many times in the course of the research I've conducted for my Harvard Business School case studies and after the lectures I've delivered to hundreds of health care groups. I know from decades of interactions with business organizations that when colleagues cannot communicate with each other without rancor and misunderstandings, when competence and motives are questioned without cause, the organizational culture has gone terribly wrong. In successful organizations, confrontations of this sort lead to intervention and analysis by upper managers, and ultimately to a plan to correct the problem through new processes, incentives, or education; but in most managed care organizations, this kind of culture does not exist.

If Paul and his HMO gatekeeper had been in a success-oriented work environment, they would have met, perhaps with a manager, to clarify the source of the problem and develop a remedy. Likely they would have agreed that their confrontation occurred because the surgeon and gatekeeper lacked a clear organizational relationship and common information. But these two were not working in this kind of organization.

Here's how a successful health care organization handled a similar problem.

Joan is the Oklahoma-based technical specialist for a firm that manufactures life-support equipment. She is notified that the device in a Louisiana hospital is not working properly. The hospital has no backup and has tried all the usual remedies to no avail. This too is a life-or-death situation that calls for immediate action. But, unlike Paul, who had to "consult" the PCP before he could act, Joan can proceed to do what she knows to do: she e-mails a request to her manager for permission to ship an expensive replacement device ASAP. Permission is expeditiously granted. She also knows that if she does not receive a response within 15 minutes, she is authorized to proceed on her own. Here, everyone cooperates: all efforts are properly focused on the right and expeditious thing to do for the patient's well-being.

Why are these two situations so glaringly different? It is not the existence of clear procedures in one case and not the other. They could have made a difference, of course. But the core difference is that Joan's organization has a culture that lends itself to the development of such protocols and Paul's does not.

People in an organization whose culture relies on a shared vision are positive and action oriented rather than negative and blame oriented. They want to work things out, find solutions, and serve their customers. The culture promotes a shared vision of the beliefs, goals, and activities of the organization. The culture helps them realize that a confrontation is not a clash of personalities, but rather a sign that something deeper is going wrong and a signal that it must be fixed to preserve the organization's ability to perform its mission.

In health care, a productive organizational culture means finding ways to help patients. But such cultures have become rarer and rarer in managed care organizations and hospitals for reasons that we will explore in this chapter and throughout the book.

Jack Morgan died while he was enrolled in an HMO, the kind of health plan that was once widely touted as the model for the rest of the world's health care systems. The HMO endlessly delayed his transplant. A culture that had lost its focus was responsible for his death.

The Death of a Man Who Should Have Been Saved

As you know, Jack Morgan is an amalgam of many patients. I was inspired to create him after I read about the momentous failure of the California-based Kaiser HMO kidney transplant program in 2005 and 2006 in the federal government's reviews and California news sources. The failure paralleled Kaiser's transformation from an efficient, caring organization focused on delivering high-quality health care at a reasonable price to a confused, bureaucratic business. In 2005, 112 of Kaiser's kidney transplant candidates died.

The disaster began to unfold prosaically, as most disasters do. Kaiser decided to perform kidney transplants in its own hospitals instead of continuing to send its patients to the non-Kaiser kidney transplantation programs that it had been using, such as those of the University of California (UC) San Francisco and Davis hospitals. (At the time, Kaiser had empty beds and operating rooms because minimally invasive surgical techniques had decreased the demand for them.)[1] As a vertically integrated organization, consisting of a health insurer, 30 hospitals, and 12,000 doctors under one umbrella, Kaiser felt it could do a better job of coordinating care by working within its own network of hospitals and doctors. This kind of decision arises so routinely for vertically integrated firms that it is often referred to in business shorthand as the "make-versus-buy" decision: Do I make something myself, using my own facilities, or buy it from an outside vendor?

The HMO notified the more than 1,500 patients awaiting transplants of the change in mid-2004. Ironically, the head of Kaiser's transplant service noted at the time, "We should be able to achieve higher outcomes."[2] Instead, outcomes (health care speak for "results") dramatically worsened. Kaiser's new program performed only 56 transplants in 2005, while in the previous year, when transplants were still being outsourced, it had performed 165. Twice as many of Kaiser's patients died as had transplants, while in the rest of California, twice as many got their transplants as died.[3]

Here is one patient's view, as described by the *Los Angeles Times* in its Pulitzer Prize–worthy coverage of this scandal:

> *"I don't know what's going on here," Bernard Burks wrote to Kaiser Permanente's kidney transplant program last October, "but whatever it is, it's wrong."*
>
> *Burks, 56, was among hundreds of patients forced to shift to Kaiser's new San Francisco program about a year earlier. . . . He feared that his chances of getting a kidney were slipping away.*
>
> *His daughter was willing to give him one of her kidneys—a good match—to rescue him from grueling rounds of dialysis. But no one at Kaiser seemed to care.*
>
> *Months passed and he grew increasingly agitated. The transplant coordinator handling the case "is worth about two dead flies," he wrote in March to the program's medical director.*
>
> *Kaiser staff hadn't read their own files, he continued: "You stated in your letter, 'If you have a family member or friend who might want to discuss donation of a kidney for you, please have them call us.' Check your damn records. It appears you are a bunch of incompetents who fail to communicate with each other."*

News about the flawed start-up of Kaiser Permanente's Northern California transplant program . . . has unleashed bitter recollections and powerful emotions among patients who say that for months they have had their appointments inexplicably canceled, records lost and pleas met with eerie indifference. . . .

"I don't want those guys cutting on me now," said Burks, a real estate appraiser in the Sacramento area. "I'm afraid. . . . I just don't trust them."

. . . Burks' daughter . . . said she didn't mind the repetitive tests and screenings she had to undergo to be his living donor.

"Now," she said, "it looks like they were stalling."

She began questioning what was going on at Kaiser after she learned that transplant staffers were trying to convince her father that she didn't really want to donate a kidney to him, citing her move to Texas.

"My dad didn't even want my kidney, and that made me want to give it to him even more," she said. "They're trying to make him think I don't want to do this."

Like her father, she no longer wants the transplant performed at Kaiser. When a Kaiser representative called this week, she said she told her: "I'm not doing it with you guys. We'll mortgage the house, and we'll just get it done elsewhere."[4]

In May 2006, the *Los Angeles Times* reported that Kaiser caused many patients to miss opportunities for a transplant solely because of improperly handled paperwork: fewer than 3 percent of those on Kaiser's waiting list got transplants, as compared to 12 percent elsewhere in the state.[5] One hundred twelve people died while waiting on its transplant list. Some of those waiting for a transplant had offers of kidney donations from relatives, so there was no need to wait for a donor kidney to become available; but UC San Francisco alleged that in 25 cases of a perfect match, the Kaiser HMO refused to outsource the transplanting procedure to avoid the delays occurring in Kaiser's own system.[6]

There were warning signs. UC Davis had warned Kaiser officials that the switch would require patients to wait longer, from 1.5 to 3.6

years, for a transplant; but Kaiser allegedly failed to notify its patients of this observation. Instead, it informed them that they could obtain transplants only at Kaiser facilities (even though Medicare enrollees were insured for transplantation elsewhere).[7]

When the smoke cleared, the federal government overseers investigating the case concluded that virtually every part of Kaiser's program failed patients.[8] A clerk with no written evidence of training, for example, was responsible for coordinating highly complex information with organ banks that procured the kidneys for transplant candidates.[9] At one point, there were 1,000 incomplete records of the medical history of these gravely ill kidney transplant patients. Three RNs had little knowledge of the care required for pretransplant patients.[10]

The report especially faulted Kaiser's quality control.[11] "There was no evidence that operations and other components of the program were being reviewed and evaluated to ensure the delivery of quality care to patients."[12] Insiders who complained were fired or placed "on leave." One kidney specialist simply walked out and never returned.[13] By May 2006, only one specialist was left, a doctor-manager who had been relieved of the administrative responsibilities she once held. Other hospitals typically employed at least four to five transplant nephrologists for this patient load.[14] The HMO's leadership seemed unaware or unconcerned that its critically ill transplant patients were at risk.[15]

The head of the transplant program's lawsuit for wrongful termination was settled by Kaiser without comments.[16] The complaint states that he "discovered that the program was so poorly organized and unprofessionally managed that it failed to comply with state and federal requirements and was compromising patient care, leading to unnecessary suffering and possibly deaths." After his numerous complaints went unheeded and he was terminated, he felt compelled to alert the media and state and federal regulatory agencies, including the California Department of Managed Health Care, the U.S. Department of Justice, and the Medical Board of California. Lawsuits followed.[17] In early 2007, as I write this, the story is far from over. One other plaintiff alleged that when he expressed his fears about the damage the delay was causing him because he had already been a dialysis patient for six years, a Kaiser doctor advised him to obtain his transplant overseas.[18]

The steady bombardment of media stories and government requirements eventually prompted Kaiser to shut down the transplant program in May 2006 and transfer the patients awaiting surgery back to the UC Davis and San Francisco Medical Centers.[19] Kaiser was also required to pay $2 million to the California Department of Managed Health Care, the largest fine in the department's history, and $3 million to an organ-donation organization.[20] But where was the care and concern that should characterize a health service organization? Where was Kaiser's soul?

The evidence suggests a failure of the managerial system at Kaiser, a failure I attribute to the erosion of the culture of excellence that once made Kaiser a model for the managed care movement in the rest of the industry.

What Happened to Managed Care?

All great organizations—families, tribes, companies—are made great by their culture—a shared set of values, expectations, and modes of behavior—forged by a long, closely examined history of successes and failures. In the beginning, Kaiser's culture was dedicated to delivering high-quality, efficient care to its patients. Its doctors, executives, and enrollees understood that this was not a mere business; it was a movement in which they would jointly manage health care.[21] But by the time people like Jack Morgan needed their help, HMOs like Kaiser were more businesses than movements.

Initially, Kaiser was a classic entrepreneurial nonprofit—it did good and it did well. Like so many other social innovations—the environmental movement; the women's and minorities' liberation movements; the Salvation Army—it began with the best of motives: to provide cost-effective health care. It managed care through two important innovations: an unusual organizational structure, which vertically integrated physicians, hospitals, and insurance firms with each other, and prepayment.

Kaiser's novel integration of providers and insurers was crucially important to its success: it aligned their separate interests in providing good health care and in doing so at an affordable price. (In contrast, as we saw in Paul's case, independent insurers and providers are typically at each other's throats because their aims conflict: health insurers that do not own hospitals or employ an exclusive team of doctors aim to minimize medical costs, while health care providers that are not integrated with an insurer want to maximize the use of their services.) Kaiser's integrated structure helped to align the hospitals', doctors', and insurers' interests in the overall welfare of the organization—good medical care at a reasonable price.

Prepayment was novel and important too. Kaiser's founders believed that prepaid health care would induce doctors to provide preventive measures and wellness so the enrollee would not get sick. Typically, physicians and hospitals are paid only for treating sick patients, not for keeping them healthy. In contrast, the idea behind the HMOs was that providers who were prepaid for their services would have a financial incentive to keep their patients healthy.

Kaiser was widely cited as the model for the managed care organizations that proliferated in the United States in the late 1980s. Yet, although a few vertically integrated Kaiser clones already existed, most of the new managed care firms were no Kaisers. For one thing, they were not integrated. Instead, insurers merely cobbled together a disparate network consisting of physicians and hospitals that were willing to accept their low payments. The health care providers continued to work for themselves. They were, in effect, contract workers paid to perform particular services who had no allegiance to the insurer. Indeed, providers frequently resented the insurers as a result of the treatment they received, including late and stingy payments and "gatekeepers" to ensure that enrollee patients were not referred to "unneeded" services.

Although the insurers were prepaid for their services, most of these independent providers were not. They had no financial incentive to promote wellness. And even in the cases where the providers were prepaid, the payment was sometimes so stringent that providers felt pressured to skimp even on medical therapies.[22] A doctor who receives an adequate payment per patient is motivated to keep patients healthy. But if the prepayment is too stingy, he may reluctantly decide to skimp on this kind of preventive care.

Some of these kinds of HMOs transformed the managed care movement from social entrepreneurship into the worst kind of business—the kind that injures its customers. Meanwhile, their CEOs became dazzlingly wealthy, with compensation topping even that of other corporate CEOs. Dr. Norman Payson, the CEO of Oxford Health Plans, a firm notorious for its mismanagement with regulators, the health care industry press, and physicians,[23] earned $73 million when the firm was finally sold.[24] I do not begrudge Bill Gates his billions from Microsoft—or any other corporate leader's compensation from creating wealth and opportunity. But I do begrudge the millions earned off the backs of patients, who were denied the services that are rightfully theirs, and doctors, whose autonomy and spirit were broken.

At their end, managed care executives believed that their networks—that is, groups of doctors and hospitals—were the keys to their success. With the right network, groups to which they paid relatively low prices and that were acceptable to enrollees, the managed care firm would flourish.

No. Wrong.

By accepting this simplistic abstraction, the insurers ignored the many complex, diverse interactions that must guide the applications of medical principles to an individual.

And in the process they helped Jack Morgan to die prematurely.

It's the Culture, Stupid

George H. W. Bush began his 1992 reelection campaign in the warm glow of a dazzling U.S. military victory in the Persian Gulf War. He was a sure bet. After all, Bush was a military hero, a patrician

Yale Phi Beta Kappa, a true public servant, whereas his opponent was the virtually unknown governor of one of the nation's poorest states, tarred with unsavory allegations of sexual and financial transgressions. But Bush lost the election to his opponent, William J. Clinton.

What happened? As Clinton's political advisors crowed, Bush missed the obvious: "It's the economy, stupid." The U.S. economy was in the doldrums, and Americans vote for their pocketbooks.

Many smart people replicate Bush's mistake: they miss the obvious. Those who believe that mere organizational structures and characteristics such as a network are *the* key to performance similarly miss the obvious. It is, above all, the culture that counts.

In many organizations, the culture—an attitude, a way of doing things, a set of values—is so deeply internalized that it is not readily observable. Nevertheless, it is the key to their success. The Salvation Army, for example, has survived for more than a hundred years as a missionary organization that provides loving care to the destitute in part because of its culture—many of its members consider themselves soldiers in God's Army.[25] When cultured organizations become uncultured—by distancing themselves from their internalized values, attitudes, and approaches—they fail. Consider Enron, which drove amazing growth through its entrepreneurial culture as an energy trading firm. But when its executives fell in love with their bonuses, their skyrocketing salaries, and their images as portrayed on Wall Street and elsewhere, they sought endless expansion in earnings, leading to the erosion of their culture.

When health care organizations lose their culture, they can kill people in the process.

The Care and Feeding of Culture

What is culture? Where does it originate? How does it sustain itself?

All cultured organizations are essentially religious—they may not revolve around God, but they hold a core set of spiritual values that inform their actions. What can we learn about the formation of culture from the formation of a religious organization? How does a group of people come to share a set of values that are so powerful that they can be maintained across centuries and geographies?

As one example, let us examine the history of the Israelites, a group whose culture has long survived despite its members' geographical dispersion and nomadic existence. This culture was forged during the 40 years that Moses led the Israelites in the desert.[26] It was strengthened by successful responses to external and internal challenges.

Consider, for example, the effect on the Israelites of the pursuit by the Egyptians. At first, they cry:

> Let us alone that we may serve Egypt!
> Indeed, better for us serving Egypt
> Than our dying alone in the wilderness!
> (Exodus 14:12)

But after Moses leads them to safety through a sea, "the people trusted in God and in Moses his servant" (Exodus 14:31).

The desert itself, parched and desolate, helped to forge the culture. So did responses to internal challenges. When the monotheistic Hebrews strayed and worshiped multiple gods in heathen fertility rites, for example, the Bible approvingly recounts that one of Moses' followers thrust a javelin "through the man of Israel, and the woman through her belly" (Numbers 25:8).

Culture does not inevitably require charismatic leaders. When God commands a stuttering Moses to lead the Israelites out of Egypt, for example, he pleads:

> Please, my lord,
> No man of words am I. . . .
> For heavy of mouth and heavy of tongue am I!
> (Exodus 4:10)

But Moses is a good leader—one with a steadfast vision. Born an Israelite, raised as an Egyptian prince, forced to flee Egypt to maintain his identity, Moses had the clarity of vision of those who define themselves. And, as in all successful cultures, he did not work alone. He forged powerful alliances with people who had complementary skills: his eloquent, weak brother Aaron and his ferocious enforcers, the sons of Levi. His ultimate ally becomes his successor—the clever, courageous Joshua, who leads the Israelites out of the desert.

Myth or reality? Considerable archeological evidence supports the major elements of the story told in Exodus; but even if the physical evidence were absent, the psychological elements of the story ring true. It seems right that cultures are formed from an unusual point of view, refined and strengthened by external and internal challenges, and led by a group of people with complementary skills. Failures and hardships define a culture as much as its successes. The culture survives its immediate leaders and is passed on from one generation to the next, in part through continual repetition of the pivotal events in its formation.

The Cultured Kaiser Permanente

All of the key positive elements of culture were present in the early days of the Kaiser Foundation Health Plan. It too was founded in the desert, in the 1930s, by flawed leaders who had complementary skills. It too was strengthened by numerous internal and external challenges. By 1992, Kaiser was so widely admired that it served as the model for President and Hillary Clinton's national health care reform initiative.

Sound evidence supported their enthusiasm for Kaiser. It was among the largest health care providers in the United States— covering more than 9 million people in 1995[27]—and it was rated among the country's best HMOs by popular consumer publications.[28] Kaiser's excellence was also evidenced by its size: had it been a public corporation, its 1992 revenues of $11 billion and profits of $796 million would have placed it forty-third on the list of the Fortune 500.[29]

Out of the Desert

The early version of Kaiser developed its culture the old-fashioned way: it earned it, building it up over the years and supporting it with the investment of billions of dollars. Its founders had a long and productive history of collaboration, as did its other principals. Like the Israelites, who, after 40 years of wandering in the desert with Moses, developed a clear, cohesive identity, these early Kaiserites literally lived together in the desert for five years in the 1930s and in geographically isolated sites during World War II. External challenges from hostile medical associations and Communist witch hunter Senator Joseph McCarthy, as well as internal challenges from dissident physician groups, strengthened the organization. Failures helped to clarify its culture as much as successes did.

As told by John G. Smillie in *Can Physicians Manage the Quality and Costs of Health Care?* the story begins, in 1933, with Sidney Garfield, an entrepreneurial physician who, in the Mojave Desert, built a hospital and employed doctors to provide health care for the workers who constructed the Los Angeles aqueduct. Virtually from the inception of his career, Garfield was a practical businessman. He insisted, for example, on prepayment for his services: "The insurance companies held the money but they were anxious to keep it. We would treat a patient with tender loving care and, more often than not, the (insurers) would discount our bill, saying we had treated the patient too many times."[30] Later, Garfield learned that prepayment also motivated doctors to try to correct problems that could create the need for more expensive health care in the future. This mindset applied even to safety concerns outside doctors' usual realm of activity. For example, to avoid head injuries caused by loose rocks in the aqueduct, Garfield convinced the contractors to shore up areas he identified as dangerous.

At the end of the aqueduct project, Garfield had managed to accumulate $250,000 in profits (at a time when the average annual wage was $1,350). Garfield's tight rein on the purse strings was legendary. For example, "employees could obtain a new pencil only if they turned in a pencil stub of three inches or less. A Pencil Stub Club rewarded those who had served the organization for 35 years with a stub-shaped lapel pin." Recalls an observer, "This period of stringent economy established a pattern of frugal allocation of resources that persisted even into more prosperous years. Formed by these early economies, the physicians and staff, as a matter of institutional culture, continued to abhor waste."

Garfield imbued this culture in the physicians who worked for him, some of whom he had met as fellow medical students. For example, Garfield's physicians worked six days a week on one project, but "there was no complaining." For one thing, the physicians formed a tight social group: "We picked people who liked each other—we felt like we were enjoying ourselves." For another, Garfield was one of the guys; he worked alongside the other physicians and continually sought out their advice about new ideas. Garfield understood the importance of this culture, although likely he didn't use the word. For example, he attributed the failure to provide cost-effective health services in one project to people who "were not interested in making our plan work."

The five-year sojourn in the desert laid the foundation for the organization's culture, which balanced health care quality and costs, and for the lifelong business partnership between Garfield and industrialist Henry J. Kaiser. They joined forces after the aqueduct project when Kaiser tapped Garfield to set up a similar project during construction of Grand Coulee Dam. Garfield, a reserved, enigmatic physician, was drawn to the ebullient, expansive Kaiser, a man who claimed he could accomplish the seemingly impossible. Kaiser, who saw himself as a benevolent employer, wanted Garfield to provide health care to his workers in various geographically isolated construction and World War II defense contract sites.

Both men were self-created. Garfield was the son of Jewish immigrants whose self-creation even extended to fashioning a new surname. Kaiser, for his part, had abandoned his home and school after the eighth grade to seek his fortune. He ultimately built an empire based on his organizational skills: construction, ships, steel, cement, autos, hotels—he did them all. "Rome wasn't built in a day," he bragged, "because the Romans didn't give us a contract."

The bond between the two ran deep, so deep that it cries out for a Freudian analysis. Garfield always referred to Kaiser as "the boss" and docilely concurred with Kaiser's critiques of his management style: "Mr. Kaiser doesn't have any confidence in my ability to manage the program, and everyone agrees [that] . . . strong leadership hasn't emerged yet." Eventually, he even became Kaiser's brother-in-law, despite the 24-year difference in their ages, marrying the sister of Kaiser's second wife.

After Garfield successfully provided health care to Kaiser's workers during World War II, he established a private prepaid group practice. Only the true believers joined him: in Northern California, that meant a scant 13 physicians who would form the core of the new practice. In 1945, the nonprofit Permanente Health Plan was formed. Garfield, who owned the physicians' group and headed the hospitals owned by the Permanente Foundation, effectively ran the show, although the Henry J. Kaiser Company had formal control.

Garfield's unilateral management became increasingly untenable as the organization grew. In 1948, he withdrew from administration of the medical group. He noted, "I did this with complete faith—blind faith—that these changes would not alter the situation. We doctors had conceived the plan, developed it, sacrificed for it, made it work, and believed that it was going to remain in operation." Garfield knew he had developed a culture that would survive him.

Strengthened by Fire

The belief in the virtues of a prepaid managed care group was strengthened by the attacks of medical societies that routinely rejected Permanente physicians for membership. The independent doctors viewed the Kaiser physicians not only as economic threats but also as compromisers of physician independence because they permitted a nonphysician board to control them. The societies also questioned whether prepayment would motivate physicians to provide fewer services than needed. These attacks backfired, however. For example, Paul de Kruif, a well-known author whose son was a

Kaiser doctor, defended the organization in a series of widely read *Reader's Digest* articles, thus bringing it to the sympathetic attention of the public.

The charges of Communist ties among Kaiser physicians, which began in the late 1940s and intensified during the Senate investigations chaired by the Communist witch hunter Senator Joseph McCarthy, also strengthened the organization. When Henry Kaiser fired three physicians because of his concern that the charges levied against them would compromise the Kaiser Company's defense contracts, the medical group urged increased self-governance. As one physician skeptically observed, the Kaiser higher-ups "were telling us what a good job we were doing but [that] really we ought to spend our efforts in taking care of the patients . . . and they would run the business. We had sense enough to feel this wasn't quite right. Providing medical care was itself a business."

Yet the medical group's attempt to build its own vertically integrated system in San Diego, complete with hospitals and health plan, floundered. The physicians learned that they needed the culture engrained in Kaiser's hospital and insurance arms to succeed. Similarly, when Henry Kaiser tried and failed to replicate the system in Hawaii by converting five successful fee-for-service physicians to a medical group style of practice, he was forced to bring in the true believers—Garfield and his prepaid group practice acolytes from California.

These failures were deeply etched into the organization's consciousness: the three components of the organization understood how much they needed each other and forged ways to work together.

Kaiser Permanente's Culture Disintegrates

The founders of Kaiser Permanente and its culture had a novel vision: prepaid health care services delivered by an integrated troika of insurers, medical groups, and hospitals. This cultured organization achieved great financial and medical success. And deservedly so.

Kaiser's 1992 selection by some health care reformers as the model for the U.S. health care system seemed like its apotheosis. Instead, that year marked the beginning of a period of turmoil and decline for the organization.

By October 1997, Kaiser's chief financial officer announced the company's first-ever loss, which she estimated at $30 to $50 million. She proved embarrassingly wrong. The loss for the year turned out to be $270 million.[31] An organization's inability to forecast its earnings correctly is usually viewed as a serious problem, perhaps even more serious than a loss in itself, because it frequently indicates a fundamental lack of managerial control.

And indeed, there were other signs at that time that the fabled Kaiser had lost its way.

To implement an ambitious growth strategy, Kaiser had abandoned its adherence to prepayment, to integration, and to physicians and hospitals who believed in managed care. In 1994, the organization's chairman deplored legislation that would have required Kaiser's plan to abandon its medical groups and include any provider willing to accept Kaiser's fee, noting that it "would seriously undermine or eliminate our ability" to provide high-quality, cost-effective care.[32] But by 1998, he introduced a systemwide health insurance plan that enabled enrollees to visit non-Kaiser doctors for additional fees. Indeed, in some areas, Kaiser's insurance plans had no doctors who were exclusively affiliated with them.

To staff its growth, Kaiser sought out new managers (one estimate placed 50 to 60 percent of its top managers as new to their positions and 20 to 30 percent as new to the organization) and new acquisitions.[33] For example, Kaiser purchased health plans from public for-profit HMOs, like Humana, that had little ideological kinship with its nonprofit insurance plan. By 1998, Kaiser's chairman acknowledged that many of these expansions were spin-off or sale candidates because of substantial losses, up to a billion dollars.[34]

Kaiser's problems were not solely financial. The quality of care in its Texas plan triggered a critical report by the state insurance department, later settled by a fine. Kaiser subsequently sold the plan.[35] When the Texas plan's assets were sold in 1998, the buyer did not pick up obligations for its malpractice suits. A California state inspection found serious deficiencies in its hospitals. Labor problems abounded too. Thousands of unionized Kaiser workers picketed the organization. A nurse at Kaiser's Oakland facility who was not bound by gag rules noted, "We've watched the quality of care go downhill." The California Nurses Association successfully struck against Kaiser, in part because of its concern that the organization was spending $60 million on marketing while laying off nurses. Doctors were unhappy too, some even proposing affiliations with other plans.

Kaiser's explanations for these problems followed the PR 101 lines of firms that are in denial: the loss? "We missed the price turn in the industry."[36] Employee and quality problems? "That's a flat lie. These are human systems. . . . They don't work because there are honest mistakes."[37] Problems in Texas? "The media often focus on isolated incidents that are unrelated to the things being done to make the organization stronger."[38]

But Kaiser's problems indicated a profound problem, one much more fundamental than errors in human systems or forecasting costs: Kaiser had strayed from its cultural roots. Kaiser's growth strategy caused membership to soar, but it nearly lost its soul in the process. The culture-imbued physicians, the hospitals man-aged directly by Kaiser, the seasoned insurance officials who worked with the providers to balance health care quality and cost, the tense interplay among the three elements of the system—all of these were diminished in a growth strategy in which Kaiser embraced physicians it did not know, hospitals it did not manage, and geographical regions whose politics and populace it did not fully understand.

Do not get me wrong. I do not question the intelligence, energy, honesty, or motives of Kaiser's management. But growth at the expense of culture vitiates the elements that establish a company's success. It is like building a flashy home extension without a foundation. Absent the financial and health care quality controls internalized by the Garfield-era doctors, managers, and their progeny, their shared history and sense of purpose, such losses and allegations of quality problems are no surprise. As Sidney Garfield prophetically noted: "If you don't have the . . . groups who have it in their hearts to make it work and who believe in prepaid practice, it won't work. This is the thing that makes me wonder about HMOs all over the country. They aren't going to work unless they get men who really believe in giving service to the people."[39]

Corporate Managed Care: Straying from the Kaiser Culture

As it matured, the managed care movement cast Kaiser's integrated model by the wayside. After all, building hospitals and financing doctors' groups, as Kaiser had done, required billions of dollars of investment, and developing a corporate culture required decades of time.

The new moguls of managed care did not have this kind of time or that kind of money: they could not rely on a deeply embedded culture and an integrated doctor-hospital-insurer organization to craft better, cheaper ways of delivering health care. Instead, they controlled costs by "just saying no": no to payments to providers; no to requests from enrollees for referrals to specialists; no to hospital admissions—no, no, and no some more. At the peak of managed care's sway, in 1999, far more physicians were financially rewarded for productivity by the insurers than for patient satisfaction.[40]

A managed care organization with the unintentionally ironic name of U.S. Healthcare exemplified this new breed of HMO. Formed as a nonprofit organization funded by a government loan, it did not take long for its CEO to figure out that there was gold in them thar managed care hills. Six years after its founding, U.S. Healthcare was a publicly traded company, renowned for its low prices, attained with the metaphorical brass knuckles it wore when reimbursing providers. In a key market, its practices so worried a competitor, a traditional health insurer, that it took out ads to decry U.S. Healthcare's strict, severe gatekeeper rules for referrals to emergency rooms and specialists. Bad mistake. When U.S. Healthcare sued, guess who won?

By 1996, Aetna, another traditional health insurer worn down by competition with these managed care start-ups, purchased U.S. Healthcare for $9 billion. U.S. Healthcare's founder, a pharmacist, earned nearly a billion dollars in the process.[41] Aetna was so confident that its purchase would enable it to expand U.S. Healthcare's success that it exited all other product lines, such as property and casualty insurance.

Although these new managed care organizations were no Kaisers, most of the academic health care policy world was delirious about their prospects. The academics believed that big systems and big organizations were needed to oversee individual physicians. They questioned the health care quality and cost controls of doctors who worked for themselves in small groups. The new organizations' just-say-no version of managed care met the academics' view of appropriate health care because it meshed with their technocratic skills of evaluating the cost-effectiveness of medical care.[42]

In November 1999, *Health Affairs*, a leading academic health care public policy journal, published a lengthy, fawning interview that allowed Aetna's CEO to share his wisdom with its academic readers.[43] The interviewer seemed oblivious to the fact that Aetna's hardball managed care practices were widely excoriated by patients and providers. As Aetna's reputation soured, along with those of other managed care players, its share price tumbled.[44] Very soon after the laudatory *Health Affairs* interview was published, Aetna's CEO was forced to resign.[45]

The academic touting of the virtues of managed care convinced politicians as astute as former President Bill Clinton and his wife, New York Senator Hillary Rodham Clinton, for a while to go out on a limb in support of plans like U.S. Healthcare; but doing so turned out to be a costly mistake. They did not appreciate the public's and doctors' disdain for this kind of "just-say-no" health insurer. They failed to achieve their plan to offer universal health care coverage in the United States, in large part, because they chose managed care as its centerpiece.[46]

HMOs Are Market Driven? Huh?

To promote their adoption by a skeptical public, managed care firms like U.S. Healthcare were touted as "market-driven" clones of Kaiser that would compete with each other to make health care better and cheaper; but, in truth, most of them were controlled by third-party technocrats rather than entrepreneurial providers. They were miles apart from the original version of Kaiser, whose providers were intent on re-creating health care so that it responded to consumers' needs for efficient, personalized services.

Market-driven industries rely on interactions between customers and providers, supply and demand. Picture the dynamic retailing industry as a model of this interaction. In retailing, companies have succeeded when they have paid attention to some unfulfilled consumer need, such as Target for fashion-conscious budget shoppers and Whole Foods for the organic set, and they have failed when they have stopped listening, like Kmart. But with this new breed of managed care, patients and doctors were minor players. Nobody listened to them. Instead, a third party, a gatekeeper, controlled all the action.

Technocrats can only ration what exists; they typically lack the business and medical skills, vision, and daring needed to create new, better ways of delivering health care. They are not entrepreneurial: technocrats can say yes or no, but they cannot create innovations. The technocrats' notion of managing health care involved reducing payments to hospitals and doctors and weaning consumers away from wasteful, expensive specialists. As one analysis noted, "Most (but not all) HMOs have not accomplished what their proponents had promised: changing clinical practice processes and improving quality of care relative to the existing system."[47]

These technocratic managed care policies were so widely deplored that they became the stuff of humor. For example, one Web site posted the following satirical headline:

> ### New HMO Strategy: Pay Health Claims
> ### *Analysts Skeptical; Doubt Insurers Equipped to Handle Job*
> Minneapolis, Minn. (SatireWire.com)—Moving into what insurance executives concede is "uncharted territory," five of the nation's leading HMOs announced yesterday they will begin paying health insurance claims for sick and injured people.[48]

To most Americans, HMOs had the cold, hard heart of an under-ripe cheese.

Managed care's just-say-no strategy is generally conceded to be a failure. Nevertheless, academic die-hards continue to point to past reductions in the annual increases of the insurance premiums paid by employers as evidence of managed care's efficacy. For example, some attribute the drop in premium inflation from 1993 to 1996 to the effect of managed care.[49]

But the role that managed care played in causing this reduction is questionable. After all, many other cost-reducing events occurred during this period too. For one, general inflation dropped dramatically—the consumer price index declined by nearly 50 percent from 1993 to 1998.[50] And, from 1997 to 1999, the U.S. government's massive Medicare health insurance program for the elderly put harsh new payment rules into effect, which caused providers to decrease their costs substantially. For example, Medicare's payment rate per beneficiary declined by about one-third for home health costs and by 5 percent for outpatient hospital costs.[51] These payment declines caused suppliers to reduce their costs, not to shift them to other insurers. To the contrary, during this period, Medicare paid providers 100 percent or more of its costs.[52] Last, to gain market share, some insurers incurred significant underwriting losses during this period, effectively decreasing their prices by absorbing cost increases.[53] For example, the Blue Cross and Blue Shield plans that earned a small profit in 1994 experienced losses of 1.2 percent in 1997.[54]

In other words, the 1990s reductions in the inflation of health insurance prices paid by employers should not be credited solely, or even primarily, to the impact of the just-say-no managed care insurers. The reductions were also affected by the generally lower level of inflation in the economy, cost-reducing pressure on providers from Medicare, and price competition among insurers, who were willing to incur losses in an attempt to gain market share.

The Managed Care Phoenix: Rising from the Ashes

It did not take long for the just-say-no version of managed care to unravel. Health insurance plans that provide easier access to specialists and hospitals now dominate. These preferred-provider-organization (PPO) plans enable enrollees to use the doctor or hospital of their choice for a higher price or use the "preferred providers" for a lower price.

Yet even as their just-say-no strategy was coming apart at the seams, managed care organizations retained a considerable part of their expensive gatekeeper infrastructure. This time around, they promise to control costs by actually managing care, especially for the victims of chronic diseases and disabilities, rather than just saying no. "Disease management" is their new mantra.

But the current version of managed care is unlikely to manage health care any more effectively or efficiently than the old just-say-no one. There is no accepted evidence of the cost effectiveness of disease management.[55] Managing the delivery of health care services is the right idea, especially in the case of sick people, like Jack Morgan, because most health care costs are incurred by people who suffer from chronic diseases and whose care is mismanaged.[56] There are considerable opportunities to innovate medical care, as described in Chapter 7; but insurers are unlikely agents of these changes. The fundamental premise of a top-down strategy in which an insurer manages how hundreds of thousands of independent physicians, multi-billion-dollar medical technology firms, and thousands of hospitals deliver medical care to millions of people is dubious. It is as questionable as the premise that automobile insurers can rescue the U.S. automobile industry by telling manufacturers how to make better, cheaper cars.

Can you imagine GEICO, the automobile insurance company, asserting that it can manage the sickly automotive manufacturers, Ford and General Motors, back to health? Of course not. GEICO may be a wonderful automobile insurance firm, but its executives would probably quickly admit they do not know how to make cars. Health insurance executives and their academics groupies, however, lack this kind of self-awareness and humility. Filled with hubris, they moan and groan about the providers' "low compliance" with the insurers' care management advice, mysteriously baffled by the reluctance of independent professionals who are legally liable for the quality of care to "comply" with the strictures of health insurance officials who not so long ago made these professionals' lives a misery.[57]

Productivity gains arise primarily from innovations driven by entrepreneurs. Productivity rises organically, not technocratically. We celebrate Thomas Edison, Henry Ford, and Sam Walton because they transformed how energy was used, cars were manufactured, and goods were sold. We do not celebrate them because they muscled down their suppliers' prices and barred consumers from needed goods. Entrepreneurs, not bureaucrats, create the innovations that increase productivity.

At this point, reductions in health insurance premiums are a relic of the past. The underwriting losses incurred in 1998, 1 percent in the case of the Blues, were the last straw. Health insurers have since raised their rates in successful efforts to restore their underwriting profitability.[58] Meanwhile, underlying health care costs have shot up once again.

Back to Basics: What Is Health Insurance All About?

If the just-say-no policies and other costly, ineffective, top-down strategies of the managed care form of health insurance help to kill patients like Jack Morgan, what are the alternatives? We cannot do without health insurance. We need it primarily to protect us financially if we incur medical costs that are catastrophically high.

The first health plans for U.S. workers were designed to do just that. They compensated victims for loss of income when an accident or illness caused extended disability. In 1863, Travelers Insurance Company offered death or permanent disability benefits, and in 1899 Aetna and Travelers sold a temporary disability plan "occasioned by all diseases except tuberculosis, venereal disease, insanity, or disabilities due to alcohol or narcotics." The first business-based group plan, organized by Montgomery Ward in 1910, was cut from the

same cloth, intended to protect workers from the financial consequences of loss of income due to catastrophic illness.[59]

How can we get health insurance plans that protect us against
bankruptcy without subjecting us to the oversight of managed care
gatekeepers? One simple way is to change their coverage.

Recent innovations in the design of health insurance policies illustrate the potential impact of this different kind of health insurance.
A 2006 analysis of new health insurance plans that required the
enrollees to pay up to $2,000 out of their own pocket before insur-
ance coverage began found that their premiums were up to 35 percent lower than plans that offered comparable benefits and that their
costs grew at significantly lower rates.[60] Separate analyses revealed
that enrollees in such plans—called "high-deductible plans"—used
health care resources in significantly different ways, when compared
to their usage patterns before they were enrolled in a high-deductible
plan and to a matched control group: they used less of the emergency room and hospital and fewer drugs and yet engaged in more
preventive care, such as yearly physical examinations. Those who
had chronic diseases complied more with the drug regimens that are
key to their health status.[61]

When the consultancy McKinsey asked the enrollees in these
high-deductible plans why they had improved their health care
behaviors, they answered, "If I catch an issue early, I will save money
in the long term" at significantly higher rates than a matched sample of those with conventional insurance plans.[62]

Traditional plans were called "first-dollar coverage" because they
paid for virtually all the expenses of the care provided by doctors and
hospitals, not only the expenses that we could not afford. These
insurance plans were begun during the depression to protect the
providers' income, not ours. At that time, several hospitals initiated
prepayment plans to guarantee their revenues, and, in 1939, doctors
organized the Blue Shield insurance plans to pay for physician fees
in hospitals.

But as these plans proliferated, concerns began to arise that these
"first-dollar-coverage" health insurance policies disconnect the user

from the cost of health care. Fully insured patients might feel that their health care is free and become careless about how much they use or whether a provider gives them good values. After all, the nation's largest health insurance plans, Blue Cross and Blue Shield, were created by doctors and hospitals to protect their income. Yet, the conventional wisdom among health economists was that insurance had little to do with the growth in the cost of health care. Two analysts, for example, concluded that technology was the primary cost driver. They pegged the impact on the costs of health care on pocketbook issues, such as prices or income, at only around 20 percent.[63]

But a recent analysis, conducted by MIT economist Amy Finkelstein, suggests quite the opposite. She found that the increased availability of Medicare insurance funds accounted for more than half of the growth in health care spending between 1965 and 1970. Medicare increases caused new hospitals to enter and existing hospitals to expand their capacity. Further, the increased supply of hospital capacity may well have spilled over to those enrolled in other forms of insurance and increased their costs as well.[64] (Her results differ from the conventional wisdom because she examined the response of supply to increased demand, over a longer period of time.)

What did we receive for the increased expenditures induced by increases in health insurance? Finkelstein's analysis reveals no impact on death rates.[65] The only benefit she found was that out-of-pocket spending by the heavy users of health care declined substantially.

In other words, the increased availability of first-dollar-coverage insurance induced a large increase in spending with no discernible impact on death rates. The only corresponding benefit of providing the insurance was that of reducing out-of-pocket spending by the heavy users of health care. Had we simply paid their out-of-pocket needs directly, rather than with Medicare insurance benefits, total health care cost increases would have been significantly lower.

Finkelstein's analysis has important implications for the design of health insurance policies. It suggests that an alternative strategy to managed care is to permit consumers to manage their own demand by exposing them to more of the costs of health insurance, while protecting them against catastrophically high expenses.

What do you prefer? Insurance plans that motivate consumers to manage their health care or those that rely on third-party technocrats to do so?

High-deductible plans are only one example of health insurance plans that rely on consumers and doctors, rather than on technocrats, to manage their health care. In Chapters 7 and 8, we will examine the rich variety of consumer-driven health insurance plans that already have been created, even though the U.S. consumer-driven health care movement is in its infancy.

For Want of a Nail, Jack Morgan Died

At one time, the fabled HMO Kaiser exhibited a corporate culture that enabled it to offer high-quality health care at a reasonable price, and Kaiser still does a good job for many of its patients. But when Kaiser's managers decided to grow the organization, they wore down the foundations of this culture and lost a fortune in the process.

In all human activities, God is in the details, especially when it comes to taking care of seriously ill people. The management of the Kaiser HMO allegedly neglected these thousands of details in its kidney transplant program: it reportedly understaffed the program, fired or ignored employees who complained about its quality problems, and provided little support or training for those who remained. In 2006, after more than a hundred of the patients awaiting kidney transplantation died, Kaiser performed one merciful act: it closed the program.

Jack Morgan had little choice. He did not want to enroll with an HMO; but his only alternative to it was to become uninsured because his state regulated small business's health insurance heavily. Jack purchased insurance so that the HMO would keep him alive if he became sick.

But, instead, he got death. The insurer simply did not perform the transplant.

But why did Jack not simply pay for the kidney transplant out of his own pocket? After all, he was a solidly middle-class guy.

Jack knew that he could not afford to pay the price of a kidney transplant out of his own pocket. U.S. hospitals are far more expensive than those in other parts of the world. He knew that these hospitals charge their highest prices to the uninsured and that requests for discounts are often ignored. To the contrary, the hospitals would likely confiscate everything he owned if he failed to pay these high prices.

The story of how our hospitals, most of them nonprofit, became so bloated and greedy is told in the next chapter.

CHAPTER 3

KILLER NUMBER 2:
THE GENERAL HOSPITALS
Death at the Hands of
Empire Builders

T he general hospitals are both Dr. Jekyll and Mr. Hyde.
In the Dr. Jekyll role, their skilled, dedicated, often heroic personnel perform amazing surgeries and medical procedures that help many people to stay alive, frequently without pain or disability.

But then there is the Mr. Hyde side of these hospitals. Some charge uninsured people the very highest of prices, hound them for payment, and are so erratic in their quality that hospital patients feel they need to bring a loved one with them to oversee their care and protect their interests. All too many people die from an illness caused by the hospital.

The Mr. Hyde side helped kill Jack Morgan.

To comprehend the Dr. Jekyll side, consider the commonplace open-heart surgery and the astonishing skill and coordination it requires.

Imagine your chest caught in a vise. This pain is endured by people with blocked-up coronary arteries (the arteries that supply the heart muscle itself with oxygenated blood). If these symptoms are not relieved, they may well die.

The surgical procedure to bypass the blockage, called a *coronary artery bypass graft*, also known as a CABG and pronounced "cabbage," replaces the clogged-up portion of the artery with a section of a healthier blood vessel, taken from a vein in the leg or an artery beneath the breastbone. If the leg vein is to be used to bypass the coronary artery, one surgical team opens the leg from the groin to the ankle to remove the vein, hands it to the operating team, and then carefully closes the long incision. Another surgical team exposes the heart by cutting through the fat, muscle, and skin of the chest wall and sawing through the large breastbone that pro-tects it. Retractors forcibly hold the chest open as the gunked-up portion of the coronary artery is bypassed by segments snipped from the leg vein. The surgeon completes the procedure by closing up the chest.

During the procedure, the patient is one power shortage away from death. Because the vibration of a beating heart does not allow the exquisitely careful snipping and stitching that this procedure requires, the patient's heart is usually stopped for the duration of the surgery and an external heart-lung machine takes over its function. After the procedure is completed, the stilled heart is spurred back into action with warming or electrical shock.

These CABG patients may display two badges of their courage: a scar on their leg and another scar on their chest. They sometimes carry a third memento: a scar on their throat, which marks the site where a ventilator tube was inserted to help them breathe after the operation.

A CABG usually requires a surgical team consisting of a heart surgeon and resident, an anesthesiologist, a nurse anesthetist, a perfusionist to oversee the heart-lung machine, and at least two other nurses or technologists; three to four hours in the operating room; recovery in an intensive care unit staffed with highly trained nurses and cardiologists; and a minimum of two to five days of recuperation in the hospital.

Pretty awesome, no?

But a CABG is expensive. Indeed, on the Mr. Hyde side, U.S. hospitals are so expensive that even a solidly middle-class guy like Jack, with a good job and some retirement funds, could not possibly afford to pay the hundreds of thousands of dollars his kidney transplant operation required out of his own pocket. The expense would eat up his savings and take every penny he could squeeze out of his house. As the owner of a small business, Jack could obtain only HMO insurance because of the health insurance regulations in his state. And, in a complete Catch 22, his HMO insurer did not give Jack access to its own hospitals for a transplant.

So the general hospitals—meaning the kind of hospitals that do everything for everybody—helped to kill Jack Morgan because of their bloated costs. Most of us simply cannot afford to buy their services without health insurance. But even if Jack could have afforded the hospital costs, he might have died solely because of the mistakes they often make, like transplanting the wrong kidney, giving him a deadly infection, or simply ignoring his needs.

It does not have to be this way: U.S. hospitals are substantially more expensive than those in other countries that have standards of living comparable to ours, such as Germany.[1] And they are enormously more expensive than hospitals in developing countries, like India or Thailand. A kidney transplant in an Indian hospital would cost only $7,000 in 2006, for example, and Thailand offers first-rate care at prices as low as 10 percent of those of U.S. hospitals.[2] And they are lower cost because they use innovative organizational structures, not only because they are lower-wage economies. Innovative managerial practices enable health care facilities in the United States to achieve far better quality for the money than the general hospitals.

Why Are U.S. Hospitals So Low Quality, High Cost?

At nearly a trillion dollars in 2006, hospitals and their affiliates are the biggest and most rapidly growing part of the U.S. health care system. In the first half of 2004, their costs grew by 8.6 percent, accounting for more than half of total health care cost increases.[3] Yet their mammoth size and rapid growth are puzzling: the demand for their services has grown far more slowly than their costs. In 2003 and 2004, for example, hospital prices grew at least six times more than the growth in their utilization.[4] There are no noticeable commensurate increases in quality either. To the contrary, the hospital is an increasingly dangerous place for a sick person. "Adverse events," bureaucratese for mistakes that gravely injure the patient, affected nearly 400,000 cases in 2004. Between 1998 and 2004, tens of thousands died because of hospitals' "failure to rescue" and 32,000 had an "infection due to care."[5]

One analysis concluded that hospitals accounted for almost 50 percent of the excessive 2003 health care spending in the United States, relative to its wealth, versus other developed countries.[6] For example, U.S. per capita costs for hospital care, in 2004, exceeded Germany's by 34 percent.[7] Some claim that the U.S. hospitals incur higher costs because their patients are sicker than those in hospitals elsewhere. But U.S. per capita outpatient costs are four times those of Germany too. (The outpatient departments are often operated by hospitals for services, such as minor or minimally invasive surgeries, that require a hospital infrastructure if problems occur.) And the Germans have more beds available for their citizens and allow them to spend more time in the hospital.[8]

Bottom line? U.S. hospital beds cost more than those in Germany and other developed countries because we have allowed our hospitals to become fatter than hospitals elsewhere. Their sheer size and massive scope surely contribute to their quality problems. The scope of a general hospital is akin to that of a single company that manufactures computers, electronics, and agriculture. U.S. expenditures for cancer, for example, are roughly equal to spending of the manufacturers of computer and electronics products, while expenditures for diabetes exceed those of our mining sector.[9] These are but two of the thousands of problems confronting hospitals. It is virtually impossible for one organization to effectively manage such a large range of sizable activities.

You might think that I do not admire the people who work in hospitals. But, to the contrary, I greatly admire those who provide the medical care—nurses, doctors, aides, technicians, administrators of wards and clinics, and so on. They are generally skilled, compassionate, dedicated, and hardworking. So are the administrators who manage logistics, finance, supplies, accounting, and quality control, among other support functions. There are some great CEOs too, such as Paul Levy at Boston's Beth Israel Hospital. But some of the top executives of U.S. hospitals are cut from a different cloth. They are, purely and simply, empire builders. To support their empire building, they have suppressed the kind of competition and important managerial innovations that could control costs, and they have acted less than charitably toward the poor uninsured.

Hospitals have noble, charitable origins. In Medieval times, for example, they were operated by religious orders, in various parts of the world, to provide care for the poor. They were "hospitable" in all senses of the word. U.S. hospital executives continue to flaunt this religious, charitable background and their "nonprofit" status as evidence of the hospitals' sanctity and selfless service mentality; but the behavior of some of these hospitals hardly qualifies them for sainthood. Like the managed care insurers, these general hospitals have lost their souls.

Jack Morgan knew from his own experience that nonprofit hospitals charged their uninsured patients higher prices than they charged their insured patients and that they used hardball tactics to collect these inflated charges. Jack Morgan and his wife, a two-career couple, had employed a housekeeper, an immigrant to the United States, for more than 20 years. They treated her well: they had sponsored her citizenship, hired her immigration lawyer, and paid her middle-class wages. They even offered to pay for three-fourths of the cost of a health insurance policy or her actual health care expenses.

But the housekeeper, who was in her sixties, chose to work only half-time. Her income qualified her for care at her local "safety-net hospital." She turned down the insurance, reasoning that her 25 percent share of health costs would be low at this institution, which received almost half a billion dollars annually to provide care for the uninsured at reduced prices. Wrong!

She paid sky-high prices—$450 for a shoulder X ray, for example. Nobody except the uninsured was charged such high prices. And she had to pay $1,400 out of her pocket before she qualified for any care. If she failed to pay any of this, the hospital denied her access to the drugs she relied on for her chronic disease.

But the hospitals' outrageous treatment of the uninsured is not the worst of it. Hospitals have actively squashed the innovative competitors that threaten them. Hospitals induced the U.S. Congress to pass laws that inhibit competitors. And they have crafted consolidations, ostensibly to create economies of scale, that suppress competition. Rather than reducing costs, they have added to them. The added costs caused by hospital mergers from 1990 to 2003 have caused the loss of five million life years of private insurance.[10]

All this legislative activity is supported by millions in political contributions from U.S. hospitals, most of them nonprofit. In 2006, the American Hospital Association (AHA), which represents nonprofit hospitals, donated $1.8 million to federal candidates.[11]

Don't let them kid you. Some nonprofit hospitals earn considerable profits: the University of Pittsburgh Medical Center (UPMC) earned more than half a billion dollars in operating income, and a Catholic hospital chain had stashed away $4 billion in cash as of December 2006.[12] The profits earned by UPMC roughly equaled those earned by the world's largest drug distribution firm.[13]

Being "nonprofit" means only that hospitals cannot funnel profits to owners or shareholders. Instead, they plow their profits into cash reserves and massive building plans: hospital construction spending doubled from 1998 to 2005, and 85 percent of all nonprofit hospitals plan not only to replace what exists, but to add capacity.[14]

Last, with that kind of money floating around, nonprofit hospitals' CEOs can be a little less than saintly and selfless when it comes to their own salaries. The CEO of the safety-net hospital that Jack's housekeeper used, the hospital that charged her prices higher than any other class of patient, earned over a million dollars in 2005.[15] These sky-high salaries, profits, and cash balances, as well as the money dedicated to overly aggressive expansion, represent funds that could have been spent to pay for care of the poor uninsured or returned to us, their consumers, in the form of lower prices.

Most hospitals do not have massive profits, but that does not mean they are efficient. They may be bloated and inefficient, using their money for self-entrenchment or for services not in the public interest. If the hospitals were more efficient, millions more Americans could afford to buy health insurance, and people like Jack Morgan, whose insurer denies them needed services, could more readily afford to pay for these services out of their own pockets.

How Nonprofit, Charitable Hospitals Stop Competition

A shortage of competition enabled hospitals to become so big and fat.

Here's how they did it.

Let's walk through the huge oak doors of one hospital boardroom and visualize for a moment the hypothetical discussion that took place before its latest merger:

The chairman of the board sits at the head of an exquisite conference table, crafted, at exorbitant cost, of recycled materials, and nestled in an opulent corporate suite. Large, sparkling glass windows look out at the busy street below, while Oriental rugs with gently faded colors cushion the polished hardwood floors.

He is a short, squat man, his football playing muscles long ago turned to fat. When he was the CEO of a major advertising firm, he was much valued for his political skills, which are fully on display during this meeting:

"We are at war," the chairman declares, the folds on his face rippling with indignation. "Our biggest customer, the Blue Cross health insurer, is telling us that unless we cut our prices, they will give all their business to our rival hospital across town, St. Luke's. The Blues must think we are stupid. They think they can play our competitor St. Luke's off against us, getting each of us to cut our prices by threatening to go with the other hospital. Let's show them just how stupid they are.

"I propose we merge with St. Luke's. We will become the biggest hospital system in town, so big that the Blues will have to have us be part of their network. If they dare to exclude us, their enrollees will complain about lack of access. The move will not only keep our price structure intact, it may even allow us to gain some pricing power [a corporate code phrase that means "we can raise our prices without fear of price cutting by our competitors"]. I see big benefits in this for all of us."

The hospital's CEO nods in agreement. He is one of those hospital million-dollar babies. The board members nod too, although they are not well versed in the ins and outs of the hospital business. By and large, they are social arrivistas, newly successful corporate executives and lawyers who want to meet their city's elite, old-money, social strata by joining the board of a local nonprofit hospital. While their motives in joining the board are social, not substantive, they clearly understand the strategy the chairman begins to outline.

The strategy is simple: the firm "merges" with its rival hospital across town to control prices by suppressing competition. Not to worry—this will not be a real merger with the kinds of massive upheavals and layoffs that usually occur when two merged firms slim down to become an efficient one; it will be more of an unconsummated marriage whose purpose is other than conjugal. This merger will create a bargaining unit that can withstand the pressure of powerful insurers that are demanding price discounts.

Doesn't sound much like a warm, fuzzy, nonprofit institution, does it? Sounds more like one of those predatory Industrial Revolution companies that inspired "trust-busting" because they gobbled up other firms and formed cartels to limit price competition, doesn't it?

The boards of similar hospitals approved this strategy all across the country. Our little hospital boardroom scenario repeated itself in one form or another thousands of times. In a six-year period, 900 merger deals occurred, from a base of 6,100 hospitals.[16] Additionally, 2,700 hospitals affiliated with each other to become part of a megasystem.[17] The total number of hospitals decreased by more than 20 percent between 1970 and 2005.[18]

Hospitals gained approval of these mergers by claiming that they would bring about economies of scale,[19] but the promised economies have yet to appear as reduced prices to insurers or patients. To the contrary, consolidation has led to price increases of at least 40 percent and reduced quality.[20] Thus, hospital mergers increased the number who could no longer afford health insurance by nearly 700,000 people in 2003 and 5.5 million between 1990 and 2003.[21]

How could these mergers reduce costs when the careful, painful managerial rationalizations needed to reduce costs did not take place? The number of hospital systems organized with the sort of tough, centralized management that can squeeze out excess costs decreased sharply, while those with laissez-faire management increased.[22] Give the management of these integrated institutions credit for one thing: they were good at increasing prices.

Virtually overnight, the number of hospitals shrank dramatically.

Two or three hospital systems now dominate the markets in many large cities. How can you negotiate with a supplier who controls nearly all the capacity in an area?[23]

The government is supposed to protect us against suppliers' artificially constraining supply. Trustbusters usually judge undue concentrations in a market on the basis of the so-called Herfindahl-Hirschman Index (HHI). In many hospitals' markets, the level nearly doubled from 1990 to 2003.[24]

Were our overseers asleep at the switch? Well, yes and no. The feds tried to break up or nullify these mergers; but they failed. Between 1994 and 2000, one federal government agency lost a string of seven hospital merger cases.[25]

The nonprofit hospitals charged in the lawsuits wrapped themselves in a cloak of sanctity as their defense. They frequently averred they are nonprofit, they have no greedy owners who demand dividends, and they are doing the Lord's work. How can one dare to allege that they would engage in profit-maximizing sorts of activities? How can you doubt the word of a hospital called something like "Mount Sinai" or "City General" that has been a cornerstone of your community forever? Their presentation of their sanctified behavior was supported by an academic literature that assumes selflessness on the part of nonprofit organizations.[26]

Hospitals assured the public that the mergers had only the purest of motives: economies of scale would lower costs and enable the hospitals to provide more community benefits. Many local judges and juries bought the argument and permitted the mergers. Virtually overnight, in some parts of the country, the mergers almost eliminated any competition among hospitals.

But, far from providing more community benefits, the mergers created massive increases in prices and probable diminution in quality. One study showed that severely ill Medicare heart attack victims' expenses and mortality decreased in areas with more competition.[27]

Both nonprofit and for-profit hospitals acted alike in raising prices: one analysis revealed no difference between the willingness of nonprofit and for-profit hospitals to "exploit merger-related market power."[28] Nonprofits set lower prices but had higher markups.[29] (But nonprofits should have lower prices because the costs of nonprofits are lower. After all, because they are nonprofit, they do not have to pay income taxes, are usually excused from sales and real estate taxes, and can borrow with tax-subsidized municipal debt.[30] U.S. congressional staff members have estimated that these subsidies lowered the expenses of nonprofits by $13 billion in 2002.)[31]

One group was clearly reaping "community" benefits, however: the CEOs of some of the combined firms were earning multi-million-dollar salaries. But the other community benefits were so murky that a major Senate investigation of their existence was launched.

When Senator Chuck Grassley from Iowa, as part of this investigation, asked 10 nonprofit hospital systems if their charity policy requires providing certain amounts and types of charity care, an astounding 70 percent said "no."[32] A 2004 congressional comparison of nonprofit and for-profit hospitals found that, on average, nonprofit hospitals provided only 0.6 percent higher levels of uncompensated care than did otherwise similar for-profit hospitals. (Their analysis included bad debt as well as charity care. With this measure, every business whose customers do not pay their bills should qualify as a charitable institution.) Nonprofit hospitals were more likely than otherwise similar for-profit hospitals "to provide certain allegedly unprofitable specialized services, but they were found to serve fewer Medicaid-covered patients as a share of their total patient population. On average, nonprofit hospitals operated in areas with higher average incomes, lower poverty rates, and lower rates of uninsurance than for-profit hospitals."[33]

Indeed, the uninsured, the most financially vulnerable part of our health care system, encountered the very obverse of community benefits: ruthless collection tactics if they failed to pay their bills. The hospitals' collection agencies did not break legs, but they did confiscate homes and other personal assets. And the uninsured, many of them poor, were billed at the very highest prices the hospital charged. One uninsured man was billed $37,000 for hospital activities for which Medicare would pay $15,000. He was charged, for example, $1,050 for a medical device whose list price was $250 to $300.[34] Hospitals joined the credit card companies in lobbying for amendments to the Bankruptcy Code that have made it much harder for the working poor to extinguish their liability for unpaid hospital bills in bankruptcy.

It is not as if the hospitals needed the money collected from the uninsured: a number had earned substantial profits and had huge cash reserves and ambitious building programs. But sadly, all too few shared this wealth with the poor uninsured. Unfortunately, the Internal Revenue Service encouraged this lack of altruism in a series of revenue rulings commencing in 1969 that replaced the requirement set in 1956 that a nonprofit hospital seeking tax-exempt status must operate "to the extent of its financial ability" to provide services to those unable to pay[35] with one mandating only that the hospital promote health for the benefit of the community as a whole.[36]

There is a ray of legal sunlight, though. Notes my HBS colleague and lawyer, Professor Constance Bagley:

> *The government will finally break this losing streak if it wins the case it brought in 2004 to undo the acquisition of Highland Park Hospital by Evanston Northwestern Healthcare Corp. (ENH) in 2000. Seizing what he characterized as a "rare opportunity to examine 'the actual effect of concentration on price in the hospital industry,"*[37] *Judge Stephen J. McGuire ordered ENH in October 2005 to divest itself of Highland Park Hospital after concluding that the merger had substantially lessened competition in violation of Section 7 of the Clayton Act.*
>
> *The merged firms' market share had increased from 35 to 40 percent post-merger even though ENH had raised its prices by more than 9 percentage points in excess of the increases by hospitals in the control group. Managed care representatives testified that they had to accept these price increases because employers demanded a plan that*

included a local hospital where their employees' physicians admitted patients that was close geographically and in travel time. Citing the statement . . . that the "adoption of the nonprofit form does not change human nature,"[38] the judge rejected ENH's argument that its non-profit status and deep community roots reduced the potential for competitive harm. ENH had, in fact, raised prices more than its competitors and the senior executives responsible for those price increases received enhanced compensation agreements and higher awards after doing so.

As of December 2006, ENH's appeal to the commissioners was still pending. Even if the commissioners uphold the administrative law judge's decision, a judicial appeal is virtually certain. One can only hope that the commissioners and the courts will use this case to send a strong message that attempts to drive up prices by buying the competition will no longer be tolerated.

Orville Redenbacher and Francis Ford Coppola's Love Child: Vertically Integrated Health Care Systems

Some hospitals not only merged with each other but also bought the practices of independent physicians and hired salaried doctors. The number of self-employed doctors dropped sharply, while those salaried by a hospital increased.[39] The strategy of owning the sources of your customers and your suppliers is called *vertical integration.*

By hiring salaried doctors, hospitals acquired their sources of customers. A physician who works for herself will refer patients to the hospital that she believes will best meet their needs, but a salaried physician in a vertically integrated hospital system is more likely to refer patients to the hospital that employs her. In other words, you lose.

Vertical integration is an old business strategy. For example, in the early days of Hollywood, movie producers owned theaters so they could guarantee that their films would be shown and that their rival producers' movies would not. Although vertical integration is an old strategy, it is not a good one. For one, it may work against the public interest by restraining competition. And second, it is very hard to implement. Any business requires a particular set of skills: making movies requires creative people; operating theaters requires excellent service and food management. Mixing these two skill sets in one organization is like marrying Francis Ford Coppola to Orville Redenbacher.

The managerial problems created by vertical integration in health care are illustrated by the saga of a physician who was, at one time, part of a doctors' group practice owned by a hospital. He was pressured by the hospital to increase revenues by upping the number of patients he saw to 32 and working 12-hour days. But he felt the hospital itself was inefficient: medical files were stored in 39 different places, three people often had to be consulted before an appointment could be set, and the hospital paid 6 percent of its gross revenues to an outside bill processor, despite the fact that many bills were not collected.

The physician felt frazzled, and his patients complained. In despair, he quit and opened his own practice. His efficiency zoomed with an office now so highly automated that it was virtually paperless. Almost three-quarters of his patients were satisfied with their care and its timeliness, as compared to 30 percent nationwide.[40]

The Power of Innovation in Health Care

All of us benefit from a continual flow of innovations, both technological and managerial. They drive what the economists label as *productivity*: innovations improve the quality and/or lower the prices of the things we buy.

Yet some economists believe that it is impossible to improve the productivity of service organizations.[41] "You can't make an orchestra play any faster," they aver. This economic argument is important to the health care sector: if you believe it, then the only way to control health care costs is to ration health care. If hospitals cannot become more efficient, the only way to control their costs is to make sure that you and I do not use them so much. In other words, hospital costs are not the problem. You and I are the problem because we use hospitals inappropriately.

Although this argument is widely held, it is profoundly wrong. The retailing industry provides important evidence of how wrong this argument is. Retailing, which is a service sector like health care, was identified by the consulting firm McKinsey as *the* leading cause of the remarkable burst in U.S. productivity for 1995 to 1999.[42] As we shall see, it increased its productivity primarily with managerial innovations.

Technological innovations are important sources of productivity too. We see their impact most clearly in the computers that have become a ubiquitous feature of our daily lives—in our programmable coffeepots, cell phones, and PCs. I have personally witnessed their evolution. Before I was allowed to graduate from MIT, my *alma mater*, I was required to program a new, low-cost minicomputer to solve a trivial problem. I could have easily solved the problem with paper and pencil; but programming this machine to solve it was far from trivial. The computer was a prima donna: it had to be kept in a clean room, free of dust; its vacuum tubes required gentle cooling; it could be programmed only with a complex language of its own; and it was a fussy eater, with a diet restricted to punched cards, laboriously typed by people like me.

Although the minicomputer was substantially cheaper than its predecessors, it still cost $150,000. Today, the Treo phone-computer combination that I casually toss in my purse has more computing power than had the minicomputer, and the Treo can be easily programmed in a natural language, like English, and costs less than $300. Technological innovations such as microchips have made computers simultaneously cheaper and better.

Like every other organization, hospitals can benefit from innovation too. To their credit, they adopted key technological innovations in advances such as minimally invasive surgical procedures. You can read more about them in the appendix to this chapter. Yet, unlike other parts of the economy, hospitals have increased their prices despite the cost-reducing impact of these technological innovations. They have done so by suppressing important managerial innovations.

The Power of Managerial Innovations in Service Organizations

What were the managerial innovations that made retailing so productive?

The answer contains important lessons for the managerial innovations that could enhance hospital productivity.

Innovation in retailing required one bold sweep—massive restructuring of the sector—bolstered by millions of other innovations.

Today, hardworking, two-career families, frantically sandwiched between the needs of their children and elder loved ones, demand convenience. To fill this demand, retailers have radically redefined the very process of shopping by introducing a considerable choice of shopping sites. Merchandise that was once available in a store can now be bought through mail-order catalogs, the computer, or television. Consumer purchases from the home grew sharply.[43]

Savvy merchandisers also increased convenience. A large variety of shopping sites are newly available, ranging from neighborhood stores that stress service and minimize travel to shopping malls that are anchored by huge stores with a vast array of merchandise to an array of stores located in office buildings and transportation terminals, where busy people work and travel.

Retailers also reorganized their stores' contents to increase shoppers' convenience. Instead of providing a jumbled array of merchandise that once required cartographical skills to navigate, many stores are clearly organized around lifestyles. Focused stores provide an abundance of merchandise and choice in one location. They include Staples for office equipment; Lowe's for building supplies; and focused women's clothing stores such as The Limited, clearly targeted at young adults, Ann Taylor for young careerists, and Chanel for hugely successful older women.

Retailers in successful stores accentuate service by training employees in new, clearly defined roles. Stores like the venerable Sears, hard hit by declining sales, no longer require their salespeople to restock merchandise—now they can concentrate on serving the customer. Catalog sales employees are also trained in telephone skills. For example, they are trained to respond quickly to the magic words, "Can I speak to your manager?"[44]

In these stores, you know what the store contains and you can usually get what you want. The competition among them controls costs. Increased productivity means that the customer is getting more for every dollar spent. For example, prices at the ubiquitous Wal-Marts are as low as or lower than those in local stores. To further enhance convenience, Wal-Mart's concept of everyday low prices has freed customers from the need to hunt for special sale days. Many other stores have adopted this form of pricing.

Accomplishing these changes in the mammoth $3 trillion retailing industry has been like turning a battleship around in a pond.[45] And yet, to meet customers' needs for convenience and control, retailers have created substantial managerial innovations: they changed shopping sites, reorganized their organizational focus to meet lifestyle needs, and trained and motivated employees to emphasize service.

To calibrate the difficulty of making these changes, consider the $20 billion Kmart chain. Here, one change after another met with disappointment and evaporating profits. Yet while Kmart floundered, Wal-Mart, a similar kind of retailer, achieved fabulous success. From Wal-Mart's inception in the early 1960s, it grew to about a $350 billion sales retailing giant in 2006. How did Wal-Mart do it? With millions of superlative management innovations: vast stores, smart buying, well-trained and motivated employees. No single factor explains the success of Wal-Mart, but thousands of details are crucial, including its choice to locate in rural America; the precise information systems that enabled virtually instantaneous restocking of inventory; the revolutionary contracts that forced suppliers to meet Wal-Mart's own stringent quality and price terms in order to obtain its huge volume of business; and the training programs and generous profit-sharing plans that made millionaires of many Wal-Mart store personnel.

Don't get me wrong; I am no apologist for Wal-Mart's labor practices. But there's no arguing with the success of its managerial innovations.

The leadership of Sam Walton, its brilliant founder, was key to Wal-Mart's success. Predicting which entrepreneur will succeed is exceedingly difficult. Before he started the Wal-Mart chain, Sam Walton's résumé did not show him to be an obviously natural winner. After all, he had been only a local Arkansas storeowner, and he could easily have been taken for a hick, whereas the managers of his retail store competitors had long experience in running big businesses.

Competition in a consumer-driven system sorts out winners from losers by permitting the customers to pick their favorites. Consumers vote with their dollars, choosing the innovators that best meet their needs. Those who succeed are handsomely rewarded. Those rewards are well earned—after all, the innovators take tremendous risks to ferret out the best ways to satisfy demanding, assertive consumers. Responding to the needs of the consumer requires a daring, visionary businessperson—not a bureaucrat, a political manipulator, or a social engineer. Yet retailing does not pick its customers' pockets to earn these handsome rewards. The fact that their ventures increased productivity means we got more for our money as a result of their innovations.

Where Are the Sam Waltons and Managerial Innovations in Hospitals?

Affirming the sovereignty of the consumer and rewarding skilled, visionary risk takers are the keys to successful transformations in the economy.

Can this kind of a revolution be accomplished in the hospital sector? Can we obtain better and lower-cost care? As the remaining sections in this chapter demonstrate, the answer is a resounding yes, but only if we permit competition to flourish. If we can break the hospitals' lock hold on competition, technological and managerial innovations will work their magic on health care, just as they have elsewhere in the economy.

In other industries, entrepreneurs can effectively compete with established firms that control a market by creating technological and managerial innovations that bring consumers more value for the money. This is how we got innovations in personal computers and retailing, for example, despite the one-time dominance of IBM and Sears.

But the hospital sector is notable for its lack of managerial innovations. Although you may hear about efforts to improve quality within existing hospitals—*Newsweek* devoted a whole issue to the subject in 2006[46]—you don't hear much about the results of these efforts. The reason is simple: incremental tinkering with the existing hospitals will not make them significantly better or cheaper. They need the same kind of radical surgery as the retailing sector underwent: they need to create health services that are clearly focused on customers' needs, for example, newly situated in convenient locations. We do not need more hard-to-reach, giant, everything-for-everybody hospitals. We do need integrated centers for victims of chronic diseases and disabilities, such as diabetics, cancer victims, people with AIDS, and those plagued with "bad backs," that are located in places that patients can easily reach.

But hospitals suppress managerial innovations like these with tactics akin to a mugging. Consider the case of specialty hospitals that perform only a narrow range of surgical procedures, such as those for cardiovascular disease or orthopedic repairs of banged-up bones, muscles, and joints. These specialized hospitals are typically very good at what they do. The heart hospitals are lower cost in part because they are focused on one class of procedures, and also because they are typically at least partially owned by their doctors.[47]

The physicians who own and/or practice in these facilities play a substantially different role in them from physicians salaried by a general hospital or loosely affiliated with it. The doctors play a pivotal role in designing and operating the specialty hospital. For example, in one heart hospital, the doctors created a size and layout that corrected the design shortcomings they experienced in general hospitals. The CEO of an orthopedic surgery practice noted: "Orthopaedists . . . in a hospital . . . work in the same operating room [as] general surgery and obstetrics. Orthopaedics is nuts-and-bolts-equipment intensive. It drives them crazy to have a staff that's not familiar with a tray of multisize screws and nuts and bolts."[48]

The physicians in specialty hospitals are also involved in all operational issues, such as developing clinical care protocols, selecting new hospital managers and surgical supplies, scheduling patients, setting nurse staffing levels, creating the marketing plan, and devising community outreach programs. For example, the physicians in one specialty cardiology hospital designed a new clinical procedure to recognize and intervene in cases of dangerous, erratic beating of the heart that may occur after heart surgery. These new steps, incorporated into the standard protocol through a "best-demonstrated-practice" process, led to a two-thirds reduction in this dangerous aftermath of surgery.[49]

Physicians also help govern the specialty hospital. Their increased influence and autonomy address some of the frustrations they had felt in their professional associations with large, traditional hospitals. Some specialty hospital physicians feel that traditional hospital administrators have been making unilateral decisions, perhaps to the detriment of physician productivity and patient care.[50] For example, because the administrators of one particular Arkansas hospital were closing three of its four heart surgery facilities in midafternoon to save labor costs, substantial delays resulted, with patients and physicians alike waiting all day for access. Noted one cardiologist: "I did angioplasty [a heart procedure] at 11:30 p.m. one night on a patient who had been waiting all day."[51]

Physicians' perceived lack of influence in a traditional hospital has also extended to capital investment. In a large hospital, administrators can delay approval of new capital spending and the capital budget is rationed among many divisions. According to one cardiologist, such capital investment decisions that often take two years in the general hospitals could sometimes be accomplished in less than three months in the specialty hospitals.[52]

Last, as their incomes have been squeezed by managed care insurers, physicians have become increasingly interested in the financial rewards of ownership.[53] They want to share in the economic rewards of providing lower-cost/higher-quality patient care. And, as we saw in retailing, these kinds of profits do not come about by suppressing competition and raising prices.

The Managerial Innovation of Health Care Focused Factories

Specialty hospitals are a subcategory of a more general class of business, called focused factories. For example, Ken Iverson, a technology entrepreneur, almost single-handedly revived the moribund U.S. steel industry with Nucor, the steel-focused factory he managed. Nucor differed from the everything-for-everybody steel behemoths of yore, like Bethlehem Steel, with Nucor's specialty products, relatively small mini-mills, and egalitarian management practices. Nucor paid its non-unionized workers like owners, primarily with productivity-based incentives. In contrast, Bethlehem Steel's unionized workforce was paid wages, largely regardless of their productivity.

The results? Nucor required 1 man-hour per ton of steel and Bethlehem 2.7; Nucor's workers earned $60,000 ($40,000 from bonuses), and Bethlehem's $50,000;[54] and Nucor earned $42 million in nine months of recessionary 2003, whereas Bethlehem lost $2.3 billion.[55]

Nucor's focused factory success contains important lessons for health care. Many agree that the health care system, too, should provide focused, integrated care—especially for the victims of chronic diseases and disabilities, who account for the bulk of costs.[56] When focused health care is permitted, the results are impressive. For example, when Duke University Medical Center offered an integrated, supportive program for congestive heart failure, annual treatment costs per patient declined by $9,000, nearly 40 percent. Duke's new model achieved these cost reductions by improving participants' health status—hospital admissions and lengths of stay dropped—and not by reducing providers' payments or restricting access to needed care. To the contrary, this managerial innovation increased visits to cardiologists sixfold.[57] In these ways, focus helps both patients and physicians, but the big, politically powerful empire-building, everything-for-everybody general hospitals stand in the way.

David versus Goliath:
The Suppression of Specialty Hospitals

The specialty hospital sector is minuscule relative to the general hospital sector: there are only a hundred or so specialty hospitals versus thousands of general hospitals. Yet the general hospitals have been worried about competition from this less costly provider. The hospital industry, sensing correctly that this is an innovation that could really do it in, has gone to all-out war against the specialty sector.

To defeat this threatening innovator, in some areas the general hospitals have refused to sign contracts with insurers that also have the specialty hospitals in their network. They have pressured the physicians affiliated with them not to refer their patients to the specialty hospitals. The joint effect of these two moves has been devastating. They bankrupted the Heart Hospital of Milwaukee, for example. Here's what Dr. Bruce Wilson, a physician-partner, had to say:

> The big, bloated U.S. everything-for-everybody hospitals use anticompetitive tactics to kill off competitors that threaten them. I know their tactics well because I was the physician CEO and part owner of the ship they torpedoed—the Heart Hospital of Milwaukee.
>
> While hospitals claim that it is a conflict for doctors to own hospitals, nobody seems to be saying that it is a conflict for hospitals to own doctors. About 90 percent of the primary care doctors in southeastern Wisconsin are owned by the hospitals.
>
> As in virtually all cities with heart hospitals, Milwaukee's general hospitals told their "owned" physicians whom they could and could not use as heart specialists. They removed my partners from their emergency room on-call lists, and in some cases they instructed

emergency room doctors to call other cardiologists, even if the patient was ours. Those with a financial interest in the Heart Hospital were told they would never again receive referrals from doctors with whom we once had close personal and professional relationships. Pressure was exerted on large insurance companies to exclude coverage for our hospital. Although hospital administrators denied all this, it's true.

My hospital is shipwrecked. Because of the tactics employed by the local hospitals, . . . we never generated enough volume and revenue to stay afloat. I lost essentially all my investment. When I invested, I understood that it would take years before I would see returns. That didn't matter. We were looking for a new model where efficient, data-driven health care practices would set a new bar for excellence in cardiac care.

Financially, we may recover, but we can't imagine going back to huge systems that weren't designed for efficiency and don't want our input. We can't imagine working for organizations that depend on negative PR to generate what are often huge profits, even though many enjoy "not-for-profit" tax exemptions. . . .

My colleagues and I felt the power of ownership. Because we are expert physicians and designed how our service was delivered, we had great results in an environment never before encountered by our doctors, nurses, and especially patients.

How does it feel to know that the person who manages the general hospital is choosing your specialist for you and denying you access to focused programs?

Competition brings innovation and better products and services. Don't we need innovation in health care?[58]

How the U.S. Congress Is Threatening to Help Goliath

In a blatant display of their self-serving agenda, the general hospitals convinced the U.S. Congress to ban further expansion of specialty hospitals. Although this "moratorium" was rescinded in the fall of 2006, it serves as a chilling example of their awesome ability to suppress competition, and Congress is threatening to reinstate this "moratorium."

Usually when a government deters something, it acts to protect the consumer—for example, banning a product that explodes, catches fire, poisons people, and so forth. But no one alleged that the specialty hospitals were *bad for the consumer's health*. No, instead, the general hospitals alleged that the specialty hospitals were *bad for their health*.

The general hospitals were using an unusual argument. Suppose Hewlett-Packard tried to stop the expansion of Dell into the printer business by alleging that Dell's success in printers would hurt Hewlett-Packard's computer business. We would find the argument laughable. After all, if Dell succeeds because it gives the consumers better value for the money, we all benefit. And if Hewlett-Packard fails in the computer business, it is because it is not as efficient as other manufacturers.

But that is exactly what the hospitals alleged about the impact of the specialty hospitals. And the U.S. Congress bought their views hook, line, and sinker.

But the arguments used by the general hospitals to convince Congress to suppress competition were sheer sophistry.

They're Cherry Picking. First, the hospital lobby argued that the specialty hospitals are serving only those with milder problems, leaving the harder cases for the general hospitals. Since hospitals get paid pretty much the same no matter how severely ill their patients, the general hospitals were clearly going to make less money than the specialty hospitals.

Let us suppose this allegation that specialty hospitals are treating healthier patients than general hospitals is true, although the evidence is ambiguous.[59] If we were designing a health care system, would we not want more complicated cases to go to a hospital that has all the bells and whistles and less complicated ones to go to a specialty hospital? Do we want to service a Daytona 500 car at the corner garage? No. We want the racing car looked after at high-tech garage facilities. Our Toyota will fare just fine at the corner garage. A system that consisted entirely of units capable of servicing the racing car would clearly cost much more than one composed of a combination of high-tech facilities and corner garages.

The real problem is not the existence of the corner garage but the price the hospitals are paid. Would we expect the price for servicing a racing car to be the same as the price for servicing a Toyota? Of course not. So why not change the pricing, paying more for more severely ill patients, rather than banning the corner garage out of existence?

Of course, the general hospitals do not like this option. They do not want the insurers to change their prices. They have invested billions of dollars in building capacity to treat corner garage problems. No, they prefer to legislate a lower-cost competitor out of existence.

They're Killing Us Financially. To achieve their goals, the general hospitals used another variant of this competition-is-killing-us argument. They alleged that the specialty hospitals are focusing only on high-profit procedures, leaving the general hospitals with the money-losing dregs. Absent these profits, the hospitals, most of them nonprofit, alleged that they would no longer be able to serve the uninsured.

There are some troubles with this argument. For one, the ostensibly injured nonprofit hospitals are earning good profits, even in areas where they compete directly with specialty hospitals. They either have become more efficient as a result of competition or else have been so profitable that the competition with the specialty hospitals has not really hurt them.[60]

But even if this allegation were valid, the problem again is with a pricing system that permits some lines of business to remain high profit. In a normal market, high-profit areas, say, software, attract competitors. Sooner or later, the competitors start to slash prices, and what was once a high-profit area becomes a normal-profit one. But hospital markets are so concentrated that abnormally high prices can be maintained. In a free market, suppliers succeed because they are productive, not because a third-party insurer has mistakenly set their prices too high.

The Uninsured and the King of Torts

To help suppress specialty hospitals, the general hospitals claimed that they helped the uninsured, while the specialty hospitals had no such obligation. In fact, general hospitals often screw the uninsured, charging the very highest prices and generally treating them like deadbeats or criminals.

Here is an example of the behavior uncovered in Fort Myers, Florida, by Consejo de Latinos Unidos, a group that *60 Minutes* has highlighted as dedicated to protecting the uninsured from hospital price gouging. In this example, the victims used hospitals operated by Lee Memorial Health System.

> *Donna was sick. They had taken a third of her colon. She had to go back in from being constipated. She always went to Lee Memorial. She accumulated approximately $57,000 of bills. These bills financially ruined us; we filed bankruptcy last year. . . . I have been a cook for almost 7 years. Donna has been a waitress. The hospital never sat down and spoke to us. We tried paying our medical bills; we never refused to pay. I worked very hard. We lost a home because of this lawsuit.*[61]

In response, Lee Memorial reviewed its payment policies. As of 2004, it had 42 lawsuits outstanding against its delinquent patients.[62] This general story attracted the attention of a person who might generally be classified in the category of "your worst nightmare": Richard "Dickie" Scruggs.

Scruggs looks like the Navy flyer he once was: trim, purposeful, well tailored, and reserved. He likes to affect a good-old-boy act, describing himself as an "ambulance chaser from Mississippi." Hardly. Scruggs is an ambulance chaser like a tiger is a vegetarian. Scruggs, the architect of the $240 billion tobacco lawsuits, was allegedly the model for John Grisham's *King of Torts*. Scruggs is a master of political connections—although he is a Democrat, his brother-in-law is a former Republican Senate Majority Leader.

Although he has many detractors, Scruggs has a terrific nose for newsworthy lawsuits. He does well for himself too, having earned some $300 million for himself from the tobacco cases.[63]

Scruggs has set his sights on hospital overcharges to the uninsured. He claims that the hospitals' tax-exempt status requires them to provide charitable care. His lawsuits have been bolstered by the Illinois government's revoking of the tax-exempt status of the Provena Covenant Medical Center in Urbana.[64]

By October 2006, Scruggs had filed over 52 lawsuits but had scored only 1 victory; but do not count him out. Notes one lawyer of Scruggs's tobacco victories: "He . . . litigated and litigated and litigated and lost and lost and lost until he found a defendant too weak to litigate who agreed to a settlement. He was able to establish a precedent, which he used like a shoehorn to extract other settlements and ultimately bring down the industry. I can't argue with his success."[65]

Hospitals Try to Bury the Evidence

There ought to be a law that makes public the prices that hospitals are paid by their customers so that the uninsured customer does not get screwed. But the hospitals have staunchly resisted even this minimal transparency. Once again, their arguments are mind-boggling: they allege that public posting of their prices would lead to collusion, so that there would be even less price competition.[66] Somehow, they get away with it.

If this argument were valid, we would have no price transparency elsewhere in the economy, and in fact it is everywhere. Suppose the makers of raisin bran types of cereals—Post, Kellogg, and local store brands—argued that if they posted their prices, it would lead to all the manufacturers' and stores' colluding and fixing the price of the cereal. The cereal manufacturers would be hauled into court in a second with this kind of argument. The daily media would have a field day with their outrageous behavior.

But so far the kind of price transparency that we have elsewhere in the economy is notable for its almost complete absence when it comes to hospitals. Instead, they want you to just trust them to maintain a fair price, which they will set in secret. This type of behind-the-scenes pricing is not benefiting anyone, and consumers need price transparency. Chapter 10 discusses how we can attain it.

A Glimpse of the Future: Global Competition for Hospital Services

The hospital was beautiful, in the way a Four Seasons hotel is beautiful—spacious, airy, sparkling clean, with gorgeous stuff lying around. In fact, it made you feel as if you actually were in a Four Seasons hotel—pampered, elegant, really cool. The staff was Four Seasons caliber too. They could not do enough for the patient, including giving her an up-to-date copy of her medical record and a schedule. Everything was done right on time—bam, bam, bam, no waits—including the diagnosis of the source of her foot pain by an Ivy League–trained doctor and the creation of some specially fitted orthotics for her aching feet.

The price was a tenth of the thousands of dollars charged by the hospital that I had personally experienced—one of the great Harvard University hospitals in Boston. The Boston hospital was dingy, cramped, ugly, ugly, ugly. While I spent an eternity in waiting room hell, with a TV blaring *General Hospital*—funny to see the attractive, sex-addled hospital personnel it depicted in comparison to the rumpled real thing—I was privy to a display of Rudeness 101:

> *"Hey, Cathy, come here," yelled a twenty-something receptionist to a crippled woman in her sixties. Cathy hobbled up to the receptionist's desk. She knew the receptionist would not come to her.*
>
> *"You have to go to the Orthopedics section. You know where it is, right?" said the receptionist, without deigning to look up. But few visitors know where other services are located in the mile-long hospital because it has so few signs.*

I finally escaped waiting room hell when the great man—the orthopedic surgeon—burst in, two hours late. Never mind: he was really good. He diagnosed the source of my foot pain in a few minutes. He also arranged appointments with a radiologist to inject a steroid to reduce the inflammation that was causing the pain and an orthotics manufacturer. The injection was to be done under an X-ray screen because it had to be placed in just the right spot.

Weeks later, when the date for my injection appointment finally arrived, I got a Fellow (a doctor who is receiving further training in a specialty—these guys are training on your body). He anesthetized my foot because bone-related procedures really hurt. But when I looked up at the X-ray screen, I saw he had placed the long needle in the wrong spot. He had to do the whole thing over again, and the anesthesia was wearing off. "Sensitive, are we?" he asked tactlessly as I grimaced in pain. The orthotics maker, located in an entirely different part of Boston, was no better: he mismade the orthotics and billed me for an unusable product. Two visits later, I finally got what I needed.

Oh yeah, my feet hurt less; but total elapsed time?

Ever wonder why you are called a patient?

Their time is valuable; but you? You just be patient.

Here is why I am telling you this story—the first hospital is in Thailand. There are millions of elective surgical procedures done in the United States every year in places just like the Harvard hospital. There will be millions of U.S. surgical procedures done in Thailand or India real soon.

These institutions outside the United States provide better value at much lower cost, even after allowing for transportation. A $60,000 open-heart procedure costs only $15,500 in the first-rate Thai Bumrungrad Hospital, in which half of the cardiac surgeons are U.S. trained.[67]

Their lower costs come about in part because of lower wages. But these foreign hospitals also feature the kind of managerial innovations that enhance productivity that are absent in the U.S. system. For example, some are organized in nonconventional ways— they may be focused on areas such as heart disease or built with a "hub-and-spoke model" in which a high-tech hospital serves as the hub and lower-tech, community hospitals as the spokes.[68] Unlike U.S. hospitals, they are transparent—if you want to know their prices, just look at their Web sites.[69] The focused heart hospitals in India even publish their results. One Indian heart hospital claims, for example, that its mortality rate from open-heart surgery is only 0.2 percent more than the U.S.-based Cleveland Clinic, while it performs three times the number of open-heart procedures.[70]

To gauge their human impact, consider this paean from a U.S. veteran of the Vietnam War, fully insured by the U.S. Veterans Administration:

> *I'm 58 now, [self-employed], and insurance costs have been out of my price range for several years now. . . . I'm a Vietnam War veteran so I have been going to the V. A. the last years, but they are so full with people from the Iraq war and all, that it takes forever to schedule anything besides blood tests and prescription refills.*
>
> *I have been having problems with my hip and lower back and had thought that I had a heart attack a few months back. . . . A friend who lives in Thailand suggested I go there. . . . I had seen the 60* Minutes *show on Bumrungrad Hospital in Bangkok and thought to go there for additional opinions. . . .*
>
> *I went to Bumrungrad Hospital for all my tests. It is one of the largest, busiest hospitals catering to an international clientele in the world. . . . It looks like a 5-star hotel instead of a hospital. . . . I had the comprehensive checkup and a full orthopedic exam. I also ordered and had [a la carte] eye and hearing tests, some skin growths removed and tested. . . .*
>
> *I was not pushed into any kind of treatments. . . . I had been thinking of hip and/or back surgery, angiogram etc. The doctors instead suggested diet and lifestyle changes. . . .*
>
> *I was treated like a VIP everywhere. . . . All the various doctors I saw had studied and or interned in the states and spoke very good English. They spent so much time with me going over all my tests, X-rays and all, that I felt they really cared. . . .*

I spent around $10,000 for everything—including all the medical and dental work [$2,600], my airfare, 3 weeks hotel, great food, entertainment, and lots of shopping. . . .[71]

Thirty years ago, the executives of GM and Ford never for a moment imagined that their lunch would be eaten by car companies with funny names like Toyota and Honda. They were wrong because they were blinded by greed, hubris, and a parochial, U.S.-centric view of the world. In the new global marketplace, anything is possible, and organizations, whether they provide cars, computers, or health, should face the fact that competition can make them as obsolete as a Chevy Corvair.

If U.S. hospitals are not radically restructured, future Jack Morgans may simply hop a jet to another country to avoid the expense, the wait, and the horrible possibility that their illnesses may kill them before they obtain the care they need. Already, insurers like the brilliantly managed Blue Cross Blue Shield of South Carolina are investigating this option for their members.[72] Our big, greedy hospitals and their overpaid, politically manipulative executives may soon find themselves with big empty waiting rooms and depleted bank accounts.

How Hospitals Helped to Kill Jack Morgan

Jack Morgan desperately needed a kidney transplant. His HMO insurer delayed and delayed in performing the procedure, and Jack simply could not afford to pay for it out of his own pocket. U.S. hospitals hide their prices, so Jack was not sure how much it would cost; but he knew it would be a hundred thousand dollars or more.

Jack also knew that if he went to a hospital as a self-paying uninsured patient, they would likely charge him their very highest price, and if he could not pay, they would hound him, perhaps taking everything he had worked so hard to acquire and bankrupting him in the process. It did not matter if the hospital was nonprofit or carried a religious name.

So Jack Morgan did without a kidney transplant, and he died.

Yet there is no reason for U.S. hospital costs to be as high as they are. A kidney transplant in India, for example, costs only $7,000, and U.S. hospital care is also far more expensive than that in developed countries with standards of living similar to ours. Further, technological innovations, especially in the techniques of minimally invasive surgery and imaging, have substantially lowered hospital costs: they have enabled many of the procedures that once could be performed only in expensive hospitals to be done in far less expensive out-of-the-hospital, ambulatory settings.

These technological innovations have greatly reduced the need for hospitals. Yet U.S. hospitals have not only maintained their high prices but also continue to increase them at rates that outstrip the increases in inflation of any other part of the health care system.

U.S. hospitals have maintained their bloated costs by shamelessly manipulating their nonprofit image—draping themselves in an undeserved mantle of sanctity. Yes, some of them teach, do research, and perform unprofitable services; but they used this mantle to protect themselves from competition through mergers, which they claimed would reduce costs. But, instead, the mergers have increased costs and may have reduced quality too, due to lack of competition. Armed with millions of dollars in political contributions, the mostly nonprofit hospital sector also convinced the U.S. Congress to suppress specialty hospitals—viable competitors that provide cheaper results that are at least equal in quality—by arguing that the specialty hospitals rob them of the monies they need to provide "free care" to the uninsured and other vaguely defined community benefits. But the truth is that among the primary beneficiaries of this are not the uninsured or the community but the empire-building nonprofit hospitals and their overseers.

Like other sanctimonious, self-serving, insular U.S. industries, the hospitals have created an environment in which viable foreign competitors can flourish. How long will it take before they once again turn to the U.S. Congress to protect them by prohibiting travel for health care services? The hospitals may argue that they are a better value for the money, but, because they do not publish any meaningful data about their results or even their prices, this assertion is hard to prove.

"Dickie" Scruggs, the King of Torts, is fighting to ensure that this mantle is ripped away with lawsuits on behalf of the uninsured. Don't get me wrong: Scruggs is no angel; but, in this case, if he prevails, hospitals will not only lose considerable funds, billions of dollars, but, more importantly, they will be stripped of the undeserved sanctified image that they have manipulated to suppress competition and innovation.

Had hospitals been as competitive and productive as the rest of the vibrant U.S. economy, Jack Morgan could have paid for his kidney transplant out of his own pocket.

Jack Morgan would still be alive.

But why was Jack Morgan forced into a managed care plan that denied him access to the health care he needed?

Because as an owner of a small company living in a state that aggressively oversees health insurance prices and the design of their policies, he had no other choice. But had he been employed by a larger company, he would not have fared much better. Most employers wrongly believed that limiting choice to managed care policies was the best way to control health care costs and quality. And because they select our health insurance, we have no recourse but to accede to their faulty judgment. In an ultimate irony, these employers use our money to buy the health insurance policy that helps to kill people like Jack Morgan.

TECHNOLOGICAL INNOVATIONS THAT REDUCE HOSPITAL COSTS AND IMPROVE HOSPITAL QUALITY

The decline in the need for hospitals has been driven partially by a relentless flow of technological innovations. Some of the innovations are so complex that their innovators have won a Nobel Prize, such as that awarded for developing the process that automates the replication of DNA. But among the most important innovations is the simplest—a catheter, a plastic tube.

In the late 1960s, President Lyndon Johnson pulled up his shirt to display the scar left on his ample belly from a gallbladder operation. President Johnson was as justly proud of his scar as the other survivors of the grueling surgical procedures of that time. Perhaps you have heard your elderly relatives' vivid and lengthy recollections of their own operations.

Most surgery is performed to remove a diseased, unnatural, or debilitated part of the body—an inflamed appendix, a malfunctioning kidney, the stretched-out part of a blood vessel, or the calcified section of a joint. Sometimes its purpose is to insert a replacement part—an artificial hip, a new heart valve, an elastic tube or piece of a blood vessel, or, as in Jack Morgan's case, a new organ.

Why were these operations so traumatic? Because clever Mother Nature designed our bodies to foil invaders. To protect us from disease-carrying injuries, she buried key parts of our anatomy; covered them with a sturdy sheath of skin, muscle, connective tissue, and bone; and cushioned them with a layer of fat. She even installed an alarm system, made up of our nerves, that triggers a pain signal whenever the security of this protective sheath is breached.

Mother Nature does not take kindly to violations of her defenses. When deft inventors developed anesthetics to knock out the body's alarm system, Mother Nature retaliated: early anesthetics induced virulent responses, including acute nausea. She punished patients who permitted surgeons to probe inside their bodies with daunting mementos: trauma to surrounding tissues, infections of the open cavities, and ugly scars. Those who endured operations thus learned painfully that it is not nice to fool with Mother Nature.

No wonder President Johnson was so proud of his scar. The removal of a gallbladder was a big deal in those days, and it cost a lot of money. In 1984, a surgeon charged $1,000 for a gallbladder operation, to which the hospital would likely add $2,000 to $4,000 for the use of the operating theater and a semiprivate room.[73] The resulting expenditure of up to $5,000 equaled about a fourth of the median income of American households in that year.[74] Surgery was not only expensive; it required lengthy hospital stays that busy and burdened consumers found increasingly difficult to manage.

The New Technologies: Lights, Camera, Action

People were once forced to endure traumatic and expensive surgeries or face death, functional impairment, or unbearable pain. But recent technological innovations dramatically changed all that, greatly reducing the trauma of surgery, the time needed for recuperation, and its cost.

The key innovation came from an unexpected source—the plastics industry.

Plastics revolutionized surgery through small plastic rods that are inserted through catheters (tubes) into natural openings in the body—such as the mouth, penis, vagina, and nose—or into small holes punched into the body. These rods are fiber optic light sources that illuminate the surgical site for miniature cameras (endoscopes) and small surgical instruments. They too are inserted through catheters. When these lights and cameras reach the surgical site, the surgeon can spring into action, using small instruments to operate, while watching an image of the surgical site on a screen.

The plastic tubes that enabled these minimally invasive surgeries were as revolutionary as the canals that ushered in the Industrial Revolution.

Other technological innovations also helped to reduce the trauma and costs of surgery. Computer technology automated not only the tiny camera sent down the catheter but many other devices that can diagnose or monitor the body's functioning without violently breaching its defenses.

New diagnostic instruments produce clear, crisp pictures of the soft tissue buried deep within the body that once could be seen only during exploratory surgery. Powerful computers reconstruct the information produced by the different forms of energy sent into the body to diagnose its contents. Sonar instruments can distinguish a malignant tumor from a harmless growth, a healthy embryo from a malformed one. CAT (pronounced *cat*, an abbreviation for *computerized axial tomography*) scanners use X rays to detect subtle differences in tissue densities. And magnetic resonance imagers (MRIs) use electromagnetism (or, more precisely, the interaction between external electromagnetic fields and those of the atomic nuclei of body tissues) to image tissues. Small chips and other electronic instruments power miniaturized monitoring devices, such as the noninvasive pulse-oximeters that can monitor the patient's blood oxygenation without puncturing the skin.

These computer-based devices have eliminated not only many exploratory surgeries but also some of the world's worst diagnostic procedures. For example, the late, unlamented pneumoencephalogram, used to detect masses growing in the brain, began with an injection of a gas into the patient's spine. The patient was then strapped into a chair and catapulted into various positions that caused the gas to flow into the normally fluid-filled cavities in the brain. The gas-filled cavities were then visualized. As one radiologist put it, this procedure "almost inevitably resulted in the mother of all headaches." This ghastly diagnostic technique has been completely replaced by MRI and CT techniques.

A Tale of Cabbages and Angioplasties: An Example of Minimally Invasive Surgery

New forms of surgery were made possible by fiber optics and computer-based and miniaturized instruments. Minimally invasive surgery (MIS) techniques rapidly supplanted many older invasive ("open") procedures. The pace of change was staggering. For example, 80 to 90 percent of all gallbladder removals are now performed laparoscopically.[75]

Because MIS procedures do not require long periods of recuperation, they are typically performed in sites other than the in-patient section of a hospital. Of the estimated 28 million surgeries in 2005, 63 percent were completed outside the hospital walls.[76] An increasing number of these out-of-the-hospital surgeries are conducted in doctors' offices or in freestanding facilities that are not affiliated with a hospital. In 2005 more than 17 million surgical procedures were performed in outpatient sites.[77]

Why has MIS diffused so quickly and widely? Because it has greatly reduced the trauma, cost, and recuperation time of surgery.

Its appeal can be clearly illustrated by comparing two procedures to unclog coronary arteries and enhance the flow of blood to the heart: the old open CABG procedure, described earlier, and an MIS one performed with a catheter.

With a catheter-based procedure, also used to improve blood flow through the coronary arteries, called *coronary angioplasty* (or *percutaneous transluminal coronary angioplasty*, that is, PTCA), a radiologist or cardiologist snakes a catheter through a tiny opening, made in the artery in the groin, up to the artery in the heart. Contrast media enable her to watch the catheter's progress through the vascular system to its destination. When the catheter reaches the gunked-up portion of the coronary artery, a collapsed balloon, cleverly furled along the catheter, is positioned so that it straddles the blocked-up section of the vessel. *Poof*—the balloon is then inflated to distend the artery at the plaque. It is then deflated and removed along with the catheter.

The total time required for an angioplasty ranges from one to two hours. It is typically performed in an outpatient facility—that is, outside the hospital walls—and requires only mild sedation and local anesthesia.

The cost differentials between CABGs, in the $60,000s, and angioplasties are significant, if somewhat eroded by the reclogging of the artery that sometimes follows angioplasty and, less frequently, CABG procedures. (The reclogging requires additional procedures.)[78] But a 2003 study concluded that angioplasties cost less than CABGs and drugs and have better outcomes.[79] This cost differential is likely replicated for many other surgeries. After all, many MIS procedures require fewer resources than open ones: less time in the hospital, less time for recuperation, a smaller team of assistants, and even a cheaper outpatient setting for many procedures.

But lower costs are not the sole economic difference between the two types of surgeries. More important, MIS procedures, like angioplasties, enhance national productivity because they enable people to return to work more quickly.[80] For example, newly introduced MIS hip replacement surgery can be done on an outpatient basis. If performed in a hospital, it reduces the length of stay by more than half.[81]

KILLER NUMBER 3: THE EMPLOYERS
Death at the Hands of a "Choice" of One

A few years ago, I went food shopping with a new immigrant from the Caribbean. We went to a supermarket in the middle-income, blue-collar community of Waltham, Massachusetts. I had liked the place since my first visit there. When I asked a young man who was stocking shelves where I could find bulgur wheat, he not only knew what it was, he actually accompanied me to its location. But more startling was the beauty and variety of the food displays: gorgeous, crisp red-leaf lettuces nestled in pristine crushed-ice beds; orange carrots arranged in a sunburst pattern, cleverly reflected in an angled overhead mirror; pyramids of polished apples radiating light. The fish and meat counters too were mosaics of color and texture, displaying their firm-fleshed and obviously fresh wares. Even the prepared food line was stunning.

Because this supermarket was located in the People's Republic of Massachusetts, we went prepared to laugh at the veggie burgers, and yes, they were there. But so were glistening, crisp roasted chickens; wonderful melted-cheese-oozing pizzas, quiches, and pasta; and dozens of delicious salads and fragrant spiced ethnic foods. There was fresh-brewed dark roasted coffee too, along with the chicory and carob drinks. My friend marveled at the beauty, choice, and quality of the merchandise. "What a difference," she said, "compared to the limited choice and sullen service of the markets back home. You have to beg for everything, even for a bag to put your groceries in. And the prices here are much less too."

The American consumer experience is about choices—a dizzying array of choices is available to us nearly everywhere we shop. Go to a supermarket and you will find shelves that groan with choices. You buy what suits your tastes, your dietary needs, your pocketbook. And you can choose from a large variety of markets too, ranging from your local convenience store to your metro high-end purveyor of gourmet foods. Shop for a car and you can select from hundreds of foreign or domestic makes, fuel-efficient or gas-challenged models, large or midsized or small, sports cars or family vans. Four-wheel drive? Sure, if you want it. Colors? Accessories? Options? You buy a car based on your desires, your needs, and the amount of money you are willing to spend. And you can buy your car from many different car dealers.

Yet all this consumer choice does not come at an increased price. To the contrary, the prices for consumer goods, such as cars and food, have steadily decreased as a percentage of income, while their quality has steadily improved.[1] The reason is that choice enables competition, and competition fuels innovation, and innovation increases productivity. In other words, we all get more for our money because of choice.

But when it comes to health insurance, there is little choice and few options. You take what your employer gives you and you go away. Want your human resources department to reward you with lower insurance premiums for not smoking and for working hard to stay fit? Want to increase your deductible and pay less for your health insurance? Want to strengthen the dental coverage in recognition of your lousy teeth and gums? "I'm a diabetic. Could my coverage include this specialized facility for diabetes . . . ?" Forget it.

Even if your employer offers a "choice" of more than one policy, the choice is often illusory. Current insurance plans are overwhelmingly identical. If you are willing to pay a little more, you get to choose from a wider array of doctors and hospitals. If you want to pay less, you get an HMO, as Jack did, or a narrow group of doctors and hospitals. That's choice, health insurance style. What a contrast to the choice we have in items that are not so central to life or death as health care, like food or cars.

After all, "We're paying," your employer will tell you. But, in fact, they're not. You are.

Your employer uses your money to pay for your health insurance. In a global competitive economy, your employer can pay you only some total sum in salary and benefits, say, $50,000, and remain competitive. You can receive that $50,000 totally in salary, or you can receive it in some combination of salary and benefits. To receive health insurance, your employers likely commandeered a lot of what would otherwise be your salary, up to $15,000, and then used it to give you what they claim is an insurance "benefit."

Employers do not buy our clothes, our food, or our cars. We would not want them to. How can they possibly know our preferences and the prices we are willing to pay? So why in the world are we willing to give them our money to buy something much more important, our health insurance, for us?

Our employers have become our health insurance buyers because Congress willed it to be so. By jiggering the tax codes, Congress enabled corporations to buy health insurance with pretax money; but in the same breath and in the same tax codes it required that if you or I bought health insurance on our own, we could use only after-tax money.[2] A policy that costs us $7,500 a year when purchased by our employer would cost us $15,000 if we purchased it ourselves, assuming for simplicity that we are in a 50 percent tax bracket (including federal and state income tax and Social Security taxes). Not much of an option. (These and the other fatal contributions that the U.S. Congress provided to speed along Jack's death will be explored further in Chapter 5.) Some estimate the 2006 value of this tax subsidy at hundreds of billions of dollars.[3]

Employers have a business to run. Senior managers cannot spend a lot of time in selecting health insurance. So they have turned the job over to their human resources (HR) staffers—a really bad decision. HR personnel have many good qualities—they are well-meaning, able people—but they are not trained as business managers with numbers to meet and markets to conquer. Their motivations are paternalistic and bureaucratic rather than competitive and entrepreneurial.

HR staffers were mandated to cut costs, and they felt they could accomplish that only by limiting options, not by expanding them. They thought that by giving all their health insurance business to only a few firms, they would receive volume discounts on the price. Thus, HR staffers that were involved in purchasing health insurance for employees decided to narrow the health insurance choices the company would offer. Like typical corporate bureaucrats, they did not believe in competition, choice, and entrepreneurialism. They also mistrusted their employees' ability to choose among many options that might have been offered.

The paternalistic HR types also advocated managed care plans. You don't have to spend much time in an HR department before they tell you how irrational employees are and what terrible choices they make. Many in the HR community believed that insurance firms would do a better job of managing medical care than incompetent employees and their greedy doctors.

By limiting choice and making the health insurance policies virtually identical, HR simplified the job of comparing their costs. Their decision to limit the choice of insurance vendors and insurance plans so that their jobs would be simpler, once again demonstrated the truism that when agents serve your interests, they frequently also pay considerable attention to their own needs.

Most big businesses do not really buy insurance. They are large enough to insure themselves against the high odds of a few of their employees' becoming really sick. Instead, they self-insure; that is, they pay all of their insured employees' health care expenses. They hire insurance firms solely to administer their health insurance plans. But small businesses, like Jack's, cannot self-insure. They have to buy an insurance policy from an insurance plan. As an owner of a small business, Jack's average annual health insurance cost per employee was $4,000, while a large business's cost per employee was $3,300—

nearly 20 percent less.[4] Jack was discriminated against. But this is only the beginning of the problems of small businesses in the health insurance market.

Many states mandate the benefits that health insurance policies must contain, thus increasing their cost. State governments have the power to regulate health insurance; but self-insured employers are free from this regulation because they do not buy health insurance. New York state legislators, for example, require that all insurance policies contain benefits for chiropractic therapy and in vitro fertilization. Whether enrollees want these benefits or not, all New York state insurance policies must contain them. State governments also license and regulate the insurers who are permitted to do business in the state, thus potentially limiting competition. In massive New York state, in 2006, there were only 29 such firms while the much smaller, but less regulated, state of Indiana had 77.[5] Some state governments force health insurance firms to charge the same prices for everyone, sick or healthy, causing many insurers to avoid doing business in them. Last, some states prohibit the sale of cheap, high-deductible health insurance policies.

Because Jack's state government actively regulated the benefits, pricing, and coverage of the insurance policies made available to small businesses, he could not find anything other than an HMO policy. Although Jack was a benevolent owner, his employees, most of whom earned less than $40,000 a year, could not afford the $10,000 price tag of the HMO policy for a family, and he could not afford to subsidize them.

So, as the owner of a small business, Jack wound up with only one HMO option. In theory, if Jack had worked for a large corporation, his employers could have offered him considerable choice; for example, they could have offered him a health insurance policy that would have enabled him to choose his health care provider from a broad range of doctors and hospitals, including some that specialized in the treatment of kidney disease patients like Jack. But the HR staff in the large firms would likely have forced him to accept only managed care options for his health insurance. They too would have contributed to his death.

Why Does Your Boss Buy Your Health Insurance?

My former boss, Harvard University's President Lawrence Summers, is a brilliant economist (despite occasional gaffes, such as questioning women's innate scientific ability and the worthiness of collegiate departments for African-American studies). But, although Summers is a great economist, and economists study financial resource allocation, I would not allow him to select my house, my car, my refrigerator, or my children's education.

As brilliant an economist as Lawrence Summers is, how could he possibly know what I want, need, and am willing to pay for in my health insurance coverage? After all, I am only one of Harvard University's thousands of employees. As a result, he did not offer me what I want in health insurance. Worse yet, I do not even know how much of my salary he commandeered to buy this health insurance, although I too am an economist.

Yet I allowed him to choose my health insurance. A historical accident explains why people like you and me sit back while our employers misuse our money to choose and buy our health insurance coverage. File it under the heading of "be careful what you wish for."

Employer-sponsored health benefits grew rapidly in the 1930s and 1940s, in part because several attempts to provide government-sponsored health insurance failed—Theodore Roosevelt's 1912 election platform included national health insurance. Private-sector insurance companies preferred to sell insurance to employed people because they were thought to be healthier than the unemployed, and it was easier to sell to one large company that represented thousands of employees than to sell to each of its many employees. In those early days, employees paid the full premium. Employers offered support for the purchase of health insurance only in the form of payroll deductions.

All this changed when, after World War II, the government froze wages and prices to control inflation. Meanwhile, the economy was booming, fueled by pent-up demand for goods and services from long-deprived returning soldiers and their families. Employers searching for a way to recruit workers hit on a great idea: exempt the money they used to purchase health insurance benefits from income taxes so it could be purchased with pre-income-tax money. GI Joe could buy his health insurance on his own with after-tax income or let his boss buy it for him with money that would not be taxed.

Clearly, the corporate promise to provide tax-free health insurance benefits could be a great lure to perspective employees. Another tax benefit loomed: corporations could (and still can) deduct the money they used to purchase health insurance from their income when they computed the amount of income taxes they owed, thus lowering their taxes—but consumers who purchased health insurance could not.

In the mid-1950s, only 45 percent of the population had hospital insurance.[6] But the number insured through their employers grew explosively, peaking at nearly 170 million in 2000.[7] In 2004, 64 percent of the insured got insurance through their employers.[8]

As time went on, employees tended to forget that their income was being used to buy their health insurance. Increasingly their perception was that health insurance was a freebie. But it was not and it is not.

Insured employees are effectively paying for their health insurance by accepting lower salaries than they would earn if their employer were not offering this "benefit."[9] After all, there is a market for labor. Employers whose total labor costs are way out of line cannot survive in globally competitive markets. Employers examine the total amount they pay for labor, including salary and benefits, such as health insurance. When the total sum becomes uncompetitive for employers who pay for their employees' health insurance, they must lower either employees' salaries or employees' benefits or outsource the work to an uninsured third party. But because of the tax preference for income that comes in the form of health insurance benefits, both employers and employees would rather cut some other components of the total compensation bucket.

For example, suppose an employer in the ferociously competitive global automobile industry who pays average employees a total of $90,000 in salary and benefits feels compelled to reduce this total in some way to remain competitive. If the employer cuts the employees' health insurance benefits, they will have to use after-tax income to pay for the costs of additional insurance. An employee in a 50 percent tax bracket will need to earn $2 for every $1 of health insurance he or she buys for himself or herself. On the other hand, if the employer continues to buy the employee's health insurance, the employer needs only $1 of salary to buy $1 of health insurance.

The increase in the total number of people with health insurance was not totally good news either: the very fact of being insured causes people to pay less attention to the value they receive for the money. When I gave birth to my first child, I noticed a huge charge for a room on the surgery floor on my bill; but I never made it to surgery. The hospital had put me on this floor because it had run out of regular rooms. When I called the hospital to correct the bill, the clerk said, "What do you care? Your insurer, not you, is paying for this." No wonder health care costs were soaring.

Employers are increasingly trapped between a rock and a hard place. They find it difficult to reduce significantly their role in the selection of health insurance because of the tax preference attached to employers' purchase; but employees who perceive that they are using somebody else's money do not exercise their normal shopping muscles when it comes to health care.

The rise in health insurance premiums gravely injures U.S. competitiveness. Especially hurt are old-line sickies like General Motors. GM spent $5.2 billion in 2004 on health care for employees, retirees, and their families. They claim that adds up to $1,600 for every car they made last year, more than they spent for steel. These costs, they tell us, had a "tremendous impact" on GM's billions of dollars in losses. Add lackluster sales of their products to the picture, and we can see why the auto giant is hemorrhaging money. In contrast, GM's global rivals, like Toyota, spend only $110 per car.[10] (These figures are unlikely to be exactly correct, says your author, an old accounting teacher; but they, nevertheless, illustrate the magnitude of the problem. GM is likely overstating its current costs by throwing in the unfunded expenses for its retirees' health care. Toyota, on the other hand, may be understating its costs by ignoring the increased taxes paid to fund the Japanese government's substantial role in health care. But because Japan spends about half as much as the United States spends on health care, the differences in spending between GM and Toyota are likely significant.)

Don't get me wrong. I'm not pleading the case of the poor multinational corporation here, nor am I offering to pass the hat for GM. But I am concerned about the workers who are being hurt as GM lays off employees and contemplates cutbacks on benefits, including, of course, workers' health care.

What to do? Well, one HR solution, not a great one, was to require employees to pay more of their health insurance premiums. They did that. General Motors, for example, newly required its retirees to pay $752 per family per year in 2006.[11] The second was to reduce the payment for the benefits in the insurance policies. They did that too. From 1999 to 2006, the amount that employees spent on health care out of their own pocket increased substantially. Annual spending for family coverage doubled to $3,000, while the percentage of insured workers whose plans had deductibles less than $500 halved.[12]

But these changes have not accomplished much response to the inflation in costs. Employers, still searching for new ways to control their health care costs, turned to their human resources staffs, who have come up with the ideas that many companies have tried in recent years. The results have been awful. In a bad imitation of Corporate Purchasing 101, they reduced the number of their suppliers and turned to a new breed of managed care vendors—not Kaiser, but tough businesspeople who scrutinized every health care dollar, especially those aimed at the sick.

Bad Idea 1: Squeeze Your Suppliers by Giving All Your Business to Only a Few

I can choose from 240 models of cars; 500 types of chocolate bars; 50 million blogs;[13] but my boss offers me a "choice" of one or only a few virtually identical health insurance policies. Why do corporations limit plan choice?

Employers know that, in the long run, employees will not put up with paying more and more for less and less, so they have hit on a different solution: limit the number of plans they offer employees. This idea is Corporate Purchasing 101, a strategy perfected by Wal-Mart, fabled for its supply chain management: that is, squeezing the hell out of its vendors on pricing, product, and delivery. They endure the purchaser's bear hug because it is buying so much volume. If GM applies it, for example, by offering only a handful of health insurers to its employees, it can squeeze those insurers to get greater value for the money.

But this strategy is deeply flawed when applied to health care. Remember Professor Harold Hill, the great rascal/salesman in *The Music Man?* He was teaching an important business lesson when he noted that "you gotta know the territory."

Same thing with corporate strategy: you gotta know the business environment. Corporate Purchasing 101 does not work in health care.

One reason is that people have some brand loyalty when it comes to health insurance, especially for older brands like Blue Cross and Blue Shield. The brand loyalty gives the vendor power because it is difficult to take away a trusted brand product from employees.

But an even worse obstacle to the vendor squeeze play in health insurance is the idiosyncratic history of partner-providers of insurers. U.S. health insurance programs were essentially created by health services providers who wanted assurance that they would get paid for their services. Consequently, a strong relationship existed between the providers and the insurers. Naturally, in these circumstances, insurers found it hard to press their partner-providers for price concessions. In other words, the middleman in health care—the insurer—has always had a lot to do with the doctors we could use.

In 1929, Baylor University Medical Center enrolled Dallas public school employees, many of them women of child-bearing age, in a plan that guaranteed 21 days of hospital care for a premium of $6 a year. Similar monthly payment plans to local hospitals soon became popular. Plans offered by individual hospitals eventually gave way to regional Blue Cross plans supported by the American Hospital Association. Begun in 1939, Blue Shield provided coverage for physician fees in hospitals.

The local Blue Cross Blue Shield insurers, which in many parts of the country are the largest health insurers, were thus founded by the doctors and hospitals who dominated the insurers' boards.[14] How much could the Blues squeeze the pay of their own board members?

So the dominant, trusted brand-name insurance firms could and did push back against the corporate HR demands.

Furthermore, the implementer of this Corporate Purchasing 101 strategy was no steely-eyed purchasing agent. Health care benefits are usually purchased by the human resources department. The "I don't get no respect" mantra could well be echoed by HR personnel. In most firms, their status is at the bottom of the corporate pecking order.

The managers who really run the corporations, the ones with profit and loss responsibility, view the HR focus on benefits and employee morale as peripheral to the main corporate missions of making goods, providing services, and maximizing the bottom line.[15] It does not help that most HR managers are schooled in counseling or human relations rather than in finance or accounting.[16] Toss in a hefty amount of sexism—most HR personnel are women[17]—and you can see why HR personnel are generally viewed as softies. Their history in dreaming up the Corporate Purchasing 101 did little to dispel this image.

Although this failed cost-cutting strategy did succeed in robbing employees of a choice of carriers and coverage, companies were still faced with rising costs.

Bad Idea 2: Get New Kinds of Suppliers

The academic health care public policy community has long been enthusiastic about the prospects of using your money to manage your health care, but the American public did not share its enthusiasm. Americans simply did not want to pay somebody else to interfere with something as personal and important as their health, thank you very much. They didn't want to be told what doctors they had to see or when they had to see them, nor did they want any of the other limitations placed on them by HMOs. The few HMOs that existed were stuck in the mud.

Along came an unlikely savior for the HMOs—a U.S. president, one with a distinctive voice and a big nose.

Who was this champion of HMO health insurance? Bill Clinton, promoting Hillary-care or another of his well-intended but failed health care initiatives?

Nope. It was the Prince of Darkness himself, Richard Milhous Nixon, our tormented former commander in chief.

Nixon, whose interests lay primarily in foreign policy, was instinctively interventionist when it came to domestic policy. After all, he introduced government control of wages and prices for the economy. But Nixon was enough of a political realist to understand that governmental control of health care was not going to fly with the American public. Instead of the government, he would get HMOs to effect cost controls, while the federal government would foot the bill.

What convinced the cynical Nixon to back HMOs was the idea that "the less care they give them, the more money they make," as his aide, John Ehrlichman, informed him on February 17, 1971:

Ehrlichman:	On the—on the health business—
President Nixon:	Yeah.
Ehrlichman:	—we have now narrowed down . . . problems on this thing to one issue and that is whether we should include these health maintenance organizations like (the) Permanente thing.
President Nixon:	. . . You know I'm not too keen on any of these damn medical programs.
Ehrlichman:	This—this is a—
President Nixon:	I don't [unclear]—
Ehrlichman:	—private-enterprise one.
President Nixon:	Well, that appeals to me.
Ehrlichman:	Edgar Kaiser (son of Henry Kaiser) is running his Permanente deal for profit. And the reason that he can—the reason he can do it—I had Edgar Kaiser come in—talk to me about this. . . . All the incentives are toward less medical care, because—
President Nixon:	[Unclear.]
Ehrlichman:	—the less care they give them, the more money they make.

President Nixon: Fine. [Unclear.]
Ehrlichman: [Unclear] and the incentives run the right way.
President Nixon: Not bad.[18]

Nixon's 1973 HMO act not only required firms that offered health insurance to include a managed care product, in which the enrollee must obtain a gatekeeper's authorization for the use of medical care, among their choices, but it also subsidized their price with hundreds of millions of dollars of your tax money. With their then-limited volume, HMOs cost more because they incurred substantial fixed costs and "gatekeepers." Richard Nixon effectively lowered their price by subsidizing it. Federal subsidies enabled managed care plans to attract customers by offering benefits that other insurers could not. Last, in its cruelest aspect, the act enabled physicians to be paid for not providing health care. After all, the just-say-no version of managed care was all about convincing doctors not to provide medical care.

A few wily entrepreneurs saw a substantial opportunity in all of this. If the traditional insurers were not playing ball with HR and the federal government was subsidizing the purchase of HMOs, these sharpies were going to offer a new kind of health insurance—they called it "managed care." Their pitch was that they would not be merely paying health care providers whatever they charged for whatever they did; instead, they would oversee them to ensure that they did not give more health care services than needed or the wrong kind of care.

The managed care entrepreneurs promised the HR types that they would manage the prices the doctors and hospitals received. No more multimillionaire surgeons and hospital CEOs lounging away their Wednesdays at the golf club.

This new managed care strategy was supported by the academic community. The academics cited the example of Kaiser. They talked about the importance of prepayment and the emphasis it enabled on prevention. They lauded health service providers whose interests were squarely aligned with the insurers in integrated managed care groups. What they did not talk about, but what they knew, was that this version of managed care put their technocratic skills of evaluating medical treatments front and center.

After all, the managed care health insurance firms these new guys created were no Kaisers. OK, Kaiser's CEO earned $4 million in 2005, not a bad sum for a nonprofit CEO.[19] But his millions were a pittance when compared to the gobs of money earned by the managed care entrepreneurs. Unlike the missionary Henry Kaiser and Dr. Sidney Garfield, the new entrepreneurs were clearly out for the bucks. And they were good at extracting as much money for themselves as possible. Scoundrels or not, and you be the judge, you have to admire their sheer chutzpah.

Martin "Marty" Wygod provides one example of their financial acumen. Wygod, who got his start in life by managing horses, was a little late to the managed care land grab. Instead, he focused on managing one slice of health care, pharmaceuticals. He set up a pharmaceutical benefit manager (PBM) called "Medco" that would oversee pharmaceutical expenses for the managed care enrollees. The managed care insurers were glad to offload this tedious function: people take a lot of drugs, and the information technology required to manage their prices and volume is enormously complicated. From the perspective of the managed care insurers, in a market that exceeded $1 trillion, the game was not really worth the candle: pharmaceuticals accounted for less than 10 percent of U.S. health care expenses. Pretty soon, Wygod had a big public firm on his hands.

But Wygod knew something that many people did not: a substantial fraction of Medco's profits came not only from its dazzling skill in managing drug expenses, but also from rebates the manufacturers gave Medco for favoring their drugs. Marty Wygod, no HR softie, understood Corporate Purchasing 101 very well. He threw Medco's business to those pharmaceutical firms that gave him the best prices. Not all of these discounts were passed on to the managed care firms or to their enrollees; some of the rebates were kept by Medco.

What some call a "rebate" others might call a "kickback." And when it is called a "kickback," the congressional and executive branches of government get interested. It was only a matter of time before the PBMs would be grilled by a member of Congress intent on grabbing the lead story of the 7 p.m. news.

Entrepreneurs generally sell at the top of the market. After all, they know so much more than the buyer about the enterprise. When Wygod was ready to sell, he found a really munificent buyer, a veritable fairy godmother—the pharmaceutical firm Merck.

Merck not only paid $6.5 billion for Medco, but—and here is the part that makes this whole story worth telling—it also paid Wygod, personally, a $60 million finder's fee. Get this: the guy is the chairman of Medco; it is his job to maximize shareholders' welfare; but he is so shrewd that he somehow convinces his board to allow him to pocket an additional $60 million for selling the outfit.[20]

How shrewd is shrewd? Merck ultimately offloaded Medco in an initial public offering (IPO) valued at $5.5 billion in 2003. Merck never fessed up to how much money it lost, or made, while it was running this acquisition; but Eli Lilly, another pharma that bought a PBM, lost about $3 billion when it finally dumped it.[21] Meanwhile, Medco had the dubious pleasure of explaining to the U.S. Justice Department why a rebate from a company for buying its drugs was not a kickback and against the interest of the public.[22]

How Employers Killed Jack Morgan

Our income tax codes essentially force our employers to buy health insurance on our behalf. But the selection of health insurance is not an essential business function. Executives have a business to run. So they have turned the job over to the human resources personnel. The HR crowd is made up of staffers. Unlike most businesspeople who are charged with line, or operating, functions, HR does not design, manufacture, sell, or service products. Their experiences are thus not shaped by competition. And by education, and likely inclination, they are paternalistic; they study benefit design, not supply chain management or competitive strategy.

As an examination of HR magazines and their own journals will confirm, HR professionals do not present the idea that competition among different vendors of health insurance would reduce costs and improve quality. Nor do they trust employees to make good choices. Instead, they limit health insurance choices. Faced with rising health care costs and with federal requirements and subsidies, encouraged by the academics about Kaiser, and influenced by the HR crowd, companies began to restrict these policies to ones that managed care. But the new versions of managed care that they selected bore scant resemblance to the early incarnation of Kaiser. These new versions were managed by tough businesspeople who understood that a good way to make a buck was to tightly manage the use of health care services by the sick and disabled.

We know the rest of this story. Since 1996, many employers have narrowed choice. By 2005, virtually all employers were offering only one plan, typically a managed care one.[23]

But HR staffs were not the only entity on the side of the HMOs. The U.S. Congress helped too by subsidizing the HMOs' prices with our tax money and passing legislation that enabled doctors not to provide medical care. Congressional munificence was not limited to HMOs; it also helped hospitals, as we saw in Chapter 3, and it really opened the coffers for some drug companies. Sadly, doctors are not on Congress's gift list. To the contrary, the U.S. Congress is encouraging Uncle Sam to become Dr. Sam, encroaching on the practice of medicine, and it has also limited the ability of doctors to manage the organizations in which they work.

As we will see, Congress has gotten powerfully involved in various aspects of health care. How would it behave if it had full control?

We can answer the question by examining congressional oversight of kidney care, the only disease that is almost fully paid for by the U.S. federal government.

CHAPTER 5

KILLER NUMBER 4: THE U.S. CONGRESS
Death at the Hands of Those Elected to Represent Us

In 1973, the American people generously decided that we would use our taxes to pay for the care of patients with permanent kidney failure. Before then, most patients died prematurely because they could not afford dialysis.

We could have channeled this money in a number of different ways. We could, for example, have given it to the people most directly affected by the money and the disease—the patients themselves. After all, it is our tax money that is paying for virtually all this medical care, and we could have chosen to put it directly under Jack Morgan's control. Had we given the patients the money, they could have decided who among the providers of dialysis gave them the best value.

Instead, the U.S. Congress decided to confiscate Jack's decision for itself. It did this by prescribing what kind of care he needed and then buying it, without consulting Jack or his doctor. Congress decided he would receive dialysis three times a week; that he would not have much in the way of diagnostic testing and even less in helping him to promote his health status; and that he would be given a whole lot, perhaps too much, of a hormone, erythropoietin, that controls the anemia that typically plagues the victims of kidney disease. With this set of decisions, Congress likely hastened Jack Morgan's death.

When the U.S. Congress confiscated our tax money and declared itself both our shopper and our doctor, it assumed an unusual role for a government. After all, Congress does not set the prices for your car, your clothes, your food. Yet it sets the prices paid to the doctors, hospitals, dialysis centers, pharmaceutical firms, and other providers for kidney care. Congress does not determine the size of the refrigerator in your kitchen, at least not yet; but remarkably, it did set the level of hematocrit—a marker for the amount of red blood cells in a kidney patient's blood—that must be achieved for the medical care providers to be paid. This level could best be attained through use of the drug erythropoietin (Epogen), or epo.

Did Congress really hone in on Jack and interfere with his medical treatment? No, our elected representatives in Washington didn't know Jack from a hole in the wall. That's the problem. They took it upon themselves to prescribe his treatment and that of every other kidney patient in the country without any knowledge of their individual characteristics and circumstances.

How Uncle Sam Became Dr. Sam

How did the U.S. Congress come to dictate Jack's kidney care?

In the 1950s, patients and their families were paying for the then relatively new, costly dialysis therapy, mostly out of their pockets. Although some patients could draw upon medical insurance benefits, research grants, or private donations, the high costs of dialysis in 1965 led to fewer than 150 people being dialyzed, while tens of thousands were qualified for treatment.[1] The kidney patients who were not dialyzed were essentially consigned to death. Because there were so few paying patients, there was also an acute shortage of capacity at the time. Many hospitals set up dialysis and transplant committees to select who would receive dialysis and who would not, who would live and who would die. One member of the Seattle-based Swedish Hospital's "Death Committees" has since recalled, "I am still haunted" by these activities.[2]

To dramatize the need for funding, a patient testified while being dialyzed in front of the House Ways and Means Committee. Our representatives, shocked to learn that we were rationing this life-giving form of medical care, responded. On October 30, 1972, the legislation that created the national End-Stage Renal Disease Program (ESRDP) was passed after only 30 minutes of debate with only one dissenting vote. Senator Vance Hartke (D-Indiana) declaimed:

In what must be the most tragic irony of the 20th century, people are dying because they cannot get access to proper medical care. We have learned how to treat or to cure some of the diseases (that) have plagued mankind for centuries, yet those treatments are not available because of their cost. Mr. President, we can begin to get our priorities straight by undertaking a national effort to bring kidney disease treatment within the reach of all those in need.[3]

Once again, the fingerprints of Richard Nixon, our jowly, five-o'clock-shadowed, furtive-eyed president, are all over this one: he championed not only managed care organizations but also the federal government's takeover of payments for kidney disease. Ostensibly a Republican conservative, when it came to health care, Nixon continually expanded the control of government and big bureaucracies over it.

The cost of kidney dialysis and related services for men of Jack's age, in their fifties, currently amounts to around $65,000 a year.[4] If the patients have private health insurance, their insurer must pay for 33 months of care. After that, Medicare, the U.S. government's health insurance for the elderly, pays, regardless of the patient's age. Medicare accounts for 90 percent of ESRDP payments and about 300,000 patients. People with ESRD are virtually the only non-elderly covered by Medicare.[5]

Because the U.S. Congress approves the government budget for Medicare, in effect, every senator and representative helps to determine the treatment and to set the price for Jack Morgan's kidney care.

Congressional Control of Kidney Disease

Normally, when we buy something, you and I decide the bundle of things we want and what we are willing to pay for it.

Consider life insurance, for example. We may choose different levels of insurance and buy the policies from different companies. One of them, the Northwestern Mutual Life Insurance Company, is among the highest rated of all U.S. firms for consumer satisfaction.[6] We can choose from different firms and many different insurance brokers. The competition among them gives us better service, quality, choice, and price.

But victims of kidney disease do not have any choices and can make no decisions about their treatments. They cannot select a bundle of services or the price they are willing to pay for them. Their choice is limited to the site in which they will receive their care. Once they select the site, the U.S. Congress then muscles in and determines the services they will receive and their price.

Our congressional representatives are very able people; but they are not great shoppers. Why should they be? They're spending our money, not theirs, and they have no way of knowing our needs and preferences.

Of course, the congressional act that ensured public funding for the victims of kidney disease is laudable: inspired by a grave need and paid by a generous public, it has increased the life span of the victims of kidney disease. It could have been great legislation; but because it was implemented badly, it is not. It wrongly gave control of the money to the U.S. Congress, not Jack Morgan. The congressional overseers spent too much money on drugs and too little on diagnostic tests, health promotion, and dialysis.

Congressional oversight has been costly and, in some senses, the results have been a failure: while expenditures on kidney care soared, more than tripling from $5.1 billion in 1991 to $18.4 billion in 2004, the death rates in the first year of dialysis for end-stage renal disease patients remained the same from 1993 to 2004, as did hospital admissions and lengths of stay.[7] All that money did not result in lower death rates or healthier patients. All too many patients did not receive the preventive care that could slow the progression of their diseases. And it now appears that the high levels of epo the U.S. Congress endorsed caused a significant increase in deaths and heart disease in some recipients.[8]

It is impossible to delineate exactly how kidney care would have changed if Congress had not meddled in it. Most likely, the care would have been more efficient, convenient, and focused on wellness. Had Jack Morgan controlled the payments to providers—rather than the U.S. Congress or his insurer—medical care providers unquestionably would have responded more to his individual needs. For example, they could have competed with each other by efficiently focusing on the individual needs of the patient—no cookie-cutter medicine practiced here—with an emphasis on wellness and health promotion and excellent care for the diseases that typically accompany kidney disease. They could have given him more frequent dialysis and less in the way of drugs. But because providers must follow Congress's recipe, kidney disease victims, like Jack Morgan, can die prematurely, injured by the shortage of the testing and health promoting services they need and the excessive drugs they received, and we likely paid too much for the wrong kind of care.

For sure, if Jack Morgan were a European or a Canadian, he likely would not have fared as well as he did in the United States. As Professor Eli Friedman noted in his seminal 1997 article, "Health Care Reform Engulfs All of Us," some European countries and Canada have rationed kidney care and/or penalized doctors who provided it to too many people.[9] France attempted to reduce its annual expenditure for health care "by issuing 'Health-Care Identity Cards' and tracking each physician's treatment costs.[10] . . . [P]hysicians who 'overspend' will have their reimbursement reduced—clearly a signal to ration expensive services. . . . Canadian nephrologists are fixed by hospital and personnel funding reductions that constrain their acceptance of haemodialysis patients. As recounted by one, 'Each time I present a new patient for haemodialysis . . . I am viewed as an enemy.'"[11]

Their relative performance in comparison to the United States had not improved by 2004. Although occurrences of kidney disease in the United States are only 50 percent higher than in Germany or Canada,[12] we performed double the number of transplants per million population as Germany[13] and many more than in Canada too.[14]

As for the United Kingdom, may the force be with you. The relative risk of death for a dialysis patient in the United Kingdom, with its government-run health care system, was significantly higher than in other countries where the government exercises less control, like Italy. Hospitalization rates for ESRD patients for heart disease were lowest in the United Kingdom, although its incidence was similar to those in other countries.[15] The median waiting times for dialysis with vascular access there ranged between one week and nine months.[16] The outer edge of this waiting time could be a death warrant.

Yet despite the favorable comparison of U.S. kidney care to that in other countries—more transplants, readier admissions to hospitals, and shorter waiting times—the situation in the United States is far from optimal. In the process of spending our money, Congress pumped up funding for drugs and reduced incentives for crucial therapeutic and health promoting treatments.

One group clearly benefited, however. The businesspeople who understood the care and feeding of our Congress earned millions. For example, after earning $23 million in 2004, the CEO of DaVita, a firm that owns a fourth of all dialysis centers, earned over $25 million in 2005.[17] As the head of the nominating committee in the firm that was the progenitor to DaVita, I helped to recruit its CEO, so I know that he is an able person. He revived the faltering firm. And most of his compensation came from the increases in the value of DaVita's stock during his tenure. He benefited in the same way as its shareholders.

But was his compensation appropriate? Investors evaluate businesses on the basis of the returns, the profits, they earn for their owners, the people who own the shares of stock in the company. Risky businesses, such as biotechnology firms whose science is largely unknown, should earn higher returns to compensate their owners for the risk they take by investing in them. Dialysis is not nearly as risky a business as high technology, medical diagnostics, automobiles, or many others. Numerically, DaVita's risk—as measured by a statistic called *beta*—was only 60 percent of the stock market as a whole in December 2006.[18] (At that time, DaVita's performance trailed that of its peers.) Why the low beta? Because dialysis is a business in which the government essentially guarantees payment for all your customers.

Some may find it hard to justify this kind of income for the CEOs of firms with so little risk.[19] But DaVita's board of directors went along with it. They too were well paid. Although DaVita's disclosure of its board members' compensation is murky, it appears that the one former head who sits on the board of the Medicare agency that determines payments for dialysis earned about $5 million since 2000.[20]

As for Amgen, the biotechnology firm that manufactures the drug primarily used for people on dialysis, its CEO was paid nearly $20 million in 2005, on top of nearly $50 million of options,[21] while Amgen's stock was downgraded because it has "a pipeline gap"—that is, a shortage of important new drugs.[22]

Make no mistake about who paid the DaVita and Amgen CEOs all that money. It was you and I. After all, our tax money is one of the primary sources for Medicare expenditures, and Medicare is the primary source of payment for dialysis.

To ensure that their voices were heard, the business leaders in the kidney care industry sprinkled considerable money on the U.S. Congress. Amgen spent $5.7 million on lobbying expenses in 2005[23] and made $400,000 in federal-level political donations in 2001 and 2002.[24] As for DaVita, the *Los Angeles Times* alleged that the $1 million it spent on federal lobbying in the first half of 2006 led to an annual $100 million increase in Medicare payments to dialysis providers.[25]

We are fortunate that so many able, dedicated people are willing to serve as our congressional representatives. Whenever I visit the U.S. Congress, my head spins at the range of complex issues they must review: the Middle East today, the homeless tomorrow. But congressional representatives need substantial money for their election campaigns, and they understandably pay close attention to those who donate it.

The Congressional Recipe for Treating Kidney Disease

To oversee the billions of dollars in dialysis expenditures, Congress essentially created a recipe consisting of three ingredients: dialysis services, physician services, and drugs. It determined the amount of each ingredient by dictating its price. Imagine for a moment that Congress decided to oversee the preparation of beef stew in this way. It would pay for only three items: the restaurant where the cooking takes place, the stew chefs, and the beef and other ingredients. And it would dictate the price it would pay for each—$1 per stew preparation for the chefs, $4 for the restaurant, and $1.28 cents for the beef and other ingredients—take it or leave it. Since Congress is virtually the only payer, how could anyone "leave it"?

The congressional stew turned out to be heavy on the beef—the drugs, for which it paid $93 per treatment—and light on the restaurants, for which it paid less and less.[26] Many stand-alone kidney dialysis facilities simply could not survive the ever-shrinking payments doled out by Congress. They either folded or sold out to businesses that ran chains of dialysis centers. The chains achieved economies of scale in the purchase of drugs, supplies, and equipment and in administration and billing. For example, the largest chains paid from 8 to 22 percent less for the three leading drugs than freestanding centers in 2003. Their drug acquisition costs were 6 percent less than the average; the freestanding centers' costs were 4 percent higher.[27]

Many independent dialysis centers went out of business or were essentially forced to become chain restaurants because of the stringency of congressional payment patterns. By 2005, 60 percent of all dialysis facilities were part of a chain.[28] In 2006, after many rounds of consolidation, only two large dialysis chains were left: DaVita and Fresenius, each the product of many prior consolidations.[29]

Chains, or, in economics speak, horizontally integrated organizations, generally prosper in consumer-driven markets because they can be more efficient than one-off organizations. But a chain cannot respond as readily to the unique needs of its customers.

Meanwhile, the chefs, the nephrologists, who were paid a flat sum for their services, spent less and less time on stew preparation.[30] Congress did not offer special incentives for them to initiate the testing and wellness activities that could have mitigated progression of the other diseases that frequently accompany kidney disease.[31]

The results of these recipes and payment patterns? In 2004, patients adhered poorly to drug therapy that was essential to their health, likely because of inadequate medical encouragement and education in how and why to do it.[32] In most chains and hospital-based centers, fewer than half the patients had good results for diabetes or the important tests for the heart diseases that typically accompany diabetes,[33] and two-thirds had excessive levels of protein in their urine, a dangerous sign of the lack of efficacy of the dialysis.[34] Although many patients are diabetics, less than half of these very sick patients received comprehensive diabetic monitoring in 2004[35] or flu vaccine, despite their appearance in the dialysis centers at least three times each week.[36]

Meanwhile, treatment with Epogen shot through the ceiling.[37] The average patient received $6,000 of it in 2002.[38] Congress was very good to Epogen's manufacturer. It upped epo's usage by essentially increasing the level Congress required and favoring it in the cost-plus payment formula it chose for drugs. Then it gave the company a virtual monopoly by granting the drug a special designation as an "orphan drug"—a drug with fewer than 200,000 recipients. The legislation was originally intended to encourage the commercialization of pharmaceuticals for rare diseases. As a result, the orphan drug law is a treasure trove for the industry: no similar drugs can go through the government's clearance process for seven years, and it grants a 50 percent tax credit on clinical trials and waiver of substantial user fees. With only 78,000 patients in 1989, Epogen originally seemed like a wonderful candidate for the "orphan" designation.[39] But by 2005, with sales in excess of $3 billion, epo was hardly an orphan.

The Impact of Congressional Control on the Dialysis Chains, the Doctors, and the Drug Manufacturers

Congressional control favored chains of dialysis providers over free-standing centers and the manufacturers of the drug epo. Congress reduced inflation-adjusted expenditures on dialysis, measured in 1974 dollars, from $138 per treatment in 1974 to $34 in 2002. Yet because Congress paid for epo at 6 percent over the average sales price, as computed by Uncle Sam, it was used heavily. Six percent may not sound like much; but because the average dialysis patient received $6,000 worth of epo in 2002, it amounts to a whole lot of money.

Congressional Control of Drug Companies

The U.S. Congress decided to pay for the drugs used in kidney disease treatment at cost plus a mark-up. Because biological drugs can be digested, they cannot be swallowed. Instead, they must be infused via the intravenous (IV) line used in the course of the dialysis, or they must be injected by physicians. The treatment centers are paid not only for their services, but also for the difference between the cost of the drugs and the government's price.

You don't need a CPA to figure out what happens to costs when the federal government gives you a cost-plus contract, especially when the "cost" is difficult to determine.

The price the government pays for drugs is pegged at 1.06 of the average sales price (ASP) for some, average acquisition price for others, and reasonable costs for hospitals. These numbers can be pure mumbo-jumbo. The federal government has difficulty in determining exactly how much Dr. X in Waltham, Massachusetts, paid for the drug he injected. The dialysis clinics are estimated to earn nearly 40 percent of their profits from the spread in the price of epo between their cost and the government's price.[40]

The firm that sells the biggest of these drugs—the antianemia substance, epo—would like more and more of it to be used. And it has succeeded. In 2005, epo was Medicare's single largest drug expenditure, clocking in at $2.4 billion in 2006;[41] but it accounted for only $840 million of Medicare's ESRD payments in 1998.[42]

Why did expenditures for epo grow so fast?

For one thing, Congress motivated clinics and doctors to use epo with its payment formulas. Then, the U.S. Congress began playing doctor, encouraging the use of even more epo by dictating the level of *hematocrit*—a measure of oxygen-carrying red blood cells that is directly affected by the use of epo. For example, one powerful senator personally requested that the Medicare administrators increase the upper end level of the hematocrit.[43] His request had more than a little clout because he chaired the subcommittee that supervises the budget of Medicare. In 2006, the upper level for hematocrit was increased once again. When Congress decided that the target hematocrit range should be increased by a mere 3 percent, from 30 to 33 percent to 30 to 36 percent, epo spending increased threefold, by about $500 million. The 3 percent increase required up to a 50 percent increase in epo dosage.[44]

The U.S. Congress was practicing medicine.

What scientific evidence informs the U.S. Congress in setting hematocrit levels?

Some warned the congressional doctor that he was practicing bad medicine.[45] They claimed that the evidence from randomized clinical trials demonstrates that "patients assigned to higher hematocrit target levels do not show discernible improvements in survival, hospitalization, or cardiac outcomes. In fact, they could be prone to adverse cardiovascular events that include heart attacks and strokes."[46] These warnings were prescient. An important 2006 study found that these high hematrocit levels were increasing the chances of death, heart attacks, disease, and stroke, among other serious problems.[47]

The Congressional Magi

Epogen is a great drug that improves patients' quality of life. Before its commercialization, kidney patients required blood transfusions to combat anemia. The transfusions not only were expensive and invasive but were also carriers of blood-borne diseases, like hepatitis. Epo's value was easily observable. Kidney disease profoundly affects the complexion. When epo's clinical trials began, in 1985, patients' once-ashen skin glowed pink.[48]

Amgen, a Thousand Oaks, California, firm that discovered and commercialized Epogen and a follow-on drug, reaped huge financial rewards. Its stock price grew by more than 50 percent annually in the 1990s. Its profit margin of 32 percent was bigger than Microsoft's in 2002.[49] It earned nearly $4 billion in profits in 2005.

Why?

Well, it had scientific prowess, especially in its early days; but it has also excelled as a brass-knuckled legal combatant. Amgen repeatedly sued its "partner," Johnson & Johnson, which had bailed Amgen out of financial troubles with a 1985 licensing deal, and others who dared to tread on its patents. Give Amgen an A for marketing too. It developed a new version of Epogen, whose main virtue was that it required less frequent dosing because it was more difficult for the body to excrete it through urination.

But Amgen also owes its success to the U.S. Congress. When the bureaucrats who run Medicare deemed the new version of epo as "functionally equivalent" to the old, they were decreeing that Medicare would pay the same price for the old and new versions of epo. Guess what happened? Congress ruled that the Medicare administrators could no longer use the functional-equivalence criterion.[50]

Like the Magi, the U.S. Congress gave Amgen three gifts: First, it voided functional equivalence; second, it provided for the continual expansion of required hematocrit levels; and third, and perhaps the most generous, it gave Amgen an orphan drug monopoly over epo.

Little Orphan Amgen

Congress decided that Epogen, which by 2005 had earned $22 billion in revenues for Amgen,[51] was an "orphan drug." Remember, the orphan drug designation was meant to induce pharmaceutical investment in rare diseases; but, by 2001, 50 percent of the world's best-selling biotech drugs were "orphan drugs," including human growth hormone.[52] The prices of these drugs are typically so high that they could cause patients considerable hardships; for example, one orphan drug user, an accountant who worked in a small firm, was forced to find new work as a door-to-door salesman in a larger firm because his small firm could not afford the costs of his health insurance.[53]

Typically, a high-priced product incurs high costs. But orphan drugs require lower expenses than the massive amounts that pharmaceutical companies typically spend for clinical trials and marketing for a blockbuster drug. The number of participants in clinical trials for an orphan drug is not only smaller than those for a blockbuster, but the costly trials are also easier to implement because there are fewer doctors who care for patients with the rare disease. The smaller number of patients and doctors also reduces marketing expenses.[54]

So why are the prices for orphan drugs so high? The biologicals among them are more expensive to manufacture, but the absence of competition is also a major factor in enabling the high price of orphan drugs. Of course, if the drug is truly an "orphan," with a small number of users, a monopolistic status may be needed to encourage investment in the costly R&D that drugs typically require. But Congress enabled Amgen's Epogen to maintain its orphan drug status when it ultimately commanded a huge market.[55] Would it not make more sense to designate orphans on the basis of the dollar value of their revenues rather than by the number of individuals who need the drug? After all, it is the dollar size of the market that determines whether drug companies are willing to invest in the expensive research and development required.

Amgen, which recognized the value of the gifts that Congress has showered on it, is extremely skilled in rewarding the hand

that feeds it: In 2004, Amgen's 20-person D.C. government relations office spent $122,186 in soft money contributions.[56] Former
President George H. W. Bush's press secretary headed its D.C.
office.[57]

Congressional Control of Hospitals

The U.S. Congress pays for kidney dialysis services by site of care.
If your kidneys are dialyzed in a hospital, your providers will be paid
a different, higher price from what they would be paid if you were
dialyzed in a local center. Congress pays hospitals $132 per treat-
ment and the dialysis centers $4 less.[58]

Yet a detailed government analysis has determined that, despite
the higher hospital costs, dialysis patients receive essentially the same
services at each site. Further, hospitals are less productive.[59] The hospitals cost more because they cannot attain the economies of scale
and focus of the dialysis centers.

Normally, when two places deliver exactly the same services and
one costs more than the other, the costlier one will go out of business. But Congress happily subsidizes the hospitals' inefficiency by
paying them more, again, with our money.

Do you think that maybe the $17 million that hospitals and their
kin spent on lobbying and contributions in 2004 had a little something to do with this decision?[60]

Uncle Sam Becomes Dr. Sam:
Pay for Conformance

Traditionally, the U.S. government performs three important functions: it redistributes income from the rich to the poor, in accordance
with the wishes of the citizenry; it provides public goods that could
not be delivered by the private sector, such as defense; and it protects consumers against the potential excesses of unfettered markets,
such as collusion, excessive concentration, and false advertising. But

to control health care costs and reward high quality, Congress is now practicing medicine.

In health care, governments have encroached into traditional business functions. For example, pay-for-performance (P4P) initiatives enable governments to tell health care providers how to practice medicine.

The federal government did not always play this role. Initially, it paid those who provided services to Medicare enrollees for their costs. Not surprisingly, the costs of health care providers increased substantially. To control them, Congress used a system through which it determined fixed prices for the procedures performed by doctors, hospitals, and other suppliers of medical care, such as home health.[61] But this system was flawed: the incompetent was paid the same price as the superb. To reward those who provided higher-quality medicine, Congress turned to a new pricing system, which it dubbed "pay for performance." The higher the performance, the higher the pay.

We normally think that "performance" means quality. A high-quality car is safe, reliable, environmentally friendly, and does not guzzle gasoline. Similarly, high-quality hospital surgeries do not kill their patients, do not infect them, and do not cause potentially deadly blood clots, but they do enable their patients to improve their quality of life. But the health care system lacks such metrics of performance.

Despite its name, P4P does not pay for *performance*—the attainment of improved health at a reasonable price. Instead, it pays for *conformance*—adherence to a government-dictated recipe for the provision of health care. The government pays for adherence to its recipes for the process of delivering health care rather than for the outcomes. If P4P were used for cars, the government would not reward a safer, more fuel-efficient automobile. Instead, it would reward automobile manufacturers who followed congressional instructions on how to build a car.

Government P4P recipes, like those for kidney care, are specified as if they were the 11th commandment; but there is no *one* recipe for medical care. Treatments must be tailored to the patient's unique characteristics. Are drugs that lower blood pressure as mandatory for heart failure patients as one government recipe avers? Not to the observant doctors who keep some elderly patients' pressure slightly elevated to help the blood circulate in their rigid vessels. These doctors will be penalized under cookie-cutter government recipes. Further, medicine is the youngest science, studded with frequent flip-flops in accepted treatment. Yesterday's must-do painkillers, such as Vioxx, are today's tort lawyer bonanzas.

Government recipes for medical care are delineated largely through "peer review" and statistical "meta-analysis." Those jaw-breaking titles imply saintly physicians who use the rigorous tools of science to dispassionately evaluate the merits of each other's work. But medical "peers" often become brass-knuckled gutter fighters when their expertise is threatened. They use consensus, rather than rigorous scientific experimentation, to inform them in developing the recommended process of medical care. The history of medicine is filled with shameful suppressions of important innovations, such as one cancer researcher's inability to gain publication of his Nobel Prize–worthy theories in "peer-reviewed" journals.[62] Cancer patients paid the price of "peer review" with a delay of nearly a decade in the use of promising drugs, such as Avastin, that his theories have since enabled.

Although medicine has long been practiced, it lacks the explanatory powers of a science like physics. Yesterday's must-do estrogen treatments for menopausal women are now considered to have caused breast cancer. Much of what is now viewed as correct medical practice will change in the future—but we do not know what will change. For this reason, some analysts view P4P process measures with concern. The focus on process may divert doctors from focusing on outcomes.[63] They also worry that the measures are too rigid and that surgical P4P process measures, for example, "could be harmful for older persons with several comorbidities [additional problems]."[64]

Jack Morgan and the Congressional Kidney Care Recipe

The government created a recipe for kidney care that consisted of fixed quantities and prices for drugs, doctors, and dialysis.[65]

But many experts disagree with the congressional recipe. A number of nephrologists believe the victims of kidney disease need more dialysis, perhaps daily.[66] Nevertheless, Congress, with its relentless eye on the Epogen meter, instead chose to continuously increase those expenditures, despite mounting evidence that the higher doses of epo are bad for your health.

Suppose Jack Morgan were given the $65,000 or so that Congress spent on his dialysis.[67] Do you think that some entrepreneurs would have offered him kidney care bundled into one package of doctors, dialysis, and drugs? Do you think he might have opted for less epo and more dialysis? Less epo and more physician visits? Less epo and more preventive care?

Would someone in the community formed by Jack Morgan and his colleagues have called the *New York Times* or *60 Minutes* to shine a public spotlight on the profits earned by Amgen, the firm manufacturing Epogen, and the dialysis chain DaVita, their CEO compensation, and their lobbying expenses and political contributions?

Would kidney care have become more diverse, more organized, more effective, more efficient as a result of these efforts?

How do you spell "you bet"?

Because the U.S. Congress believed it was a better shopper than Jack, it too helped to kill him. But how did Congress become so convinced that it possessed the skills needed to become Dr. Sam? Blame the academic policy advisors who educated and advised its members.

KILLER NUMBER 5: THE ACADEMICS
Death at the Hands of the Elite Policy Makers

The academic community that analyzes health care public policy also helped to kill Jack Morgan. Sure, they commit the usual academic sins of irrelevant pedantry—with laughable critiques of each other's work that note, for example, the failure of the author to note the reviewer's latest article. The impact of this kind of narcissistic criticism on our health care system is minimal.

Nevertheless, the academics have had important and deleterious influence on the agents meant to represent us. Their voices are ubiquitous—heard not only in academic outlets but also in the popular media when they seek "experts" to disentangle the complex world of health care. Because there is so little information available on the outcomes of health care, the experts serve as Oracles of Delphi, interpreters of murky events.

When it comes to health care, many academics favor schemes that give them considerable power over your money. A perennial favorite is a single-payer health care system—that is, the government's doling out all the money to be used for health care. Some of those educated by these academics conflate the term "single-payer" with the notion of "universal health care," in which everyone has health insurance. But the two are very different. Universal health care can be achieved in many different ways, such as enabling all consumers, rich or poor, to buy their own health insurance. I discuss these different techniques in Part 3 of this book. A single-payer system, in contrast, achieves universal health care solely through the government.

Academics favor the single-payer solution for many reasons; but surely one of them, acknowledged or not, is that it puts them, as advisors to the government, in charge of spending $2 trillion. Failing that, managed care is the academics' next best solution, where they argue that it takes a lot of talent to manage your care, namely, *their* talent. And failing that, various "pay-for-performance" schemes are popular favorites.

The intellectual rationale for third-party control is the belief that productivity in service organizations, like health care, cannot be significantly improved. If this is valid, then the only way to control costs is to ration care through central control; but this view is badly mistaken. There are so many ways to increase productivity that service organizations, such as retailing, provided the mainstay for this country's productivity boom in the late twentieth century.

To be fair, the complexities of health care have defied so many reforms so often that a big, sweeping universal "reform" can seem appealing. But a single-payer system managed by Uncle Sam will kill many of the most promising innovations taking place in health care and medicine, just as it distorted kidney disease care. Don't forget that over the course of industrial history, our most important productivity-enhancing innovations earned little respect from the experts until they succeeded. When Henry Ford introduced the Model T Ford, he promised to make it the best *and* the cheapest, and he targeted customers in the middle class, not the rich who owned most of the automobiles back then. As with health care today, most observers who thought they knew something about the subject scoffed. At the time, a car in the United Kingdom cost more than many houses.[1] Yet in eight years, Ford slashed the price of a Model T by more than 50 percent. As the price dropped, volume soared— from 6,000 in 1908 to nearly 600,000 in 1916.[2] In 20 years, Ford's good car at a good price enabled ownership of automobiles to climb from 1,770 to 1,870,000.[3] So much for the doubters.

The academics' praise for managed care and other top-down, technocratic health care "reforms" tilted the board in favor of disastrous policy decisions. These broad, utopian solutions for the cost and uneven quality of our health care system glossed over inconvenient facts: If Kaiser is so universally wonderful, why did its growth plans fail? If managed care is a panacea, why did many patients and health care providers deplore it? How will innovations in medicine be initiated and used in a top-down health care system? Then too their dismissive disdain for the competence of clinical physicians and for the ability of people like Jack Morgan to choose and manage their health care depressed and constrained both doctors and consumers and the public policy initiatives that could have empowered them.

There may be some legitimate intellectual reasons for the academics' favoring solutions that give them power over 16 percent of the GDP and disdaining solutions that grant power to the people or to creators of managerial or technological innovations. But let's be clear here: a major motive for academics' support of third-party management of the health care system and for technocratic, contentless solutions and their dismissal of the consumer's role is pure and simple self-interest.

How Academic Education Caused Ambitious, Well-Intended, Smart People to Go So Wrong

In considerable measure, the U.S. Congress's paternalistic, autocratic oversight of kidney dialysis, discussed in the last chapter, reflects the academic training of its members and staff. Two trains of thought permeate public policy higher education in this country, and they have had a major effect on the health care debate: one is a relentless focus on the importance of statistical analysis, and the other stresses the shortcomings of business as opposed to nonprofits, governments, and nongovernment organizations (NGOs).

Statistical analysis—the ability to find patterns in data—can cause a smart person to believe that she can detect things that the experienced practitioner in the field misses. The ramifications of analytic techniques for the creators of public policy are clear: you do not need to be an experienced clinician to craft effective public policies. Indeed, the absence of experience or special skills honed in the health care arena may well enable you to see the forest for the trees and observe patterns that the expert misses.

But it is all too easy for these analysts to see connections that don't really exist, especially if they lack any practical experience in the subject they are analyzing. Statistical correlations are meaningless or misleading, absent an experienced person's insight into the subject being analyzed. For example, the tides in the Atlantic Ocean correlate with peak flow of traffic on our highways. What does one have to do with the other? Do tides cause a high flow of traffic? Of course not. But tides do correlate with the movement of the moon—that is, morning and evening hours. And the flow of automobile and truck traffic is, of course, determined by the time of day.

Notes 1988 Economics Nobel laureate Maurice Allais: ". . . All my work rests on the conviction that . . . the only two really fruitful stages in the scientific approach are firstly a thorough examination of the initial hypotheses; and secondly a discussion of the meaning and empirical relevance of the results obtained. . . . The mathematical rigour of the reasoning can never justify a theory based on postulates if these postulates do not correspond to the true nature of the observed phenomena. . . ."[4]

Yet another tenet of public policy is that businesses, funded by their owners, are thought to be less altruistic than nonprofits and governments, which are organizational forms that have no owners. But, as for the ostensible altruism of nonbusiness organizations, firms come in various shapes, sizes, and ethical flavors. For every Enron, there's a Johnson & Johnson. For every mismanaged Red Cross disaster intervention, there's the Salvation Army, one of the most effective organizations anywhere. All organizations are shaped by the rewards and penalties faced by those who lead them, not by simplistic distinctions in the sources of their funding. (Chapter 9 contains a detailed analysis of the roles of nonprofits, businesses, and governments in health care.)

But, understandably, since academics have traditionally thrived in the nonprofit sector and government sectors—universities, think tanks, government advisory panels, and so on—and have used them to advance their careers, they favor and feel more comfortable with these institutions. Successful academics know how to become powerful in these settings. This bias helps to explain some of the misplaced analyses, shallow theories, and reckless generalizations made by the academic health care community for government-sponsored "single-payer" or managed-care health systems.

The Intellectual Tools for Congressional Control of Kidney Care

The core tool that would be used to allocate resources in a single-payer or managed care system is "systems" or "operations analysis"—a set of techniques for analyzing the impact of individual actions in large, complex systems. Just as the techniques of managed care were thought to enable a group of analysts to oversee and override the decisions of practicing doctors, the techniques of systems analysis were thought to enable a group of economists to oversee the military's conduct of our war in Vietnam. I would have thought that the Vietnam experience would have disabused them of the notion, but, sadly, it did not.

Alain Enthoven, a distinguished Rhodes Scholar and Ph.D. in operations research, was the assistant secretary of defense charged with this type of analysis during part of the Vietnam War. Not surprisingly, he was one of the most visible advocates of managed care.[5]

Modern-day systems analysis began innocently enough. It was first used in Great Britain, prior to World War II, to install radar devices.[6] At one time, radar devices were installed in locations that minimized their individual chances of being jammed. The systems analysts, in contrast, successfully designed an installation process that minimized the probability of jamming the whole system. After this early triumph, systems analysts were entrusted with ever-larger problems, beginning with the development of a construction schedule for a weapons system and culminating in a plan for major military operations.

So successful were these applications that the techniques of systems analysis were brought to the U.S. Department of Defense in the 1960s by its then secretary, Robert McNamara, a brilliant Harvard MBA.[7] McNamara wanted to reshape what he viewed as sloppy, unsystematic military decision making by using a disciplined mathematical approach.[8]

Systems analysis had proved useful primarily for developing schedules, but not for determining policy. The McNamara Defense Department catapulted the techniques to new, different, vastly more important applications: determination of military strategies. In the heyday of systems analysis, brilliant, young, politically appointed economists suddenly wielded enormous military power. As one observer of the Defense Department notes, "The revolutionary manner in which McNamara made his decisions transformed the 'expert' [military] career bureaucrat into the 'novice' and the 'inexperienced' appointee into the 'professional.'"[9] Precisely because the analysts were trained in economics, operations research, and statistics and because they were not professional soldiers, they were presumed to be free of the military's parochial interests and able to attend to the best interests of the public.

The application of systems analysis was not limited to military problems. Soon its use spread to other government organizations. In 1967, President Lyndon Johnson ordered all the agencies of the federal government to adopt it. Many state and local governments fell into line too. New York City's Mayor John Lindsay, one of its many advocates, boasted in a large 1970 recruiting ad that his staff, along with McKinsey & Company consultants, was "creatively utilizing quantitative analysis and computer technology. But all the problems are not [yet] solved and we need more talented individuals."[10]

Virtually all these applications of systems analysis were disasters, most poignantly those that conducted the war in Vietnam. They brought New York City to the brink of bankruptcy too.

Yet many academics, entranced by their newfound power to determine public policy, became true believers. They perpetuated the myth. As McNamara's assistant secretary of defense, an economist, noted in *Economics of Defense in the Nuclear Age*, a widely read primer on systems analysis, "We regard all military problems as . . . problems in the efficient allocation and use of resources."[11]

Who could solve such problems better than the systems analyst? Programs in public policy analysis that trained acolytes in the field flourished in schools of government, public health, education, and social service.

Enthoven, now an emeritus professor at Stanford University, began to apply systems analysis to the problems of health care in the 1970s. His influential preferred solution of "managed competition" advocated competition among vertically integrated managed care health insurance plans, each offering identical benefits. A consultant to Kaiser Permanente, Enthoven frequently presented that giant as an example of the efficacy of managed care.[12]

The intellectual basis for his views was clear: managed care organizations place decision-making analysts in the center of power—above the practicing doctors—to determine patients' care. As the *New York Times* noted, "The fact that an HMO has a management structure . . . appealed to Enthoven's passion for rational systems."[13] He particularly admired its "set of documented practice protocols," that is, detailed plans for patients' treatment. Its triage system, which permits primary care physicians to treat most illnesses, appealed to him too because in his opinion the number of specialist physicians in the United States could be reduced by 67 percent.[14]

These systems could be wonderful if medicine were a powerful science, with a clear understanding of what causes and cures illness and disability. But currently, it is more art than science. Dictating protocols to doctors is as meaningless as forcing artists to paint by numbers.

Don't get me wrong: Alain Enthoven is a fine person; but habits of mind, no matter how inappropriate or unsuccessful, linger. Enthoven's academic successors are equally devoted to similar top-down techniques of "disease" or "case management" that enables an analyst to tell the practicing doctor what to do. They teach these techniques widely in schools of public health and health care administration. Virtually every one of these schools has many courses with titles such as "Decision-Making Techniques," "Statistical Analysis," and "Health Policy"; but only a handful of courses in the United States in 2005 focused on entrepreneurship in health care.

The *New England Journal of Medicine:* Business Is Evil

More than any other academic medical publication, the *New England Journal of Medicine* (NEJM), likely the world's preeminent medical journal, has published a steady stream of articles purporting to demonstrate the lack of charity of business and the efficiency and quality of nonprofit and government organizations in health care.

The attacks began in 1980, when its then editor, Dr. Arnold "Bud" Relman, published his article "The New Medical-Industrial Complex":

> *The most important health care development of the day is the recent, relatively unheralded rise of a huge new industry that supplies health care services for profit. Proprietary hospitals and nursing homes, diagnostic laboratories, home care and emergency room services, hemodialysis, and a wide variety of other services produced a gross income to this industry last year of about $35 billion to +$40 billion. This new "medical-industrial complex" may be more efficient than its nonprofit competition, but it creates the problems of overuse and fragmentation of services, overemphasis on technology, and "cream-skimming," and it may also exercise undue influence on national health policy. In this medical market, physicians must act as discerning purchasing agents for their patients and therefore should have no conflicting financial interests. Closer attention from the public and the profession, and careful study are necessary to ensure that the "medical-industrial complex" puts the interest of the public before those of its stockholders.[15]*

Favorable editorials in leading media, such as the *New York Times*, followed.[16] Bud Relman was suddenly elevated from an obscure, albeit able, academic doctor and journal editor to a business guru, an expert on comparative organizational forms. His opinion was regularly solicited by the press.[17]

This was heady stuff, and Relman, hardly a shrinking violet, made the most of it. His initial view, which acknowledged the likely superiority of efficiency from services provided by businesses, disappeared. Relman, whose primary laudatory interests were in protecting physicians, concluded that their interests were best served in nonprofit health service organizations. Newly anointed as a guru in organizational behavior, he began the publication of a series of articles purporting to demonstrate the lower quality and higher costs of for-profit health services providers, typically accompanied by supportive editorials, a tradition his successors continue. In 1999, for example, the *NEJM* published an article averring that patients treated in a for-profit dialysis center incurred higher mortality rates and were less likely to be placed on a list for kidney transplants than those treated in a nonprofit.[18] Yet a 2005 review by advisors to Congress on health care found no distinction in quality between the two.[19]

But the *NEJM*'s espousal of nonprofits was overshadowed by its ardent support for the government-run, single-payer health care system views of Stephanie Woolhandler and David Himmelstein. Their claims that Canada's single-payer system was administratively more efficient than ours and similar assertions appeared 17 separate times in the *NEJM*. Indeed, Marcia Angell, who became Relman's partner and briefly served as the acting editor of the *NEJM*, subsequently joined Woolhandler and Himmelstein in a "Physicians' Working Group for Single-Payer National Health Insurance,"[20] a small band of physicians who lobbied for a government-run health care system.

The Woolhandler-Himmelstein single-payer articles published by the *NEJM* were simplistic, seizing on one variable—administrative cost—to justify draconian restructuring of a $2 trillion sector. To calibrate the magnitude of the suggested government takeover they have advocated, our health care sector is about the size of the GDP of the United Kingdom or China. The single-payer group was essentially advocating that the United Kingdom turn to and China return to government-led economies because of the efficiency of having a single buyer.

One can question both the data used in these analyses and their analytic frameworks. It is difficult to compare the costs of private and government-run health care systems in various countries because of differences in their accounting practices. For example, governments do not reflect the depreciation expenses of most of their assets, whereas private firms do, and the substantial employee pension expenses of many governments are typically accounted for separately from the health care entities.[21]

But most importantly, their analytic framework is deficient. The assertion that governmental control of the health care sector would lower administrative expenses ignores all other aspects of the health care system, such as quality, convenience, and innovation. It assumes that our sole interest is minimizing administrative expenses. But our interests are much more complex: we want excellent, high-quality, convenient, consumer-responsive care, delivered at a reasonable price.

The inappropriateness of the framework is illustrated by the following question: why not have the government buy our cars? Government purchase of cars would eliminate all the dealerships and online merchants we currently use. It might lower administrative expenses. But would the government buy the cars we want at a price we are willing to pay? And how many innovators would want to enter a business in which only one customer exists, especially if that customer is a government?

Elsewhere in the economy, we typically prefer a system of diverse buyers because businesses' competition to attract those buyers creates better value for the money. Nevertheless, the single-payer ethic is deeply embedded in the curricula of schools of government, health policy, and public health. When I lectured at the Harvard School of Public Health in the spring of 2006, the students in the standing-room-only lecture hall told me it was the first time they had heard of any "reform" other than the development of a single-payer system.

Sadly, after Relman's departure, the *New England Journal of Medicine* continued its business-bashing ways. In 2004, the editor assigned the long-retired Bud Relman to review my book *Consumer-Driven Health Care*, despite his lack of experience in the subject matter—various forms of health insurance, tax laws, and recent innovations in health care information and delivery.[22] Relman, who is foremost an advocate for physicians, failed to understand that consumer-driven health care was a boon for doctors. Although the book was well received by reviewers elsewhere, his review was a mugging. When I wrote to protest the selection of the long-retired Relman as a reviewer—noting his lack of relevant experience—the editor refused to publish my letter. When I wrote again to dispute some assertions in a subsequent *New England Journal of Medicine* 2006 article on *Consumer-Driven Health Care,* the editor once again refused to publish my letter, although, unlike Relman, I am a currently active and well-recognized participant with real-world experience in the field.

Despite Bud Relman's ostensible disdain for profit-making businesses and the conflicts of interest they create, the *Boston Globe* revealed that he had options to buy 14,000 shares of a company that had obtained exclusive rights to place the content of the *NEJM* on the Web.[23] Relman had received the options when he served on the board of directors of the firm, HealthGate Data Corp. It was planning to go public with an offering slated to bring in about $200 million. Relman's options were worth a tidy sum, about $500,000, under this valuation. When the *Boston Globe* broke the story, Relman claimed he was unaware of the fact that he owned the options.

As for Marcia Angell, she accepted her job as the *NEJM*'s acting editor only after she received assurances of "complete editorial independence . . . and . . . full control over the commercial use of the journal's name and content."[24] Unfortunately, Dr. Angell's "full control" of the resources needed to discharge her editorial responsibilities did not protect her from embarrassing revelations that "nearly half of the drug therapy review articles published since 1997 had violated the *NEJM*'s own financial disclosure policy—the researchers selected by the journal to write the reviews had undisclosed ties to the drug companies that manufactured the therapies evaluated in the articles."[25]

Ironically, while these advocates of government takeover of health care had difficulty in tracking their personal finances or those of the institutions they managed, they, nevertheless, present people like themselves as the perfect managers of our $2 trillion health care system.

Single-Payer versus Universal Health Care

For decades, many have urged adoption of universal health care in the United States. I agree with them: all Americans should have access to health care. Equality is what the United States is all about.

But once more the devil is in the details.

Most of the universal health care crowd wants the government to run the resulting system, either by managing the provision of health care, as in the United Kingdom, in which most of the hospitals are operated by the government, or by determining the budget the government pays to ostensibly private providers, as in Canada and most of the developed countries in Europe. They argue that having only one payer—the U.S. government—will reduce the administrative costs incurred by having many competing health insurers.[26]

This "detail" is where they lose me. Government control smothers competition under a blanket of uniformity, but it is competition that will improve the quality of health care services and will create the best opportunities for cost control. Consumer-driven entrepreneurs will compete to offer the best health promotion strategies, the best health care services, and the best technology by creating more for less. This kind of competition ultimately controls costs and raises quality. If single-payer economies suppress the innovations that increase productivity, significant cost control can come about only by rationing health care services, an action that invariably leads to waiting lists for treatment and untold inconvenience, suffering, and even death.

In 1989, the *New England Journal of Medicine* published this paean to the government-funded health care system in Canada:

> *The large and growing gap between the United States and Canada [in the uninsured] drives home the point that . . . the form of funding adopted by Canada does permit a society to control its overall outlays on health care. Furthermore, it is unnecessary to impose financial barriers to access in the process.*[27]

But in 2005, Chief Justice Beverley McLachlin of the Supreme Court of Canada quarreled with this rosy view of the ease of access in the Canadian health care system in a decision that struck down the Quebec government's prohibition against private health insurance and payment for health care. George Zeliotis, a Quebec, Canada, resident, brought the case forward when he learned that he would be placed on a year-long waiting list for a replacement for his painful hip. The law did not allow him to pay anybody in Canada to perform the surgery. Other than waiting, his only options were to emulate the many Canadians who have escaped to the United States or to illegal, for-profit health care centers in Canada for prompt treatment, and to pay for the care himself, or to sue. In her decision, the chief justice noted that "access to a waiting list is not access to health care."[28]

This legal victory will inevitably cause other Canadian provinces to change their laws; but in some ways, it merely recognized a reality of the Canadian health care system. Increasingly, "rogue" for-profit health care service enterprises are filling the void left by the government-funded system. Perhaps "rogue" is a misleading term. These businesses are so well accepted that the president of one, Vancouver's Cambie Surgery Centre, became the 2007–2008 president of the Canadian Medical Association.[29]

The fabled equity of the Canadian health care system had also become a myth. Many of those who could afford to receive their health care elsewhere have done so. Former Prime Minister Paul Martin got his annual checkup at a private clinic, and a Quebec premier chose to have his deadly skin cancer treated in the United States.[30] Queues are routinely jumped by the well connected.[31]

At one time, the Canadians, a reserved, stoical people, were so proud of their health insurance system that this old joke was legend: "What's the difference between a Canadian and an American?" "The Canadian has health insurance and doesn't have a gun." They are not telling that joke anymore. In Toronto, a desperate father took a physician hostage in an effort to obtain quicker treatment for his sick child. He was shot to death by the police.[32]

What happened?

Stringent government funding caused the system to implode and stifled the entrepreneurs who could have made it better and cheaper.

When I lectured in Canada to the Ontario Hospital Association about one of my earlier books, *Market-Driven Health Care*, the results of their first-ever patient survey were announced. It revealed that almost half of those with a recent stay in a hospital graded their quality of care as barely passing.[33] Other Canadian polls revealed especially high dissatisfaction with waiting times for specialized surgery. And these waits were not costless. Some waiting patients suffered major and irreversible losses in health status.[34]

By 2006, the average waiting time to see a specialist was more than four months, 90 percent longer than in 1993.[35] And Canada has fewer facilities for diagnostic imaging than most other developed countries.[36] Further, existing capacity can sometimes be hazardous to your health. A deadly infection that caused the deaths of almost 100 patients in Quebec's University Hospital in 2004 was partially blamed on lack of sanitation in its old building.[37]

As for one-payer regimes in other countries, consider the cruel fate of British women diagnosed with breast cancer or those stricken with heart disease. They suffer from one of the worst survival rates among developed countries. The reason? The shortage of doctors, nurses, and beds in the British health care system and the difficulty in obtaining referrals to hospitals or specialists.[38] The World Health Organization in 2000 found that 25,000 British cancer deaths per year would not have occurred, for example, in the United States.[39]

Although the long-suffering, stoic British are so wedded to the goal of social equality that 50 percent of them have rated their medical care as excellent or very good,[40] their 2005 evaluations of their actual health care experiences belie these overall ratings: 41 percent endured waiting times of four months or more for elective surgery. In contrast, among U.S. respondents, only 8 percent have had a wait of similar length.[41]

Worst of all, like the Canadians, the deprivations the British have endured has not led to equality of health status. One English study has concluded: "Social inequalities in health care continue to be a major (and increasing) problem."[42] Similarly, a Canadian review of cancer incidence has noted, "Despite Canada's universal health insurance, . . . the association between lower socioeconomic status and the incidence of many common cancers is just as strong in Ontario as it is in the United States."[43] Providers of cardiovascular care in Ontario have concluded that preference in accessing care is given to those who are politically or economically powerful or potentially litigious.[44]

Why Current Health Care Markets Do Not Work Like Other Markets

The current health care market does not work at all like other markets. Unlike cars, computers, or retailing, for example, health care services have not become better and cheaper over time. Instead, they have become more costly, and people worry about quality too. Why? Because of gross distortions in supply and demand. Consumers, the demanders, have little of the information that interests them, cannot express their feelings about the price because they rarely see the real cost of their health insurance or health care purchases, and have an artificially constrained range of choices. And when it comes to supply, hospitals suppress competition and innovation, and health care's key suppliers, the physicians, are increasingly marginalized.

Lack of Information: Academics Who Would Like You to Think Consumers Are Dumb

Absent information, the market cannot work. How can people choose effectively if they lack the information needed to make intelligent choices? If Jack Morgan had known the prices and outcomes of different kidney transplant units, such as infection and death rates, he could have easily chosen the one that gave him the best value for his money. Although Jack was only a high school graduate, his successful career testified to his continued capacity to learn. And yet some academics staunchly believe that information will not help consumers.

Some question consumers' ability to interpret information and use it effectively. As an example of this train of thought, a professor of public health notes the following problems with consumers' use of information. First, he claims that an astonishingly high 48 percent of American adults have "inadequate literacy skills" and only about 20 percent can independently read and understand "most patient education material and consent forms." Then too he notes that because health care information is typically complex, "there is no reliable way to give consumers information adequate to clarify the [choice] among plans . . . until federal policy makers standardize benefits, proscribe risk selection, [and] enforce quality standards, and take other legislative steps to smooth the rougher edges of competition."[45]

In other words, consumers are so dumb and health care information is so complicated that it can be understood only when choice is standardized and regulators tell health care providers how to practice medicine. The "rough edges" this academic proposes so casually to "smooth" are the essential elements of a truly competitive market—differentiated products.

This critique implicitly assumes that professionally trained people are more capable of interpreting complex information than are average consumers. Yet health care policy analysts, the very technocrats who pooh-pooh the abilities of others, are hardly wizards when it comes to information. For example, in a simple algebraic test, only 53 percent of them could answer all the questions correctly.[46] After all, if the experts who control the health care system are so wonderful, how did we get into the present mess?

Yet the professor of public health is hardly alone in his assessment of consumers' limited ability to manage selection of their health care. The many studies that demonstrate consumers' ignorance of the ABCs of health care are a perennial favorite topic in the health policy journals. For example, in 1995, one group complained that only 60 percent of the public thought the health care system was changing slowly or not at all, in contradiction to the experts' view of the subject; in 1997, researchers noted that many could not explain the terms "HMO" and "managed care" to their satisfaction;[47] and a 2001 report pointed out that "fewer than one-third of all consumers accurately reported all four health plan attributes."[48] Consumers are depicted as not only ignorant but also obdurate, failing to heed useful health care information. For example, consumers are legendarily indifferent to the health plan performance data contained in the Health Plan Employer Data and Information Set (HEDIS).[49]

But these analyses ignore the fundamental tenet of consumer behavior: consumers seek only the information that is directly pertinent to their needs.

I cannot describe exactly how cars work. Nevertheless, I am an intelligent buyer of cars because I seek the information that assesses those qualities of an automobile in which I am interested. Health care consumers are most interested in provider outcome data for medical conditions similar to their own, for people like them.[50] Thus, it should come as no surprise that Americans cannot describe an "HMO" to the questioners' satisfaction or that they are uninterested in data about their health plan processes. Consumers clearly attribute health quality to their providers, not to their health plans.[51] And they are much more impressed by *outcome* data—data about results—than by reports of *process* measures, which track how the health care was delivered. Indeed, HEDIS rankings—a data set that tracks primarily process measures such as the health plans' rates of immunizations and mammograms—have no correlation with consumers' assessments of care by their health plans.[52]

The lack of use of the available information is appropriately an indictment of the irrelevancy and the poor quality of the data more than it is an indictment of consumers. The information provided frequently is not sufficiently comprehensive and relies excessively on the process of care (for example, mammograms received) rather than the care outcome (for example, breast cancer death statistics by provider). And when outcome data are available, they are "so broadly aggregated that the results may be of only limited value to consumers"—that is, they do not identify specific doctors, hospitals, or other providers.[53] Further, many users do not trust the data, which are typically not audited, and they cannot readily access them; for example, Pennsylvania's useful information about hospitals' risk-adjusted cardiac surgery outcomes—that is, the results achieved when hospitals operated on people with different degrees of illness—were mailed out only once.[54] Last, most consumers cannot act on the data because they lack choice and control.

Lack of Innovation: Academics Who Would Like You to Think Physicians Are Incompetent

Mother Nature is the best doctor. She alone understands how the kidney functions. She alone knows the consequences of the various interventions to improve its function. She alone knows the natural order of the kidney.

Many brilliant men and women have worked hard to try to better understand this natural order. Where they've succeeded, they have used their discoveries to help relieve pain and suffering to damaged individuals and to restore health to the critically ill. The unraveling of the structure of the human genome and the mapping of genes and their mutations will be of immense help to future doctors. But currently, our knowledge of cause and effect in medicine, of the natural order that Mother Nature created, remains minimal.

To improve our knowledge, we should examine a wide variety of theories and treatment protocols. For example, we should not impose simplistic recipes on the management of kidney disease. The U.S. Congress's recipe—specifying the nature and amount of dialysis services, physician services, and drugs to be used in the "managed care" of the disease—throw the whole lot out. Instead, Congress and we must permit brilliant providers to apply their differing ideas of optimal kidney care for different kinds of people and scientifically evaluate their outcomes. In the next part of this book (Part 3), I discuss how to make this happen.

But a whole generation of academics disagrees with this view. They favor "system," not "diversity"; top-down "management," not a "natural order"; their ability, not Mother Nature's. They try to impose an unnatural order on the natural chaos of innovation.

To explain why academics must play a central role in the health care system, some ganged up on its key and most vulnerable part—

the independent doctor who worked for herself or with a small group. In 2001, these doctors accounted for only 23 percent of the total, down from 41 percent in 1983.[55] Nevertheless, they remained an important access point to the health care system, and because of their fragmentation, they were the most vulnerable to attack. If the academics attacked the hospitals, they were likely to get a sharp rap on the knuckles from this incredibly well financed and organized sector. The object lesson of the specialty hospitals was not lost on them.

If you are going to tout yourself as the best, you have to show that you are better in some relative sense. And it is easy to pick on the independent docs. Notes an official at the Institute of Medicine, part of the National Academy of Sciences, for example:

> *Studies conducted by the Institute of Medicine have demonstrated a serious gap between what the American health care system provides and its full potential. . . . These developments require medical educators and health professionals to move from a 20th-century paradigm of the physician who was in solo practice, held autonomy as a central value, prided himself or herself upon continuous learning and the acquisition of new knowledge, and laid claim to infallibility when confronting patients and colleagues. The 21st-century paradigm is that of physicians who understand teamwork and systems of care in which they can provide leadership.*"[56]

Heroic Physicians

Earlier in this book you met the two genius physicians who have kept the victims of kidney disease alive. One of them invented the field of artificial organs, and the second performed the first kidney transplant from a living donor. If the academics had had their way, these two innovations in kidney disease treatment would likely never have seen the light of day.

The inventor of the kidney dialysis machine was out on the fringe—one of those obsessed, self-centered guys who jump from job to job because they do not play nicely with the other children. His personal life was no more sedate: lots of work and hard living.

The second appears more corporatized. He has held on to one job and one wife. But although his personality fits better with today's conformity-driven medical environment, his ground-breaking mind does not. His life-saving advances were simply ignored. So much so that he had to switch careers to earn a living.

Both performed their work 40 or more years ago. Would they flourish in today's medical environment, smothered by a blanket of enforced conformity—peer reviewed, evidence based, meta-analyzed—with its simplistic ideas about how to practice medicine, cooked up by the academics and implemented by the managed care and HR crowd and the U.S. Congress?

I doubt that people like these geniuses would even enter medicine today. Why should they when the intellectually wide open frontiers in fields such as biotechnology and high technology beckon?

Willem Kolff

"Kolff"—the name was elegantly engraved on the giant lintel of the building in which I met him.

But Professor Willem Kolff was packing his boxes, once more leaving his job. Or rather, his graduate students had "volunteered" to do the packing. Kolff, a thin man with a big nose and a long, bony face, was bouncing around, clad in khaki pants and sneakers, supervising the work.

"Yes, they threw me out. Just like the others, they could not bear to have me around," he noted in an accent that retained vestiges of his native Dutch tongue.

Kolff was in his eighties then, but he had the mind and energy of a 20-year-old. A new artificial organ was in the works. This one, an artificial eye, was as wonderful and gruesome as the rest. Wonderful because it would enable the blind to see. Gruesome because it required some major excavation in the skull to make room for it.

Kolff invented an artificial kidney in Holland in the midst of World War II. It failed on his first 15 patients. They died. A lesser person, one who lacked Kolff's certainty, ego, vision, and energy, would have given up; but he persisted. Kolff's first success was bittersweet: the patient was a Dutch Nazi sympathizer. She was so roundly disliked that when Christmas fell during her hospital recuperation, she received only one gift, from Kolff, dressed as St. Nicholas.[57]

His Dutch mentors urged him to leave Holland. "You are just too wild to succeed here," they advised. "Only the United States would welcome someone like you." Kolff ultimately wound up at the University of Utah.

Kolff, now 95, is building an artificial heart with the aid of a female companion who is a fellow retirement home resident. Kolff had taken over part of the home's arts and crafts room to fashion the heart, built from parts found in the local hardware store.[58]

You just have to love this man.

But his peers do not share this view.

One of the greatest scandals in the scandal-plagued history of medicine is that this great doctor has not yet won the Nobel Prize in medicine.

Joseph Murray

A hunk stands in my garden. It is a 20-foot-tall rhododendron that bears flowers as big as salad plates when it blooms. And even when it is not in bloom, it is still the majestic, gorgeous, glossy, green-leaved focal point of this corner of my garden.

I am especially proud of this rhodie because I rescued it. The rhodie was once planted under a huge, take-no-prisoners beech tree that commands every resource in its wake. It was starved of water and nutrients, dwarfish and leggy. But I admired its survival instincts and transplanted it to a spot where it could flourish. And flourish it did. Encouraged by this success, I now not only regularly transplant my plants, but I also take cuttings of those survivors I like—such as my friend the rhodie—and graft them onto strong stock.

I am an autodidactic gardener, but the idea of grafting and transplantation is so intuitive that even I thought of it. I know to respect parentage when I graft—my rhodie cannot be grafted to rose stock—but grafting is not too complicated, and most of the grafts and transplants succeed.

Doctors have long had the same grafting and transplantation ideas; as early as 400 B.C. *Samhita*, an Indian book, describes grafting skin to reconstruct noses and ear lobes.[59] Grafting and transplantation kicked into high gear in the early twentieth century with attempts to transplant organs from animals and cadavers into humans.

But humans are much more complex biologically than plants. None of these transplants worked until a couple of geniuses discovered the immune response—the ferocious defense mounted by our bodies against tissue that it recognizes as a foreign invader. In 1954, Dr. Joseph ("Joe") E. Murray and others performed the first successful kidney transplant. One key to their success was that the transplanted kidney came from an identical twin, and thus engendered a lesser immune response.

Murray won the Nobel Prize. Joe Murray is the anti-Kolff. His smiling face is kindly, his manner mild. Fellow parishioners consult him when he attends daily Mass at his local church. You want Dr. Kolff to invent the life-saving device and Dr. Murray to use it.

World War II stimulated the inventive genius of both. The ravages of war that Murray observed as a soldier interested him in plastic surgery. Sometimes scraps of skin were grafted to protect badly burned men. Murray noticed that grafts from genetic relatives adhered better than others. As for Kolff, the supply deprivation in Nazi-dominated Holland caused him to cobble together the first artificial kidney from discarded scraps.

Yet despite Murray's charm and good fellowship, the medical community of Boston and elsewhere initially dismissed the kidney transplant as an isolated event, especially considering the donor was an identical twin. "As the field of transplantation developed . . . there was no ringing endorsement of the . . . live donor program at international scientific meetings."[60] To the contrary, Murray was accused of playing God,[61] even of practicing unethical medicine. It took decades for Murray's ground-breaking work to be widely replicated. Meanwhile, to support himself, Murray became a plastic surgeon.[62]

In his 1990 Nobel Prize acceptance speech, Murray begins his thanks with a paean to a hospital: "If gold medals and prizes were awarded to institutions instead of individuals, the Peter Bent Brigham Hospital of 30 years ago would have qualified. The ruling board and administrative structure of that hospital did not falter in their support of the quixotic objective of treating end-stage renal disease despite a long list of tragic failures that resulted from these early efforts."[63]

But even then, the hospital protected itself first and foremost. And the doctors knew it. Writes Murray, "The donor asked whether the hospital would be responsible for his health care for the rest of his life if he decided to donate his kidney. . . . The surgeon for the donor said, 'Of course not.' But he immediately followed with the question, 'Do you think anyone in this room would ever refuse to take care of you if you needed help?'"[64]

The kidney's donor was made to understand that his future depended on doctors' sense of their professional responsibility. But today this sense has been eroded by a barrage of attacks from academics, hoping to supplant individual physicians' roles; from hospitals, hoping to employ and direct individual physicians; from insurers, hoping to "manage" the medical care that doctors provide; and from the U.S. Congress, which is replacing physicians' decisions with its own.

The work of both of these great doctors has been a blessing to the victims of kidney disease. Kolff's artificial kidney extends the lives of people like Jack Morgan, and Murray's transplant would most likely have allowed Jack to lead an almost-normal life.

How many Kolffs and Murrays can exist in today's environment, in which an Ivory Tower academic establishment continually denigrates the professional judgment and economic ethics of the doctors who actually practice medicine?

THE RIGHT MEDICINE: CONSUMER-DRIVEN HEALTH CARE

CHAPTER 7

HOW IT WORKS

Who killed Jack Morgan? The same people who killed health care.

As we have seen, the agents who were supposed to act on Jack's behalf sometimes acted for him, but all too often they did not. And they never consulted him about what he wanted and needed.

Because they did not, Jack Morgan is dead.

Yes, the U.S. health care system is a killer: it kills the people it was meant to keep alive, and it kills the U.S. economy, its hardworking wage-earners and taxpayers.

This system can be fixed. You and I can fix it by insisting that we take charge of it: not the HMOs that lost their soul, not the paternalistic U.S. Congress and HR staffs, not the millionaire nonprofit hospital CEOs and businesspeople, not the arrogant, self-serving Ivory Tower utopians, but you and me and the medical providers who take care of us.

We pay for health care. We need to take charge of it.

There is only one system that would have enabled Jack Morgan to live: one that would have allowed him to decide for himself how to spend his money. In this chapter, I describe the changes in demand and supply that will make consumer-driven health care (CDHC) happen, even for the poor and disabled. In Chapter 8, I analyze the evidence of the impact of consumer-driven systems elsewhere in the economy: the consumer-driven health care system in Switzerland, which has long used it, and the consumer-driven pension system in the United States.

How a Consumer-Driven Health Care System Would Have Kept Jack Morgan Alive

I call the system that would have kept Jack Morgan alive *consumer-driven health care*. How does it work? Consumer-driven health care will not reshape the health care system because of some underlying magic in the free market. That view is as simplistic as that of the single-payer advocates who allege that governmental control will make health care cheaper and better.

Ideology does not transform how markets operate. Entrepreneurs and consumers do. Consumer-driven health care will work only if it makes basic economics happen—if it affects both supply and demand—and alters the way that consumers demand and providers supply.

Consider this hypothetical but very likely scenario of how the entrepreneurial innovations of consumer-driven health care would have kept Jack Morgan alive and at the same time lowered substantially the costs of his care.

When he was first diagnosed with kidney disease, decades ago, Jack Morgan was given an account with $40,000 a year in it that he could draw down to buy kidney care, which was the average amount the federal government had spent on the kidney care needs of men his age at that time. He was legally required to use the money solely to buy health insurance that covered all financially catastrophic medical care and for any uninsured medical care needs. But if he spent less than $40,000, he could keep some of the savings for his retirement or uninsured health care needs in a health savings account. The amount Jack received increased regularly as he aged.[1]

Jack was an able man, but he had been debilitated for years by the untreated symptoms of his disease (his HMO doctor had interpreted Jack's lassitude as depression rather than kidney disease), and he wanted some help in managing the illness. He looked around for neutral, authoritative advice on how best to use this money. He found it in a firm called "Kidney Care." The firm furnished Jack with an experienced nephrologist, who counseled him on his medical care options, and a nurse and a certified health advisor—a new occupation, similar to a certified financial planner—who helped him choose the insurance. The firm received payment for its services solely from Jack, so serving him was their only agenda. Their prices were reasonable; but if, for any reason, he did not like the firm, there were plenty of others available.

The nephrologist in Kidney Care advised Jack that many patients wanted transplants after a few years of dialysis and discussed with him the pros and cons of transplantation and its timing. Following guidance from his physicians, his nurse drew up a daily regimen to help him manage the disease and the diabetes and high blood pressure from which he was also suffering. She advised him to think about likely donors now.

She set up a personal medical record on which Jack could track his progress. All of Jack's doctors could access these data too. But Jack owned this record, not the doctors, and if he switched doctors, this information would be at the disposal of his new doctor too. The nurse communicated with him daily to see how he was coping with his challenging self-care regimens. Sometimes, when he got depressed and did not do everything he was supposed to, she gave him a pep talk. Once, when the depression deepened, she alerted his doctor, who referred him to a psychologist specializing in treating patients with kidney disease. Jack also joined a support group of people at his stage of kidney disease, organized by Kidney Care.

Jack called his nurse "my lifeline." The two of them mostly talked on the phone; but she would have used the computer to communicate with him or visited him at his home or at the dialysis center, as he preferred. She knew Jack's daughter well too.

The certified health advisor was a trained professional who helped Jack sort through a number of health insurance choices. Jack ultimately chose to buy insurance from a firm that focused exclusively on victims of kidney disease and that offered him access to a number of teams, each of which contained all the many different kinds of health care providers he needed to help him manage his disease—doctors, nurses, psychologists, social workers, and transport facilitators.

The team he chose was paid $35,000 a year for providing everything Jack needed, including a transplant. He signed up with them for a five-year contract. They were not the cheapest team; but by looking at the audited information he had obtained about them, he determined that they clearly offered the best value for his needs.

An added appeal was that many of their providers were close to Jack's home. He no longer needed to travel for hours to reach his dialysis center. Last, Jack liked the long-term nature of the contract. It gave the team members an incentive to make sure that he was as healthy, if not healthier, in year 4 as in the first year. After all, they would be paid the same amount every year—so if he got healthier, they would earn higher profits. It was a classic win-win—he and the team were in a relationship, rather than on a casual date.

He understood that the team would benefit financially from his transplant. Despite the high costs of the procedure, it would make him so much healthier that it would pay for itself in two years.

His contract had clearly delineated escape clauses, so if Jack found the team did not deliver on their promises, he could easily cancel it. The contract also clearly stipulated that Jack needed to follow his end of the bargain and comply with the providers' recommendations or face financial penalties. If the arrangement did not work out, Jack could find many other teams. After all, many businesses would welcome a steady customer who would bring them $40,000 in revenues, or more, each year.

When the time came for Jack's transplant, all the members of the team who had treated him and his daughter were like family. At this point in his treatment, they had all known each other for years. They knew his daughter loved mystery novels—*Murder on the Orient Express* was her favorite—so they gave her a selection of the world's best current mysteries. The lifeline nurse cried and gave Jack a hug when he emerged from the operating room. As all professionals would, they cared deeply about Jack. But in addition, because they were paid directly by him and because their results were regularly analyzed and published, they had every incentive to make sure that Jack was as healthy as possible.

In this consumer-driven system, Jack did not place his life in the hands of a big HMO or hospital that had lost its soul, or the good graces of the U.S. Congress, or the blessings of the Ivory Tower academics. No, he and his medical providers and advisors directly managed his care.

Jack would be alive today if he could have taken part in this consumer-driven health care system.

How to Make Consumer-Driven Health Care Happen

The first and crucial step in fixing our health care system is to give the Jack Morgans the $40,000 tax free. That's right, $40,000 tax free, the amount we currently spend on male end-stage renal disease victims of his age. The money comes with strings attached: he can spend it only on his medical care. (He can also use some of his savings for his retirement, as described above.) But the important point is that he is the one who decides how to spend it.

When Jack has $40,000 to spend, the suppliers of kidney care will begin to think about him and his needs and how they can serve him best. They will no longer need to appeal to the government or to the HR people. They can give Jack what he wants: his kind of services, his kind of drugs, even his kind of transplant.

How would this work? Some providers might offer Jack a five-year contract that would pay them $200,000, equal to $40,000 a year over its five-year term. In addition to their normal professional motives, under this contract, the providers have substantial financial incentives to make sure that Jack has a transplant ASAP. After all, once he receives the transplant, at a cost of about $100,000, his annual treatment costs will drop considerably. In financial terms, this early transplant has a payback of 2.7 to 3.6 years.[2] And the providers also have a financial incentive to keep him as healthy as possible. After all, while the average kidney patient of his age costs $40,000, the really sick ones cost much more and the relatively healthy ones much less.[3]

This consumer-driven provision of health care is novel in two ways: it is long term, and it is offered by an integrated team of providers. The long-term contract motivates providers to ensure that he gets what he needs to make him as healthy as possible, as soon as possible. Further, because the contract pays a fixed price to an integrated team that provides all the services that Jack Morgan needs, rather than fees to each of its separate parts, the current destructive turf warfare among doctors, hospitals, and drug companies, each of whom is paid separately in today's system, disappears. The team members decide jointly among themselves how best to achieve their goals.

What will protect Jack (and any one of us) against their ripping him off, giving him lousy, cheap care, treating him like a slab of meat?

Data. There are excellent measures of health status for end-stage renal disease that Jack could easily obtain: death rates, ability to perform normal activities of daily life, anemia, kidney function, lengths of wait for care, and satisfaction with the dialysis center, for example.

In this system, Jack controls the money. If he does not like the care he receives, he can take his money and go someplace else. Many providers would be glad to see a customer who brings them $40,000 a year.

As the ramifications of the new system sink in, providers will start to compete for Jack's business by cutting their prices. If Jack is allowed to keep some of these savings in his health savings account, he will have additional interest in enrolling with those that give him the best value for the money.

In this system, innovators who have great ideas about how to get more value for the money will be able to enter the space without having to line politicians' pockets or to curry favor with insurers to ensure that they get favorable reimbursement.

How can they cut prices without sacrificing the quality of care? Some, for example, will inevitably provide more of the testing and preventive care that all too many current kidney disease victims do not receive. Others may opt for more frequent dialysis.[4] And, in a consumer-driven system, you can say good-bye to the $1.7 billion insurance executive, the $25 million a year dialysis CEO, and the other bloated executive compensation.

In the next few chapters, I will describe the essential elements of this new consumer-driven health care system—the role of government, the role of business, and the kind of legislation that can make it happen. In this chapter, I will describe how a consumer-led system will enable future Jack Morgans, rich or poor, well or disabled, to live.

Stick with me. The language necessary to describe—and the detail necessary to really bring to the light—a system as complex and as vast as our health care system can be daunting at times. Presenting the *problem*, as I have thus far in the book, is easier to get across than offering the elements of the *solution*, as I intend to do. My goal is to motivate entrepreneurs and affect public policy. As you have read, there are many powerful special interests who do not want these kinds of changes; they would like to keep things just as they are. I don't want to skimp on the details or give short shrift to real-world evidence supporting the consumer-driven health care ideas.

With the consumer-driven system, Jack would be alive, costs would go down, and the innovators who create more value for the money could easily enter the system.

This system would give all of us more control over our choices of insurance and providers. But it would be of special value to those with chronic diseases and disabilities. When they are given the money currently spent on their behalf, providers will be motivated to develop new services and approaches to attract business, driving innovation and cost reduction.

After working on this concept for three decades and consulting closely with elected officials and other experts, I know that two simple pieces of legislation and one complex one can make this happen.

First, enable individuals who purchase health insurance for themselves to receive the same tax advantages they now get when employers buy their health insurance.

Harvard University uses my pretax salary to pay for my health insurance. Give me the same tax protection too, and hand over to me the $10,000 to $15,000 of my hard-earned money the university now spends to buy my health insurance. Do it for those on Medicaid too—give them the money.

The academic health care policy wonks and Beltway crowd will hold press conferences and write papers about tax neutrality, and interest groups will lobby to gain some tax advantage. But the debate boils down to two approaches: a tax deduction or a tax credit for my expenditures. The only difference between the two approaches is that the deduction is worth more to someone who is in a high tax bracket, while the value of the tax credit is independent of the tax bracket.

Second piece of legislation: require all providers and payers to publish audited price and outcome statements, and make the statements easily accessible to the general public.

When I buy a car, I want to know how good it is: miles to the gallon, safety, reliability. I am not interested in how the car was made. I also want to know about the business practices of the automobile dealership that sells me the car. Similarly, when I purchase health care services, I want to know how well my provider has treated the kind of problem I have in people who are like me, not whether he follows somebody's theory of how my health care should be delivered. And I want to know how good my health insurer is in following through with its promises.

We already have a great model for how to create this kind of transparency in health care in the government agency that creates transparency in the financial markets—the Securities and Exchange Commission (SEC), discussed more fully in Chapter 10. Naturally, health care providers and insurers will resist this proposal because, like most people, they do not want to have their performance measured and made public. They will come up with many reasons why it is destructive, infeasible, and bad for your mother, but the bottom line is that transparency is essential in every aspect of our lives. Nothing can work properly if those who create the goods and services are not measured on their performance.

The third piece of legislation is not as simple, but it is nevertheless essential: the providers must be paid *more* for treating those who are sick than for treating those who are well or relatively healthier.

This process is called *risk adjustment*. In its absence, if providers are paid the same amount for every class of patient, their economic incentive is to target the healthier patients and to avoid the sick ones. On the other hand, if they are paid appropriately for how sick the patient is, they may well have the reverse incentive and seek out the sick, specifically if they think they can reverse or diminish the progress of illness. Switzerland, Holland, and our own Medicare system already have considerable experience with health care risk adjustment.[5]

Risk adjustment can be accomplished by risk-adjusting transfers of funds to consumers or by risk-adjusting insurers or providers. If the funds were transferred to consumers, the cross-subsidization of the sick by the healthy would become transparent; for example, I would learn that my health care expenses were only $2,000 a year, but that I had paid $15,000 for my health insurance. Thus, although risk adjustment of consumers motivates them to find the best value for the money, employers and governments may not be comfortable with such transparency. Employees may not be pleased to learn how much of their salary and wages has been used to subsidize the health care expenses of their sick coworkers. Risk adjustment of insurers would avoid this problem. Under this system, insurers who enrolled sicker enrollees would receive more funds, and those with healthier enrollees would receive less. But risk adjustment of insurers creates other problems. Insurers may retain too much of the risk adjustment for themselves and pass too little of it on to the providers. Risk adjustment of providers avoids all of these problems; but it will burden them with substantial additional information processing needs so they can track the severity of illness of their patients.

Risk adjustment is best performed by a coalition of those affected, rather than by the government. In Switzerland, for example, the insurers risk-adjust one another. Insurers perform risk adjustment intelligently because they know best how to detect and value the level of illness of the enrollees. They also know that if they do not make the risk adjustment process work fairly and smoothly, the government will supplant them.

Some governmental officials—like Massachusetts' former governor Mitt Romney and officials in Switzerland—advocate a fourth piece of legislation: a requirement that everybody has to buy health insurance. The Commonwealth of Massachusetts' novel universal coverage plan, for example, requires citizens to buy health insurance

and subsidizes those who cannot afford it. The money for the subsidies comes from the funds once given to hospitals to pay for their
"free care" to uninsured patients.

But this approach has its critics. Some object on the grounds of
ideology. They argue that people should buy health care because
they want to, not because the government forces them to do it. Others also question the practicality of enforcing this requirement: states
that require the purchase of automobile insurance have virtually the
same number of people insured as states that do not, for example.[6]

How Consumer-Driven Health Care
Lowers Costs and Raises Quality

Health care draws utopian ideologists of all types. The single-payer
crowd rhapsodizes about the transformative powers of government
control. But simplistic ideology is not limited to single-payer advocates. Market-oriented adherents also exhibit it.

For example, President George W. Bush's administration asserted
that the transformations of consumer-driven health care will occur
solely through the implementation of high-deductible health insurance policies.[7] They avowed that when people shop for health care
services that are not covered by health insurance—from $1,000 to
$5,000 in the typical high-deductible health insurance policy—they
will restrict their usage without damaging their health status. But this
plan is only partially consumer driven because it focuses solely on
changing demand, which is only part of the picture, and does not
allow for the impact of a change in demand on the supply of health
care services. If hospitals and other providers of health care services
are not motivated to change their ways, the change in demand will
accomplish little. After all, the potential impact of high-deductible
policies in transforming the supply of health care is limited. Once
the deductible is met, most catastrophic expenses are fully insured.
And it is the sick who account for the bulk of health care costs.

To be fair, the Bush administration was partially correct—high-
deductible health insurance policies, in which the enrollee pays for

the first $1,000 to $5,000 of health care expenses out of her own pocket, unquestionably lead to lower health care expenditures. For example, a 2006 four-year study of 1.6 million health insurance enrollees found that costs increased by only 3 percent from 2002 to 2005 among those enrolled in high-deductible plans.[8] These cost controls were occasioned by reduced use of hospital emergency rooms. Yet high-deductible enrollees with chronic diseases either maintained or improved their health status.[9] High-deductible policies are also a good choice for the uninsured, primarily because those policies cost so much less than traditional policies yet provide insurance for financially catastrophic events.

But high deductibles are not for everyone. After all, if deductibles are not adjusted for income, the average American household, whose after-tax 2004 income was around $45,000, may well struggle to pay a $2,000 deductible.[10] (On the other hand, the health savings account will enable low-income people to accumulate some much-needed assets for uninsured care.)

High-deductible health insurance policies are one important choice in a consumer-driven system, but they cannot be the only choice. Consumer-driven markets rely on considerable choice, not a choice of one. Consumer-driven health care can improve the productivity of health care only through many varieties of new insurance policies that are tailored to your needs and that increase the health care system's responsiveness to individuals. That is, by changing the form of consumer *demand*, consumer-driven health care will change *supply*.

How Consumer-Driven Health Care Will Change the Supply of Health Care Services

Consumer-driven health care will encourage three revolutionary innovations in the supply of health care: (1) Health care focused factories will bring specialists and generalists into one integrated "stop-and-shop" system of care. (2) Consumer-based medical records will create one information access point for patients and providers. (3)

Medical technology will be personalized for the needs of individual patients.

We observed two of these three changes—focused factories and a personal medical record—in the scenario describing Jack Morgan's new consumer-driven care. As we have seen in Jack's case, consumer-driven insurers will bundle these innovations. For example, victims of genetically linked diseases, such as diabetes, may be offered multiyear policies that feature focused factories and personalized medical technologies, supported by integrated information records.

Below I will explain these three innovations in some detail because they are the heart and soul of a new system that is about consumers and doctors finally being in charge.

Focused Factories

We organize our current health care system around health care providers and not around the needs of users. The result is fragmentation of care that directly and negatively affects the welfare of patients and the costs of the system.

The 20-plus million diabetics in the United States illustrate the problem. Many suffer from several diseases at the same time. Among diabetics, nearly half also suffer from high blood pressure and up to a tenth from asthma, heart disease, and behavioral problems.[11] Diabetics require a team that devises and provides appropriate plans for their complex medical care—endocrinologists, cardiologists, nephrologists, dermatologists, podiatrists, and behavioral support specialists, among others. Yet even though this integrated team represents the most sensible way to deliver treatment to diabetics, most victims of the disease cannot find it. Instead, they are treated by many different specialists spread out in several different offices and practices. As a result, many diabetics receive inadequate care. For example, only 36 percent of fully insured elderly diabetics had a crucially important test that measures long-term levels of sugar in the blood. These abysmal results are even worse for African-Americans and poor people.[12]

This kind of fragmentation of care imposes devastating consequences on patients' health and, ultimately, on costs. An integrated regimen of diet and drugs has achieved impressive results, quickly, through improvements in the signs of diabetes, including greatly reduced absenteeism, restricted activity days, and hospital stays.[13] Improvements in health would likely significantly reduce the direct costs of diabetes, $132 billion in 2002,[14] the billions more wasted in lost days of work, and the yet another $54 billion lost through premature death and disability.[15]

The mismatch between the needs of patients with chronic diseases and disabilities for integrated care and the fragmented structure of the current health care system leads to devastating medical and financial results beyond diabetes.[16] The economic consequences are suggested by the magnitude of the expenditures. Only five diseases— mood disorders, diabetes, heart disease, hypertension, and asthma— accounted for 49 percent of total 1996 health care costs and caused an additional $36 billion in work loss.[17]

We are blessed with excellent individual doctors, nurses, and researchers, but in the absence of integrated care, too many patients fall between the cracks. Integrated teams of health care providers, organized around the needs of victims of chronic diseases and disabilities, such as back pain, and other undertreated populations, such as African-Americans, Native Americans, and women, will lead to a better, lower-cost health care system.

I call these integrated teams "focused factories" because they resemble current focused, mass-customization factories that achieve higher-quality, lower-cost results by inverting conventional notions of manufacturing excellence. Old-economy manufacturers reduced costs by producing huge volumes of goods in cavernous, assembly-line factories. Individual workers created small components of the end product. New-economy mass-customization factories, in contrast, tailor products to specific customers in flexible factories so small that workers can see the whole before their eyes. One mass customization factory, for example, has been able to increase quality by 55 percent while reducing work space and capacity by 50 percent or more.[18]

I call them "focused" because they are organized to meet special consumers' needs. But a more important aspect of this innovation, one that will be inspired by consumer-driven health care, is suggested by the word *factory*. Factories scale up the work of brilliant individuals and make it available to all of us. The Ford factories scaled up Henry Ford's brilliant views on how to make cars; Microsoft scaled up Bill Gates's ideas about how to operate computers; and General Electric scaled up Thomas Edison's visions of how to light space.

Many in health care believe that the "factory" process, that of scaling up the ideas of brilliant innovators, cannot be applied to health care. But they are wrong. For example, many of our best treatment facilities, such as the Texas Heart Institute, employ the scaled-up ideas of individual doctors such as Dr. Denton Cooley, its founder. Cooley, a brilliant, daring heart surgeon, is also a brilliant manager who trained his disciples to perform his kind of cardiac surgery and created an organization that would support his work.[19]

Toronto, Canada's Shouldice Hospital provides such a classic case study example of this scaling-up process that it has been widely used in the Harvard Business School and similar schools to teach how to scale up service organizations. The Shouldice Hospital performs a surgical technique for hernias that was developed by its founder, Dr. Edward Shouldice. He trained the surgeons who work in the hospital in the technique and designed a hospital that would support it. The hospital, for example, features beautifully landscaped grounds with gentle slopes so that newly operated on patients can walk easily on them. A smiling nurse guides them through a daily aerobics routine. This ambulation and exercise speeds the healing process. You might think that Shouldice Hospital's focus on the patient would raise costs. But it is substantially cheaper than neighboring everything-for-everybody hospitals. The surgeons' exclusive focus on one surgical procedure increases quality; the hospital's focus reduces cross-infection rates; and the patients' active healing process speeds and improves recuperation.[20]

Brilliant entrepreneurial doctors, such as Denton Cooley and Edward Shouldice, and other medical personnel, will likely originate health care focused factories. Like them, the entrepreneurs will not only innovate new focused treatment protocols but also scale them up so that they can be made widely available.

A consumer-driven health care system will naturally inspire focused factories because consumers will seek them out. For example, diabetics who can freely choose among many differentiated health insurance products will likely opt out of an everything-for-everybody insurance plan system, choosing those that offer diabetic focused factories that provide integrated, demonstrably excellent diabetic care at a lower cost. These types of consumer-driven health insurance policies will no longer pay every provider the same price for a limited range of covered services. Instead, they will pay teams of providers the prices they quote for the bundle of services their team members have jointly designed. With this new reimbursement, focused factory innovators will avoid the economic consequences imposed by current, fragmented reimbursement.

When it comes to health care, the solutions conventionally suggested for the problem of fragmentation differ in scale from focused factories and instead hark back to the factories created at the birth of the Industrial Revolution. Most experts favor massive consolidation of health care through large physician group practices,[21] hospitals vertically integrated with physicians and insurers,[22] and other large-scale integration schemes.[23] What these utopians ignore is the infeasibility of their recommendations—any kind of integration is immensely difficult to pull off; the larger the scale, the larger the problems encountered.[24] For that reason, we see very little vertical integration elsewhere in the economy. For example, retailers rarely manufacture their own products. Indeed, many of the companies that design and market brand-name products, such as Dove soap, Calvin Klein jeans, and Coca-Cola, do not manufacture them.[25] Dell too relies on external suppliers, using its excellent information systems to deliver a customized product.[26]

The failures of vertical integration elsewhere led me to predict in my 1997 book, *Market-Driven Health Care*, that the then-prevalent vertical integration of hospitals and insurers with physicians, to provide everything-for-everybody health care, was a recipe for disaster.

In one area of the health care system, for example, the number of physician practices purchased by hospitals jumped from 6,600 in 1995 to 19,200 in 1998, growing at a 30.5 percent annual rate.[27] The results? In 1998, hospitals lost an average of $80,000 per physician.[28] Physicians' productivity decreased by 15 to 20 percent two years after acquisition. Low growth in referrals of new patients to the acquiring hospital failed to offset these losses.[29]

Hospitals that integrated with health plans experienced difficulties too. *Market-Driven Health Care* spotlighted the conflicts of interest and loss of focus that the then-hospital firm Humana encountered when it created an insurance division. While Humana's hospital division wanted to maximize occupancy, the insurance division wanted to minimize it. Ultimately, the firm shed its hospital division to resolve this conflict.[30]

Small wonder that by 2002, an industry journal noted, "Healthcare organizations spent a good deal of 2001 taking apart what they had previously pieced together,"[31] and a 2004 survey found that many of the integrated delivery systems were disintegrating, spurred by mounting losses from operations and anemic profits.[32]

Because health care focused factories are more modest in scale than the integration schemes typically recommended, they represent more feasible solutions. Their modest scale enables an integrated view of the patient. Yet their scale is not so modest as to make their creation financially impossible or their resources inaccessible. For example, the expenditures on diabetes in an average state would enable the construction of a number of 300-bed hospitals and hundreds of community facilities.[33]

The revolutionary promise of focused factories is indicated by one of their earliest manifestations—specialized hospitals. Although these are not true focused factories, as they concentrate on procedures rather than diseases, they nonetheless, do indicate the benefits of specialization with their increased quality and lowered costs.[34] The massive, effective resistance of status quo hospitals to specialty hospitals also indicates why focused factories can be formed only in a consumer-driven system.

Integrated Information Records

The need for a personal medical record that contains the results of every medical event of every person, from a doctor's checkup to a kidney transplant, is widely acknowledged. I first urged it in a 1978 article, for example.[35] Yet, nearly 30 years later, these records still do not exist, resulting in errors of commission—for example, adverse drug interactions from prescriptions by physicians unaware of others' recommendations—and omission—lapses in appropriate medical intervention.[36]

Currently, data are stored in the warehouses of providers and insurers, who lack incentives to integrate them. They keep only those data needed to support the bills sent to insurers. The radiologist who has records of your X rays and uses them to support his or her bill may never share them with your family doctor. Neither the radiologist nor your family doctor is paid to send or to receive your X rays from the other.

In a consumer-driven health care system, on the other hand, consumers will demand these records to help them manage their health and insurance, and innovative providers will respond. Intuit, for example, which developed Quicken to fulfill consumer demands for integrated financial records,[37] has already entered the consumer health information market. As this is being written, a consortium of several large U.S. corporations, including Wal-Mart and Intel, has announced their intention to create a digital database of their employees' health records. Their goal is to "cut costs by having consumers coordinate their own health care among doctors and hospitals." Craig R. Barrett, Intel's chairman, calls portable electronic records "the building block to modify the U.S. health industry" into a more responsive and cost-conscious system.[38]

Personalized Medicine

Personalized medicine—medical care that is tailored to your unique needs—can be applied to both drugs and devices. By drawing on advances in genetics, doctors, hospitals, and research units will discover and store in databases each patient's genetic variations and how those affect their need for specific drugs and ability to metabolize them. For example, 40 percent of asthmatics respond differently to the same medicines,[39] and drugs have already been tailored to mutations that cause some diseases.[40] Personalized medicine also includes medical devices that enable monitoring of the body's function. For example, one implanted device enables the victims of congestive heart failure to monitor their condition automatically.[41]

Personalized medicine promises to increase national productivity by preventing or curing disease. Nevertheless, some of the health policy experts we met before in this book dismiss innovations in personalized medicine as so costly that they will require rationing. One study concluded, for example, that "in an era of finite resources, the question is how to balance providing access to as many of these innovative, life-saving drugs as possible without increasing premiums beyond (the) ability to pay."[42]

The view that we cannot afford personalized medicine ignores the effects of increasing costs in one sector on the overall costs of health care and its productivity. This analytic framework is unique to health care. We do not use such narrow views of the impact of high technology, for example, because most of us recognize that increased computerization expenditures increase productivity. Although we spend more on computers, the entire economy will improve as a result.

An increasing body of evidence supports the productivity gains to be had from improvements in medical technology. One broad evaluation documented productivity and quality of life benefits that exceeded the additional costs of new technologies for heart attacks, low birth weight infants, depression, and cataracts.[43] Similarly, studies have revealed that drugs frequently cause overwhelming reductions in hospital costs.[44] Not every new technology is cost-effective; but taken as a whole, new medical technologies create benefits in excess of their costs.

The American people are unlikely to accept the experts' doubts about technology. Americans are staunch supporters of new technology; we embrace it, and large sectors of the population are knowl-edgeable about it. We persist in what policy experts view as a mud-dle-headed belief that payment for technology is feasible.[45] To meet consumer expectations, some consumer-driven health insurance policies will incorporate the personalized medicine that could sig-nificantly improve health care productivity and allow consumers to judge for themselves the value for the money that personalized med-icine creates.

How Consumer-Driven Health Insurance Will Offer Innovations in the Supply of Health Care Services

Consumer-driven health care will create substantial innovations in the supply of health care. Consumers will be offered these innova-tions through new types of health insurance policies.

As I've tried to make clear throughout the book, the characteris-tics of *control, choice,* and *information* to guide provider selection are sadly lacking in most current health insurance plans. The trends tell it all: since 1996, many employers have narrowed the choices. By 2005, 90 percent of all employers and 93 percent of small ones offered only one plan.[46]

But even when employees are offered a choice of more than one health insurance plan, they find the "choice" to be largely illusory.[47] Large employers' managed care plans are remarkably standardized—containing the same benefits, offering virtually identical coverage, reimbursing providers for a limited array of traditional services, gen-erally paying all local providers at similar rates or discounts, and last-ing for only one year. The only difference among them is found in the ease of accessing the providers—restrictive plans where con-sumers must contend with "gatekeepers" come at a lower price than the looser ones.[48]

One frustrated buyer notes that three managed care plans have most of the market, and their plans have less than 10 percent varia-tion.[49] Employees complain too. In one Democratic Party poll, 64 percent agreed that "individuals are best able to choose the health care coverage they want. . . . [T]hey should have that option and not have to take just what . . . their employer provides."[50]

Not surprisingly, Americans so strongly dislike the health insurance industry, which gives them virtually no choice, that consumer satisfaction with the U.S. Postal Service exceeds that of health insurance.[51]

These one-size-fits-all insurance plans leave important needs uncovered. Some of the many new kinds of health insurance policies that a consumer-driven system will offer are described below.

Health Insurance Policies That Offer Integrated Medical Care

People like Jack Morgan with debilitating, chronic diseases, such as kidney disease, AIDS, diabetes, or asthma, frequently cannot find integrated care because individual providers are paid for fragments of care. Payments for fragmented care cause a great many problems: they deter innovations that would integrate care and they encourage turf warfare. As we saw in Jack Morgan's case, the drug companies appear to have out-lobbied the doctors in getting an ever-bigger share of the money spent on kidney care, and because patients don't pay directly, they lack the clout to get the type of medical care they really need, as opposed to what the government says they need.

While providers wage turf warfare, chronic disease patients must wend their way from one provider to the next to obtain full treatment. Focused care providers have little chance to compete and survive, despite their ability to provide better comprehensive care. When Rush Presbyterian's CEO instituted a comprehensive facility for AIDS—with all the many services that AIDS victims needed, including primary and complementary care, diagnostic facilities, and behavioral support—he confronted the irony that the healthier his patients, the lower their utilization of his hospital, and the worse his bottom line. In today's topsy-turvy system, he had to find a substantial endowment to compensate for the losses he incurred from improving the health status of AIDS patients.[52]

In a consumer-driven health care system, provider teams will name their price for bundles of care they create, reversing current, insurer-dictated prices for fragmented care and enabling consumers to reward excellence. The sick will, thus, have access to integrated teams. For example, Jack will be offered a bundle of kidney care services from teams that offer him everything he needs for appropriate care for his disease. The team members will jointly figure out what treatment and care options are best for Jack.

In contrast, under today's system, what is good for the transplant surgeon is not so good for the dialysis center or for Amgen. After all, once Jack receives a transplant, he will not need so much dialysis or epo, if any. But if these providers are all members of the same team, the aim will be to maximize their joint profits by improving Jack's health. The healthier he is, the better off they are.

Health Insurance Policies That Offer Support

These "focused factory" bundles will likely be offered through multiyear insurance policies. These kinds of policies will appeal to the sick people who now struggle to comply with their daunting, painful, minutely detailed, quotidian self-care regimens, such as diabetics' enduring up to eight painful sticks per day to determine the level of sugar in their blood. Despite the challenges of managing their complex illnesses, they typically cannot find psychological support to help them maintain their health. Insurers may not offer such support because, although the economic rewards of helping sick people adhere to their demanding self-care regimens are well known, the payoffs derived from supporting people to help themselves are thought to be generally long term.[53] Because many insurers lose 20 percent, or more, of enrollees annually, they lack incentives to invest in health promoting activities that may benefit their competitors in the future.[54]

In a consumer-driven health insurance system, multiyear insurance policies will motivate insurers to provide support that enables enrollees to comply with daunting self-care regimens over the long term.

Health Insurance Policies That Offer
Protection against Financial Catastrophes

The overwhelmingly most common answer to "What do you think is the most important reason to have health care insurance coverage?" is "to cover the costs associated with major, life-threatening illness or accidents."[55] Yet health insurance does not protect people against financial catastrophe. Despite all the money we spend on insurance coverage, middle-class Americans are left to pay for uninsured, expensive medical events out of their own pockets, such as drugs and devices labeled as experimental and medical events that cost more than $1 million, the maximum most insurance policies will pay. In 2001, 11 percent of households spent 10 percent or more of their income on out-of-pocket health care costs,[56] and 27 percent of bankruptcy filings resulted primarily from medical debts.[57] Further, 15 million, or more, Americans pay for the uninsured medical needs of their parents, such as the $74,000 of annual costs for their loved ones' nursing home care.[58]

In a consumer-driven health care system, enrollees will be able to buy insurance coverage for desired benefits, such as catastrophically expensive care, including long-term care, whose costs exceed $1 million.

Health Insurance Policies That Offer
Personal Convenience

A consumer-driven system will also help the employees and employers who now lose work time and wages because of perverse incentives in the present insurance system. Unscheduled absences for medical reasons, many caused by the present fragmentation and lack of consumer focus in the health care system, accounted for as much as 60 percent of the cost of illness in 2004.[59] Insurers and providers may be rewarded for increasing this problem. For example, because the surgical time for an open gallbladder repair can be substantially lower than that of a minimally invasive one, insurers and providers may direct patients toward it. Yet those who have minimally invasive surgery return to work much faster than those who endure open procedures. What benefits the employer and employee does not necessarily benefit insurers and hospitals.[60]

In a consumer-driven health care insurance system, policies will highlight convenience from the consumers' perspective, permitting them to trade off the cost of the more convenient care, if any, against the value of their time.

Health Insurance Policies That Offer Access to Entrepreneurial Doctors

Finally, the doctors who are shortchanged by today's insurance system in which the insurer dictates coverage and price will be able to regain some measure of control over the practice of medicine in a consumer-driven system.

Doctors are so defeated by the present insurance system that a majority of them have lied to insurers so that their patients could obtain the medical care they need. Although they worried about the consequences, physicians overwhelmingly believed that "today, it is necessary to game the system to provide high-quality care."[61] And they surely resent the fact that insurers often pay the efficient, skilled, and compassionate doctor the same as her slothful, unskilled, or indifferent colleague.[62]

In a consumer-driven health care system, providers will be free to create focused factories and to name their own prices. To be sure, providers will face increased risks with this new pricing system. Consumers can either accept or reject these newly price-differentiated offerings. But consumer-driven health care will create a corresponding benefit: the doctors will regain the freedom to provide the kind of medical care they feel is appropriate.

Scare Stories about CDHC

Whenever we contemplate something new, we give it a unique face and shape in our mind's eye, one that reflects our life experiences and world views. When I read a book that interests me, for example, I picture the protagonists clearly. My personal portrait is so vivid that I am typically disappointed when I see or hear a media version of the work. The actors rarely conform to my vision.

Joseph Fiennes was Shakespeare in the film *Shakespeare in Love*. The slim, darkly handsome, foppish Fiennes is a beauty, no question, but Shakespeare? Forget about it. My William Shakespeare is sensuous, greedy, brilliant, and sly, replete with a reddish beard, gold glints within it, who manipulates his identity, toying with his public. He cloaks his genius under the guise of a common man.

I have a vague mental picture of Shakespeare's appearance from the common image of a Van Dyke–bearded man who resembles a corporate executive—stout, well-groomed, bluff. But my mind has cut a very different picture of how the world's greatest wordsmith would look. To me, great poets, like Shakespeare, look foxy—sly, incisive, and secretive—not like golf-playing executives.

So it is with consumer-driven health care, and with the groups that oppose it. They visualize it through a filter woven by their preconceived notions.

One such filter is used by the academics. Like overly protective parents, they simply cannot accept the idea that consumers can function without their oversight. Viewed through their filter, solo consumers in the health care market are vulnerable and timid. They must be protected and informed by the technocrats' superior knowledge and strength. Another filter is used by status quo advocates, those who flourish under the present, employer-based system. We have met them all in this book—the HR crowd, the Congress, the HMOs, and the hospitals. Although their motives are professional, they must also worry that consumer-driven health care will upset their cozy, lucrative apple cart. Yet another filter is that of the universal health insurance ideologues, who typically pair access to health care with control by a central government. Looking through this filter, they likely fear that decentralization of health insurance purchasing to individuals will undermine their goals. In their world view, the ideal purchaser of health insurance is a government; large employers are next best; and a decentralized market is the nightmare that keeps them up at night.

These three groups have disseminated a number of scare stories intended to diminish the adoption of consumer-driven health care. They allege that CDHC will favor the rich; screw the sick and the poor; lead to the desertion of health insurance by employers, with venal firms entering the market; and create even worse problems than we currently have in accessing the system.

Let's take a look at a number of these more widely promulgated stories and lift the filters that shape them.

The Class Warfare Story

According to the class warfare scare story, consumer-driven health care will stratify the market, so that poor people will receive much worse health care than the rich and powerful. Exponents of the class warfare story typically espouse a classic academic solution for achieving equality—a government-controlled system with standardized benefits, overseen by selfless, superbly able elites, namely, themselves, whose sole interest is in protecting us.[63]

The class warfare story is based on three false assertions. The first is that the rich obtain better health care than others. But how do the rich know that they have received better health care? Sure, their country club buddies who are doctors or hospital trustees may assure them of the fact; but do they have any data to back up their assertions that their doctor or their hospital is simply fantastic? No. One analysis of the subject found no such differences. And the analysis required back-breaking compilation of data because the quality evaluations that we can readily obtain when we are buying any other consumer good are notable for their absence in health care.[64]

The other false assertions in the class warfare scare story are that good-quality health care is more expensive than poor-quality health care and that suppliers are interested in serving only the rich and will not innovate to reach the other, much more numerous part of the population. These assertions are mistaken too. High-quality health care—integrated, wired, and personalized—often costs *less* than poor-quality health care. As consumer-driven health care increases quality, more health care will be available at a better price. Further, suppliers are vitally interested in serving the large number of consumers who are not rich.

The automobile industry provides a good example of these points. First, consumer pressures forced continuous improvements in automobile quality. In 2001, for example, problems in five-year-old cars diminished by 9 percent.[65] As cars became better, they also became cheaper. Car manufacturers who improved quality also reduced costs.

Automobile manufacturers focus on innovations primarily for the middle-class market. Paralleling their quality and price improvements was a narrowing of the gap in quality between the best car and the average one. For example, in 2000, 88 percent of the cars tested for safety by the government were in the top two categories, versus only 31 percent in 1979.[66] Although a top-of-the-line Mercedes costs substantially more than a Toyota, by 2005, Mercedes had more quality problems than the average car.[67]

When health care is consumer driven, it too will produce better, cheaper services, and the quality differential between the best and the average will narrow. All the options will deliver safe, effective health care services, just as all of today's cars meet basic consumer and societal needs for safety, reliability, and fuel efficiency. This is not to say that all differentials will be eliminated. To the contrary, distinctive features will fulfill different consumer preferences. For example, although the retail stores Wal-Mart and Target both successfully serve the discount market, they serve it in different ways. Wal-Mart caters to the rock-bottom-price crowd, and Target serves those who are willing to pay a little more for cutting-edge style.[68] Similarly, as quality improved and costs dropped in the automobile market, choice increased from 140 models in the early 1970s to 260 in 1999.[69]

Similar differentiation will occur in consumer-driven health care.

The Haunted House Story

A frequent image painted by the academics is of a child cast out into a mystifying health insurance market, like a babe innocently entering a haunted house. Fierce creatures jump out—health insurance policies offered by venal, fraudulent vendors. Consumers lose their tax protection and wander about aimlessly, futilely, without a map or a sense of direction—only to emerge diminished by the experience, their health insurance threatened and their confidence shaken.

This image was invoked, for example, when Xerox announced that it hoped at some time in the future to give each of its employees $5,000 to $6,000 to buy health insurance. "This could totally unravel American health care," noted one booster of a government-controlled model in response to the proposal. A chastened Xerox hastily retracted its tentative plans.[70]

This scare story misrepresents the consumer-driven health care movement in two ways. First, it sets up the frightening prospect of hundreds of millions of individuals futilely shopping for health insurance in a market that is not prepared to handle them. Second, it asserts that consumer-driven health care will cause the loss of the tax-advantaged status of corporate health insurance purchases.[71]

Neither is valid.

For the employees with health insurance, consumer-driven health care will initially be implemented primarily under the employer's umbrella. Says the CEO of the Pacific Business Group on Health, a consortium of large employers: "Virtually none of our members is looking at [consumer-driven health care] in terms of capping financial contributions and walking away."[72] The corporate umbrellas are the appropriate home for consumer-driven health care initiatives because employers have the infrastructure to nourish and support the small, innovative health insurance offerings that could otherwise get lost in the vast consumer ocean. But as these products and the measures of their performance mature, they will be offered to individual consumers as well. The uninsured will be served by large insurers; Internet- and phone-based marketplaces; and state-run markets, like those in Massachusetts, described more fully in Chapters 9 and 11.

The history of mutual funds, the innovations that enabled consumer-driven investment in financial assets, is instructive in projecting the likely dissemination of consumer-driven health insurance.

The employers who adopted 401(k) plans were a key element in the initial success of mutual funds. For example, in 1976, when the first indexed, consumer-oriented mutual fund was introduced for investors on the New York Stock Exchange, it met with a poor reception, and its founder was portrayed as a wild-eye zealot.[73] But as 401(k)s under a corporate sponsor became widespread and as excellent evaluations of mutual fund performance became widely available, the consumer-driven part of the industry flourished. By 2006, half of U.S. households owned mutual funds. Although most consumers were introduced to these investments through an employer-backed defined-contribution (dc) plan, nearly 40 million households now own mutual funds purchased outside the employer's site.[74]

As for the consumer-oriented fund company that introduced the first index fund, its name is Vanguard. By 2006, it controlled about a trillion dollars of assets, and its brilliant founder, John Bogle, was appropriately lionized.[75] (In the early twenty-first century, a number of mutual funds were found to have permitted special trading privileges to large investors, such as union executives. I view the fact that these activities were discovered as an indication of the vigor of a consumer-driven industry. Special privileges to the wealthy and powerful are granted in health care too, especially in single-payer systems, but we do not hear of them.)

Consumer-driven health insurance will likely follow the mutual fund pattern. Consumer-driven health insurance plans will be introduced under the corporate umbrella. With time, as the industry matures, highly differentiated insurance products will migrate from the corporate to the individual consumer market, along with reliable evaluations of their performance. Some of these new health insurance products will likely appeal to those who are now uninsured.

As for the assertion that consumer-driven health care will cause corporate health insurance payments to lose their tax-advantaged status, that is simply a canard. Employees are currently exempted from income taxes on their health insurance payments because the tax code does not consider them to be income. If the employer continues to pay for the employees' choice of health insurance, consumer-driven health care will not affect this situation. And, with time, the tax exemption will pass to the individual. President George W. Bush had already proposed it in 2007.

A variant on the haunted house story is that consumer-driven health insurance will cause individuals to lose the negotiating clout of big groups in determining insurance prices. But if the clout of group purchasing were actually so powerful, every consumer product—cars, homes, and food—would be purchased under the employer's group-purchasing models. The Achilles heel of group purchasing is that it inhibits product differentiation. The fundamental tenet of a market-based economy is that competition among differentiated products is much more effective in controlling costs than the clout of group purchases.

The Screw the Sick Story

The screw the sick story would have us believe that under consumer-driven health insurance, sick employees will no longer be able to buy affordable health insurance. This contention defies simple mathematical reasoning. Presently, most large employers pay the actual health care costs incurred by their enrollees.[76] The role of insurers is solely to administer the plans for the firms. This process is called "self-funding." The underlying pool of self-funded employer health care costs is unaffected by the insurance pricing formula. The self-funded employers who currently pay for the care of their employees will continue to do so under consumer-driven health care.

Indeed, the screw the sick scare story is exactly wrong. New consumer-driven health insurance will *help* the sick with innovative products that are designed for their special needs. Currently, as I have discussed throughout this book, health insurance fosters a system that is *not for the sick*. This fault can be traced directly to the absence of risk-adjusted payment. The risk adjustment of insurance prices and provider payments that is inherent in instilling competition through consumer-driven health insurance will correct this failure. Adjusting prices to the enrollees' level of sickness will reward those who attract sick enrollees by paying them more and paying those who attract well enrollees less. It is precisely by undermining the homogenized pricing of the present insurance system that the sick will, finally, receive the excellent focused care they deserve.

The Disappearance of Health Insurance Story

Some ask of consumer-driven health care initiatives, "Aren't they just obscuring a disappearance of benefits?" The disappearance of the health insurance story argues that consumer-driven health care is a wolf in sheep's clothing. Employers will use it to back out of paying for health insurance benefits. And employees will opt out of buying health insurance. They will insure themselves only if they are sick.

This scare story is promulgated mostly by those who worry that consumer-driven health care will undermine access to health insurance. Labor unions are among the most ardent advocates of the disappearance of health insurance scare story.[77]

But this scare story too is dubious because most employers do not want to back out of providing health insurance. For example, a detailed analysis of the correlation between the returns of small business owners and their health insurance benefits concluded: "The business's owner and the employees are in the venture together; . . . they jointly prosper and they jointly fail."[78] Employers understand that health insurance is a highly valued corporate benefit. For example, as one expert notes, a Generation Xer "who believes that the employer is not making a commitment to him, will leave."[79]

Employers' willingness to offer insurance is influenced primarily by their profitability. Notes one study: "As long as the economy is strong, employers do not cut back on benefits."[80] Indeed, since 1993, as the U.S. economy prospered, the number of workers who received health insurance through their employers steadily increased, and the employers' share of premiums increased from 69 percent in 1987 to 76.4 percent in 2000.[81] But since then, as the economy declined, the percentage of those with job-based health insurance slipped to about 60 percent in 2004.[82] The employers who did not offer health insurance typically could not afford it. By far the lowest insurance rates were in the trade and personal service sectors, whose paltry profit rates ranged from a loss to a maximum of 2 percent.[83]

Contrary to the disappearance of health insurance scare story, the lower-cost, high-deductible insurance options that the consumer-driven health care movement has already created may expand or maintain coverage. In tough economic times, employers are more likely to offer consumer-driven health insurance products than conventional ones because of their lower costs. The availability of this lower-cost option may even keep them from giving up the health insurance benefit.

A variant on the disappearance of health insurance theme is that employees will no longer insure themselves under consumer-driven health care. Instead, they will prefer to take the money over the insurance and will insure themselves only when they are sick.

But once again, the allegation defies logic. First, in a consumer-driven health care system, everyone will be required to buy insurance that, at a minimum, protects them against financially catastrophic medical events. Further, most people want to buy health insurance. The main obstacle is its high cost. By 2005, more than a quarter of the uninsured declined their employer's offer of health insurance, likely because it cost too much.[84] When Blue Cross of California offered 2002 plans that cost as little as $1,400 a year for a mother and her children in Los Angeles, 800,000 people signed up in one year alone. High-deductible health policies also expand the opportunities for the previously uninsured who work for firms of 2 to 50 employees. Blue Cross of California's FlexSCAPE program, for a good example, was priced at only $80 per employee per month ($960 a year). This feature created budget predictability and an affordable price for employers who might otherwise hesitate to offer insurance.[85]

As these examples suggest, rather than *diminishing* the number of people with insurance, consumer-driven health care will likely *increase* that number by offering innovative, lower-cost insurance policies.

The Limited Access Story

The limited access story, promulgated by hospitals and the single-payer crowd, tries to tell us that consumer-driven health care will reduce choice of providers and insurers.

The allegation that consumer-driven health care will limit access to providers is promulgated primarily by the hospitals because they are fixated on a bricks-and-mortar version of health care delivery, one that is anchored by a megalith hospital. In a consumer-driven health care system, in contrast, focused factories for chronic diseases will integrate different providers in many different locations—ranging from the home for continual support, to the community for checkups, to a centralized tertiary care facility for complex, high-end care.[86]

The allegation that we cannot afford this decentralization of care is belied by the magnitude of the expenditures on chronic diseases. They are so enormous per person that a relatively small number of chronically ill individuals can justify extensive decentralization. For example, the $132 billion spent in 2002 on the care of individuals with diabetes could support, in an average state, one 500-bed hospital, five 200- to 299-bed hospitals, and 30 community facilities at a cost of $10 million each. This enormous delivery system would be entirely focused on diabetes and the many other diseases associated with it. It would largely replace the current inadequate system in which patients must assemble their own care teams.

As for access to insurance, those who advocate a single-payer system question the explosion of choice of insurance under consumer-driven health care. The Commonwealth Fund worries that as the choices offered to workers grow, patients are likely to be spread out more thinly across providers, meaning less volume for each. There may not be enough volume to allow providers to continue offering discounts and they may not be willing to participate at all in health plans that have large provider networks.[87] In other words, increased choice will lead to higher costs and ultimately to reductions in choices. But health care costs have not been controlled through economies of scale. For example, the massive consolidation of the hospital sector has increased costs. The big-is-beautiful, limited choice theory forms the basis of our present, failed system.

Consumer-driven health care, in contrast, will control costs because choice promotes competition and competition promotes innovation. It is through innovations such as focused factories and integrated medical teams productivity increases can best be achieved, not through "discounts" from large networks.

The Wrong Time and the Wrong Place Story

The message of the wrong time and the wrong place story is that consumers will be forced to negotiate the price of their health care when they are at their weakest—at the point of care. To dramatize this point, consider the picture of a bullet-riddled person, perhaps the unlucky passerby to a gang war, forced to negotiate the price of admission at the emergency room desk.

But this is the wrong picture.

In a consumer-driven health care system, consumers make their choices when they buy insurance, not when they use health care. In the quiet of their homes, people review helpful information to select the policy that best meets their needs. At a time of emergency, they use the insured providers they have previously specified. Even those who have selected high-deductible plans, under which they can shop for any providers, can find ready access through the network of doctors and hospitals that the insurer has assembled. And the high-cost emergency situations depicted in the wrong time and wrong place plot are almost fully insured.

Consumer-Driven Health Care for the Disabled and Poor

Is CDHC strictly for the middle and upper classes? Could the poor and disabled also benefit from it? The answer to the second question is a resounding "Yes!" as the vignette below illustrates.

The Chicago lecture room was packed. But it was like no lecture audience I had ever addressed before: there were people in wheelchairs, walking with crutches, and expostulating wildly with what I assumed was Tourette's syndrome.

My host was a tall man with gray hair, about my age. But unlike me, he had a ponytail, and I sensed that he was more comfortable in jeans than in the suit he wore that day.

Tom Nerney is his name, and he is a missionary for the disabled. And, despite our dissimilar outer appearances, we are soul mates. Both of us are advocates for consumer-driven health care.

Nerney familiarized me with the remarkable results achieved by consumer-driven programs for the disabled. Like other health insurers, Medicaid, the prime insurer for the needs of the disabled, typically doles out money for covered benefits—a doctor's visit, home health workers, and so on. But the consumer-driven programs work differently. They typically feature individual budgets, free choice of care providers, and unbiased "brokers" to assist adults to work and contribute to the community.

The results are heartening: for example, nearly 1,800 disabled participants in Arkansas' Cash & Counseling program found greatly enhanced satisfaction with caregivers and reductions in unmet needs, without impairment of health and safety. Direct consumer control caused a 38 percent reduction in neglect by caregivers and minimized fraud and abuse.[88] What a difference from a New York Medicaid program that was characterized by a senior official as one "that almost begs people to steal."[89] Small wonder that 11 states have since adopted programs similar to the one in Arkansas.[90]

These experiments are one way the state governments have come to grips with reality. Like corporate health insurance, Medicaid needs fundamental change. Although it helps 52 million low-income people, Medicaid's price tag threatens financial stability. South Carolina's expenses, for instance, have virtually doubled in the past decade and may consume nearly one-fourth of the state's budget in 2010.[91] Nationwide, Medicaid spending grew by nearly 10 percent in 2004 alone, and it is projected to consume nearly half a trillion dollars in less than a decade.[92]

Fiscally conscious governors and state legislators have traditionally controlled Medicaid expenses through reductions in enrollment, benefits, and provider reimbursement. Tennessee governor Phil Bredesen, for instance, culled 190,000 from the Medicaid rolls. But letting consumers drive the system is better for both the health of patients and the solvency of their home states.

Oklahoma, South Carolina, and Florida have embarked on a path that is at once less draconian and yet more radical. All three states have taken the step of permitting consumer-driven Medicaid enrollees to choose health services and providers for themselves. South Carolina, for example, puts a set amount every year into each enrollee's personal health account (PHA), to be spent as he or she sees fit. In Oklahoma, the PHA would be established for annual out-of-pocket expenses without a "use it or lose it" penalty—that is, the unspent balance could be used for future health care needs. The state would not mandate a homogeneous set of benefits; instead, it would provide financial assistance and patient counseling.

With consumer-driven health care, Medicaid enrollees can shop for care and increase their chances of receiving the care they need. (Not surprisingly, current Medicaid enrollees have more unmet needs than similar adults with private health insurance.) Health care providers, compelled to compete for Medicaid customers, will likely offer more consumer-oriented services at competitive costs.

Critics of Medicaid choice argue that such plans have several intrinsic flaws. Some view the plans as wasteful, citing Medicaid's already low per patient cost. But these "low costs" come at the participants' expense. Physicians, scared off by the drastically low level of state reimbursement for Medicaid providers, refuse to take them on as clients. In South Carolina, 30 percent of physicians refuse to accept any new Medicaid enrollees. Nationally, the percentage of physicians declining to take on new Medicaid patients grew by a third from 1996 to 2005.[93] With the new consumer-driven regime, physicians will have increased freedom to price competitively.

But the real opponents of Medicaid choice inevitably trot out a familiar, patronizing argument. Medicaid enrollees, they claim, either are not educated enough to be trusted with their own health or lack access to necessary sources of information. Yet patients make intelligent decisions—when we let them do it. The disabled people in the "cash and counseling" programs consistently receive better care than those who lack discretion.

You don't need a CPA to figure out what happens when people feel a greater sense of control and ownership over their health care: they get better care at better prices. For example, health care providers who compete for Medicaid customers may offer more coordinated, responsive service—Saturday hours, more preventative care, and so on—at costs that give the enrollees value for the money. Plenty of evidence indicates that when people spend money that they perceive as their own on health care, they control costs and get better care. For example, the nearly 9 million Americans enrolled in national health savings account types of programs incur substantially lower costs, use more preventative services, and comply more with chronic care regimens than those enrolled in standard insurance.[94] All kinds of people like these programs. For example, 83 percent of the supermarket chain Whole Foods' largely blue-collar team members voted for a consumer-driven health plan in preference to the old managed care plans. After three years, the firm's health care costs increased by only 3.3 percent annually, while turnover plummeted.[95]

Conventional wisdom is usually posed against consumer-driven reform. It seems even less trustworthy regarding Medicaid. Strong-arming enrollees and providers with rationing tactics is a poor way to improve quality and control costs. Consumer-driven health care, which liberates both health care providers and consumers, is a much better solution.

CHAPTER 8

CONSUMER-DRIVEN BENEFITS: LESSONS FROM OTHER COUNTRIES AND INDUSTRIES

We were badly burned by the transition of our health care system to managed care.

Does not the monumental scale of the shift I am advocating to consumer-driven health care create opportunities for similar sizable mistakes? Is there any evidence that this consumer-driven system works? Or is it merely a utopian fantasy?

This chapter reviews the evidence available on the feasibility and impact of consumer-driven health care. It is based on analyses of Switzerland's long-standing consumer-driven health care system; of the similar shift in pensions in the United States, which migrated from a system in which employers invested funds on behalf of retirees to a consumer-driven one in which employees manage their own investments; and of U.S. firms that have already begun to create new, innovative health insurance products. I then use this evidence to respond to concerns about consumer-driven health care.

Switzerland: A Case Study in Consumer-Driven Health Care[1]

Switzerland, the only developed country with a long-standing consumer-driven health care system, provides broad evidence and important lessons about its efficacy. Unlike the U.S. system, in which employers or governments select health insurance, in Switzerland, it is the consumers themselves who purchase their health insurance. The Swiss have considerable experience with some of the consumer-driven insurance policies newly introduced in the United States, such as those with high deductibles.

Switzerland has been politically neutral since at least 1907, unlike most of its European neighbors. It is a haven of quiet in a roiling sea. Its consumer-driven health care system mirrors the country's traditional independence, as citizens may freely choose plans, and its solidarity, as it requires everyone to purchase health insurance and subsidizes the needy.[2] But it more closely mirrors its neighbors' centrally controlled health care systems in the constraints placed on insurers and providers.[3]

Swiss consumers, not employers or the government, primarily pay for the country's health care expenses. In 2000, 43 percent of consumers' payments were for insurance premiums (about 67 percent of total health care costs), 0.1 percent for deductibles and copayments (about 5 percent of total health care costs), and 28 percent for all other out-of-pocket payments, such as those for over-the-counter drugs (19 percent of the total).[4] The Swiss consumer-driven system directly subsidizes the needy and also assures that sick people do not pay more for health insurance than others. Individual cantons provide tax-financed, means-tested subsidies so low-income individuals can purchase compulsory health insurance. In 2001, 19 percent of the insured received subsidies, and 18 percent of enrollee premiums were government financed.[5] Subsidies are based on a consumer's income and assets. The subsidy typically equals the average premium in a canton.

No insurance plans offer complete coverage, and the Swiss may not buy insurance for these out-of-pocket payments. The required benefits range from hospital care to health spas. Insurers may also offer supplementary, optional policies for private hospital rooms or child care for sick parents.[6] Demand is thus constrained by governmentally controlled, mandated coverage and benefits that must be featured in all policies. Despite their mandated benefits, the compulsory policies offer some differentiation: they include plans with high deductibles, health maintenance organizations (HMOs) that tightly manage access, and bonus plans that reward enrollees who do not use insurance by reducing premiums over five years.

The health insurance plans vary substantially in price.[7] Supplementary plans feature additional differentiation. For example, one popular policy contains a nonsmoker option with savings of up to 20 percent.[8] The largest market share is held by high-deductible plans, while managed care plans have attained a relatively small market share.

The Swiss government approves insurance prices. Compulsory insurers are also risk adjusted: those with above-average medical care costs receive transfers from those with lower-than-average costs. For example, in 1999, on average, $541.40 per enrollee in a high-deductible plan was removed from insurers because their enrollees were healthier than average, and it was transferred to the lower-deductible insurers who had enrolled sicker people.[9] The adjustment is based on the insurer's deviation from the average medical costs for enrollees in 30 different age and sex categories.[10]

The Swiss health care system frees consumer demand much more than supply. The lessons we can draw from Switzerland are thus limited because the Swiss system is not a complete model of consumer-driven health care: demand is constrained by governmental regulation of the design of insurance policies, and supply is constrained by uniform prices paid to doctors. In addition, information about the quality of providers' services is nonexistent. Nevertheless, it provides important lessons about the impact of consumers' buying health insurance for themselves.

The Swiss lesson is generally a positive one. Switzerland provides universal coverage at substantially lower cost than the United States while avoiding the quality, responsiveness, equity, and provider compensation concerns of single-payer universal health care systems.[11] However, perhaps because of its constraints on supply and lack of information, inefficiencies remain.

Results of the Swiss Consumer-Driven Health Care System

The Swiss consumer-driven health care system achieves important, positive results. The general health of the Swiss population is at least as high as that of the U.S. population, while costs and rates of inflation are 40 percent lower as a percentage of the economy. Furthermore, Switzerland has universal coverage, unlike the United States, where more than 40 million people are uninsured.

Swiss health care expenses are considerably lower than not only those of the United States as a whole but also than those of U.S. states with comparable income, levels of education, and race and ethnicity—characteristics that profoundly affect health status.[12] Similarly, the Swiss outcomes for diseases like diabetes, which are linked to the socioeconomic characteristics above, are roughly equal or better.[13] Yet the Swiss generally have more of the resources that are typically considered in cross-national comparisons—such as hospital beds, physicians, and costly diagnostic and therapeutic equipment—than Canada, the United Kingdom, and even the United States. Last, Swiss physicians are well compensated, although not quite as well as U.S. physicians. (Most other comparisons of U.S. health care outcomes to those of developed European countries fail to adjust for substantial differences in the sociodemographic characteristics among them, such as levels of education, ethnic composition, and income.[14] Because health status is considerably affected by such characteristics, the value of the comparisons in isolating the impact of the health care system on outcomes is limited. The analysis herein, in contrast, compares Switzerland to the U.S. states that most resemble it, such as Connecticut and Massachusetts.)

One reason for lower costs is that competition among Swiss insurers has lowered annual insurance administrative expenses per enrollee,[15] while in the United States, they have increased.[16] The Swiss insurance industry demonstrates the viability of small insurers. In 2004, only 17.4 percent of Swiss insurance firms had more than 100,000 enrollees.[17] The administrative economies of scale used to justify a single-payer system are not readily apparent in Switzerland.[18] The administrative costs per enrollee for insurers with fewer than 5,000 members equaled those attained by the large insurers.[19] Indeed, small insurers frequently earned greater profits per enrollee than those with more than 500,000 members.[20] Another reason for lowered costs is that competition among Swiss physicians caused them to experience sharper reductions in income as their numbers (supply) increased to levels higher than those in Germany, Sweden, and the United States.[21]

Yet in comparison to the United States, resource inefficiencies appear, such as the number of hospitals, and perhaps, hospital admission rates and lengths of stay.[22] These results may be attributable to the government's excessive involvement in designing the insurance policies and subsidizing Swiss public hospitals and thus sheltering them from competition.

Lessons from Switzerland about the Equity and Feasibility of Consumer-Driven Health Care

Experts have voiced various concerns about consumer-driven health care.[23] I can dispel some of their concerns through findings revealed in studies of the Swiss health care system.

Concern: *"Fraudulent insurers will injure consumers in an individual health insurance market."* Individuals in the Swiss system can safely and effectively buy insurance from a large number of competent firms.

Concern: *"CDHC will end health insurance. Healthy people will not buy it, and sick people will not be able to afford it."* The Swiss system requires universal coverage. Prices to individuals are not risk adjusted. A sick 60-year-old man pays the same price for insurance as a healthy one. But insurers are motivated to provide policies to sick people because their premiums are risk adjusted.

Concern: *"Sick people will not receive adequate care in a CDHC system."* Sick people, fully insured in Switzerland, have excellent prognoses when compared to patients in similar countries.

Concern: *"CDHC will create multiple tiers of care, with the poor relegated to the worst."* The quality of Swiss health care is differentiated primarily by amenities such as patients' being able to stay in a semiprivate hospital room. Differences in health care utilization by income class are not substantial.

Concern: *"Residents in low-population-density areas will be denied access to insurance and/or care."* Some Swiss insurers specialize in rural areas, where, presumably, they earn sufficient profit to compensate for their smaller scale. Anecdotal evidence indicates that shortages of care do not occur there.[24]

Lessons from Consumer-Driven Financial Investments

But Switzerland is a small country. Can the massive United States achieve similar results when it transforms to a consumer-driven system?

We can address this question by analyzing the dramatic shift to a consumer-driven system that occurred in the United States more than two decades ago when employers expanded pension plans from defined-benefits (db) options, in which employers invested employees' pension funds, to consumer-driven defined-contribution (dc) options, in which employees invested the retirement funds for themselves. [The 401(k) plans, which enable tax-free investment of monies by the employee and matches from the employer, are a subset of the dc plans.]

The shift to dc options was propelled by forces similar to those prompting the shift in health care benefits. Employers were burdened by the administrative load of running db plans, and the mobile U.S. workforce welcomed the portability of dc plans and, likely, the control they enabled.[25]

The introduction of dc pension plans spurred a revolution in the financial industry. The lessons have been generally positive: on the demand side, dc plans have experienced substantial employee participation. On the supply size, the newly opened market motivated the industry to introduce differentiated mutual funds and develop reliable information sources, enabling average people to earn good returns, while reducing transaction costs.[26]

Lessons about Demand: Investors and Employers

Some worried about the investment acumen of employees and the integrity of employers, fearing they would abandon their support for workers' retirement needs. Others were concerned that low-income employees or those in smaller firms would get locked out. Some fretted that employees would misuse dc plans for frivolous purposes, such as taking out loans from their retirement funds to acquire assets for leisure time pursuits.[27]

All these concerns proved unfounded: employees invested intelligently; employers increased their contributions; and both low-income and small employers participated.

Lessons about Investors

Despite the warnings of the gloom and doom crowd, the dc option proved highly successful. In 2005, more than 47 million participated in 401(k) dc plans,[28] with an average account balance of $102,000.[29]

Worries that consumers would be pillaged[30] were unjustified. One study showed that dc returns outdid db ones, not only in the boom periods, 1995 to 1998, but also in down market years.[31] During one of the worst markets for stocks since the Great Depression, from 1999 to 2005, average account balances increased by 50 percent, from $67,785 to $102,094. The median account balance more than doubled.[32]

The returns earned by average consumers may outperform those of "expert" investors because administrators and middlemen do not necessarily work in their clients' best interests. For one thing, they cannot know individual preferences and risk tolerances. Further, their interests may differ from the clients'. Noted *BusinessWeek* of state pension funds, for example, "political grandstanding . . . mix[es] controversial social goals with their clear financial mandate."[33] Last, the absence of direct investor oversight may tempt managers to commit fraud.

This is not to say that administrators are unnecessary.[34] Investors who relied on mutual funds as agents were well rewarded; for example, a dollar invested in Fidelity's large company stock funds a decade ago was worth about $2 or more in 2005.[35]

A Fidelity Investments study of its dc plans, which it claims represent national averages, allayed many concerns about equity: overall, employee participation varied inversely with plan size,[36] with higher participation in smaller plans,[37] and both well- and less-well-compensated employees saved equal percentages of income.[38] More than half of lower-income earners saved.[39] Those who did not participate were not necessarily slighting their retirement needs: they were more likely to hold other financial assets than participants.[40] Although some worried that younger people would ignore the need for retirement savings, younger participants experienced the largest increases in account balances; between 1999 and 2005, the balances of those in their twenties increased by a staggering 700 percent.[41]

Lessons about Employers

More than three-quarters of Fidelity's plans feature employer matching,[42] independent of firm size.[43] Also, many dc plans offer convenient, fair access to their services.[44]

Nevertheless, some employers were self-serving. For one thing, they stuffed their employees' dc accounts with company stock.[45] Coca-Cola's and Procter & Gamble's dc assets, for example, were more than 80 percent invested in company stock—a concentration that most investment experts judge as excessively risky for most employees. Some firms locked employees into long-term prohibitions against selling.[46] If the market value of the company's stock collapsed, the employees' holdings in these underdiversified accounts took a nosedive. By 2005, employees had seemingly redressed this problem: fewer invested in company stock, and when they held company stock, they did not concentrate their holdings in that stock.[47]

Lessons about Supply

Employees received most of the choice, information, and support they needed from entrepreneurial, consumer-oriented mutual funds that entered the new dc market, such as Fidelity, Vanguard, and T. Rowe Price.[48] These companies competed on returns, services and costs. Vanguard, for example, found that as it shaved its operating costs to become the low-cost producer and focused on service, its assets boomed.[49] Noted one official, "The big thing we did differently . . . was to treat the participants in the 401(k) plan the same way as the other (institutional) investors in our funds."[50] In contrast, banks, their competitors, "had no culture of dealing with the individual."[51] Fund expenses declined steadily,[52] and most funds offered tailored educational assistance. American Express, for example, segmented its educational messages to 44 classifications of investors.[53] These entrepreneurial funds eventually entered the small employer market.[54] Fidelity's entrance reduced the costs of a dc plan to a small company by an estimated 50 percent.[55]

Innovations in the supply of dc retirement products continue to come forth. Lifestyle and life-cycle funds have become increasingly popular in recent years for individuals who might be overwhelmed by the large array of choices or are too busy to actively manage the asset allocation of their dc accounts. Lifestyle funds, for example, maintain a predetermined risk level and use words such as "conservative," "moderate," or "aggressive" in their names to indicate how risky they are. These funds typically rebalance their portfolios to become more conservative and produce more income as the enrollee nears retirement.[56]

Early U.S. Consumer-Driven Health Care Insurance Innovations

Although consumer-driven health care has only recently been introduced in the United States, there are already some noteworthy innovations in the coverage, benefits, and organization of medical care

providers they feature. Some consumer-driven health insurance policies enable consumers with large, uninsured, out-of-pocket expenditures to trade off insurance coverage they do not want for other
benefits. These plans feature tax-advantaged health savings or "reimbursement" accounts that enrollees can use to pay for uninsured
health care needs. In exchange, the enrollee buys a lower-cost, high-
deductible health insurance plan.

In Medtronic's version, for example, the firm contributed $2,000
to a family savings account and additionally paid for all preventive
care. The account could be used for needs such as hearing aids, prescription medications for weight loss and impotence, and smoking
cessation programs. Unspent balances were rolled over. With a
$3,000 deductible, this plan costs nearly $1,000 a year less than alternative managed care plan options, and enrollees gained greater
spending flexibility and reduced out-of-pocket maximums.[57] Large
insurers—UnitedHealthcare, Aetna, CIGNA HealthCare, and Well-
Point—offer variants of this plan.

The low price of these policies also helps the uninsured. In 2005,
for example, a health savings account plan was priced at 30 percent
less than all plans for individuals and families.[58] (A growing percentage of the uninsured reject their employer's offer of health insurance, likely because they consider it a bad value for the money.)[59]

Illinois-based Destiny Health featured preventive care guidelines
and rewards for health promoting activities, such as quitting smoking and maintaining proper weight. Noted its CEO: "We . . . are
committed to helping (our members) maintain and improve their
overall health."[60] Enrollees who follow the guidelines earn points for
higher-interest credits in their health savings account, major airline
mileage programs, and fitness club privileges, among others.[61]

The Buyers Health Care Action Group (BHCAG), a coalition of
large employers in the Twin Cities, had enabled providers to quote
their own prices, form their own teams, and determine their own
policies for the delivery of health care (for example, they establish
their own requirements for referrals to specialists). These plans were
also risk adjusted to protect against the economic penalties of sick

enrollees. An executive explains: "BHCAG employers realized that there were substantial differences among providers, but they were all being presented to consumers as one plan. There was no market incentive for good physicians to provide efficient, high-quality care because the health plan average would just be brought down by the poor performers."[62]

BHCAG contracted directly with 25 care teams, including world-famous institutions such as the Mayo Clinic and Park Nicolett Hospital. Enrollees received at least enough money to buy the group plan with the lowest total cost of care, and they were given considerable information about their peers' perception of the caregivers' quality. For example, in this system, the Mayo Clinic quoted one price and the Park Nicolett Hospital another. Enrollees chose one of the two, then received all their care from that system. If the Mayo Clinic happens to attract enrollees who are much sicker than the average and Park Nicolett those who are much healthier, the coalition paid the Mayo Clinic more and Park Nicolett Hospital less.

Enrollees responded strongly to BHCAG's price and information incentives: providers with 10 percent higher prices experienced enrollment reductions of 16 percent.[63] Four years after the initiative began, enrollees had shifted overwhelmingly from high-cost providers to low-cost ones. These shifts did not appear to affect the quality of care.[64] Employers benefited too; their costs increased at lower rates for BHCAG enrollees.[65]

Most providers liked the plan.[66] Despite BHCAG's relatively small market share, they introduced supply innovations, including increased quality of care for some chronic diseases and health promoting activities. Some providers even changed their cost structure. The brilliant CEO of Park Nicolett, for example, dramatically reconfigured its costs: his hospital, classified as a high-cost system initially, was considered a low-cost system four years later.[67]

Yet, despite all these pluses, the plan faltered because it disintermediated the insurers by contracting directly with the providers. Some employers were reluctant to cross swords with the insurers, typically a powerful force in the business community.[68] In a consumer-driven system, in contrast, the buyers will be indifferent to the insurers' political power. They will buy the best value for the money plan, regardless of whether it is offered by insurers or not.

Lessons about Swiss Consumer-Driven Health Care and U.S. Consumer-Driven Retirement Plans

The Swiss consumer-driven health care system and the U.S. consumer-driven dc plans achieved many positive results. The Swiss have universal coverage, and more than 80 million Americans have participated in the booming equity markets of recent years through their ownership of mutual funds tailored to their needs. Defined-contribution participants have sensibly invested for their future.[69] And the Swiss, who are at least as healthy as we, achieve their good health at a substantially lower cost.

The dc movement also provides important lessons about employers' willingness to support workers' benefits: employers have continued to contribute to dc plans, negating concerns about their opting out, and suppliers responded to the opportunities created by the new consumer-driven retirement system. In the United States, competent entrepreneurial mutual funds provided excellent, low-cost services to firms small and large. Intense competition caused continual cost decreases and quality improvements.[70] Last, companies such as Morningstar, which furnishes financial information, made entrepreneurial efforts to provide authoritative, objective, easily comprehended evaluations, enabling those who were not financial wizards to participate intelligently.[71]

There were lessons about what not to do, as well. In Switzerland, government restrictions on the design of health insurance policies and providers' organizations obviated the appearance of supplier innovations similar to those the dc movement occasioned. And, in the United States, corporate restrictions on employees' ability to invest freely subjected them to needless risk.

These lessons suggest that in a consumer-driven health care system,

- *Employers* will continue to offer to pay for health insurance benefits. Consumer-driven health care may well expand the number and size of employers who offer insurance, just as many small employers now newly offer dc retirement plans.
- *Employees* will purchase insurance and act to protect their health status.
- *Entrepreneurial firms* will supply the innovative insurance and information products that consumer-driven health care programs require and will force status quo medical providers to innovate. The competition among them will continually improve products and reduce costs.
- *Government* must subsidize the poor and oversee insurers and providers, but it must not micromanage them and allow government bureaucracies, who can manage only what exists or has existed, to stifle innovation and prevent the creation of new consumer-driven organizations and health insurance plans.

So what will it take to make consumer-driven health care happen? How can we preserve the positive elements of consumer-driven systems and minimize the negatives? The next part of the book addresses these questions.

HOW TO MAKE
IT HAPPEN:
THE CARROTS,
THE STICKS,
THE LAWS

THE CARROTS
Let Medical Business Entrepreneurialism Bloom

Think of any well-functioning organization that you know personally: perhaps your family, your place of worship, your favorite charity, and, if you are lucky, your work site or local government.

What makes these organizations effective? The answer to this question also reveals how to make consumer-driven health care work.

Ideological advocates of consumer-driven health care invoke the mystical, invisible-hand powers of free markets. But effective markets do not work through ideology. Culture is key, as we saw in the discussion of Kaiser in Chapter 2. But what creates a good culture? Clear values and a system of carrots and sticks that rewards adherence to them and punishes transgressions.[1]

All effective organizations make use of carrots and sticks to function productively. Effective employers offer financial and professional recognition as rewards for adherence to their values and use their absence as a punishment. Many religious organizations promise heaven as the carrot and hell as the stick. Family units use inclusion as a reward and ostracism as a punishment. Effective governments offer democracy as a carrot and civil and criminal punishment as a stick.

What are the carrots and sticks that will make a consumer-driven health care system work?

In effective economic markets, participants are given the freedom to do good and do well, and miscreants are punished. When it comes to a consumer-driven health care system, the carrot part is easy: we must empower the entrepreneurs who can make health care cheaper and better. These are likely to be businesses, rather than nonprofit entrepreneurs. After all, businesses can most readily raise the capital needed for entrepreneurial ventures and reward entrepreneurs financially. As a result, business organizations have both the means and the incentives to scale up successful entrepreneurial ventures. And businesses are clearly accountable to their shareholders, unlike nonprofits, which have no owners or sources of capital other than organizations. Last, businesses are typically more efficient than nonprofits, in part because of their accountability.[2]

But businesses cannot do everything—they cannot fund the poor. That is appropriately the role of government. And businesses have their dark side: avarice can lead them to fraud and poor quality. They must be regulated, as the fraudulent activities of businesses of the 1990s vividly demonstrated. Government must protect health care consumers from these destructive business practices, as it protects consumers in other industries.

Regulation is expensive. We pay the costs not only of the government agents who write and enforce the regulations but also of the business employees who monitor and ensure compliance with those regulations. Sometimes these costs may exceed the benefits we derive from them. What is the most effective form of stick?

Psychological experiments reveal that punishment works, especially when it is coupled with mechanisms that lead to gains or losses in reputation. Punishment is primal: responses to punishment can be traced in our brains. Similarly, concerns with reputation appear to guide social behavior.[3] In an interesting experiment in behavioral economics, when punishment and loss of reputation were combined, they resulted in the highest production of public goods.[4] ("Public goods" in this context means those activities that benefit all of us but to which we might contribute too little as individuals if we were left to our own devices. For example, when it comes to controlling environmental pollution, we may individually do less than we could because we are counting on someone else to pick up our slack.)

This part of the book discusses the carrots and sticks that will make consumer-driven health care happen. The carrots are opportunities for business entrepreneurialism, while the sticks are regulation and information that can enhance or reduce reputation. Part 4 ends by delineating the role of the state, the federal government, and Republicans and Democrats in enacting the bold legislative plan that can make consumer-driven health care a reality.

The Entrepreneurial U.S. Economy

The U.S. economy is blessed with business entrepreneurs who are very good at what they do. We feel their impact in our daily lives. For example, my new PC was built by one of them; the PC is powered by the operating system that was designed by another; and it was speedily delivered to me by the genius of yet another entrepreneur. The brilliant entrepreneurs who started the businesses whose products I use are Michael Dell, Bill Gates, and Fred Smith, the creators of Dell, Microsoft, and Federal Express. You too can likely rattle off a string of the names of other entrepreneurs who have improved your life.

Like them, most entrepreneurs are drawn to profit-seeking businesses as vehicles for their efforts. The business form of organization permits them to readily raise capital from people who buy shares of stock or lend money, which frees entrepreneurs from having to plead for donations—as nonprofits must do—or increase taxes—as governments must do. And U.S. entrepreneurs can freely manage their businesses as they see fit, within the laws designed to minimize anticompetitive and anticonsumer behavior and to ensure that corporations are transparent about their results.

Business entrepreneurs like Michael Dell and Bill Gates do good: they improve the quality of our lives. And they do well: if they are successful, they can become rich. But they do not become rich at our expense. They typically lower prices—Michael Dell—and/or improve our productivity—Bill Gates and Fred Smith.

Can you name any health services entrepreneurs?

Why does this huge sector, which so desperately needs people whose creative genius and leadership qualities can make things better and cheaper, have so few?

Entrepreneurs avoid the health care industry because the government has usurped and constrained so many business functions. As we observed in Chapter 5, the chapter that discussed how the U.S. Congress helped accelerate the death of Jack Morgan, when it comes to health care, the government sets the prices; limits the ability of doctors to enter the business; favors the nonprofit form of organization; and even dictates how health care should be delivered through pay-for-performance and similar initiatives.

A view of health care as a public good that must be actively managed by governments and implemented by nonprofits discourages the business innovation that could fill the huge gaps left by current health systems. Businesses can achieve important goals—improving access, lowering costs, improving quality, and helping the poor— while serving their shareholders. We must remove the barriers that stand in their way. But government has an important role too. It should ensure that the dark side of business—avarice and the kind of self-protecting manipulation of the laws and the legislators that we have seen with the hospitals, the dialysis centers, and the drug manufacturers—does not overshadow its ability to do good.

How Businesses Do Good by Doing Well

In September 2005, New Orleans was submerged in foul water after Hurricane Katrina shattered the jerry-rigged levees meant to protect the city from the raging Lake Pontchartrain. Thousands were left homeless, while mosquitoes buzzed through the fetid air and rats roamed the streets. The inadequate security in the shelters for the displaced allowed conditions to deteriorate into anarchy, punctuated by the roar of gunfire. Potable water was so scarce that many died of dehydration. Because the shelters lacked adequate sewage facilities, residents slipped plastic bags over their shoes to protect them from the rivers of urine. Bathroom walls were smeared with feces.[5]

Out of the tumult, an unlikely savior appeared—Wal-Mart. It had 45 trucks ready before Katrina hit land, laden with water, toilet paper, flashlights, prepared meals, and ammunition. Powered by in-house generators and informed by its satellite communications system, the firm opened its stores for important social services, including free use of its digital film kiosks to help reunite lost family members.[6]

In contrast, the disaster relief efforts of all levels of government were disastrous. Astonishingly, some New Orleans firefighters and police officers abandoned their jobs. And when the mayor opened the Superdome football stadium to the homeless, he had no plans for provisioning or transporting them. Louisiana's governor frantically yelled, "Does anybody in this building know anything about buses?" in belated efforts to convey the 100,000 New Orleans residents who did not own a car out of the city. The Federal Emergency Management Agency (FEMA) sadly became a model for governmental ineptitude as it failed to provide any relief until days after the hurricane had passed. In a massive communication breakdown, FEMA waited for specific requests for help from state and local governments, which never came.[7] Charges of cronyism—FEMA's hapless director was an old pal of President George W. Bush—and patronage were rife.

The American Red Cross, the nonprofit that received nearly 60 percent of the billions donated for Katrina's victims, fared no better. It not only failed to respond promptly, but it later faced a Senate investigation for possible criminal activities, including the disappearance of cars and other donations. Some volunteers felt that Red Cross operations were "being manipulated for private gain." The Red Cross allegedly buried volunteers' complaints until a reporter began investigating them. Noted one: "People were definitely taking advantage of huge flaws in accountability."[8] The Red Cross has since alleged that it has taken these criticisms to heart, thus obviating prosecution. But not all observers were sanguine. Noted one official of a charity watch group cautiously, "These changes were a long time coming, and we're hopeful they'll follow through. It's a shame it took Katrina to open up their eyes."[9]

As for Wal-Mart, I am no apologist for its practices—all too many of its employees are forced to rely on Medicaid, the health insurance for the poor. Yet its responses to Katrina underscored its hallmark efficiency and loyal employees. The keys to Wal-Mart's success were clear goals and expertise. When Wal-Mart's own meteorologists predicted a storm, its world-class supply chain models ordered the right mix of products for the store. Through well-established chains of command, Wal-Mart's centralized emergency operations staff, which is ordinarily assigned to routine events such as fires within their own stores and the surrounding communities, was supplemented by senior officials from each functional area.[10]

The qualities that Wal-Mart displayed—clarity of goals, well-established organizational protocols, and loyal workers—were notable for their absence in the government and nonprofit organizations. The Katrina saga exemplifies how business organizations can do well and do good when it comes to health care.

The Role for Government in a Consumer-Driven Health Care System

The government's dysfunctional role in the Katrina mess parallels its counterproductive roles in health care: passing tax laws that favor employer-purchased insurance; curtailing the development and spread of physician-owned innovations, such as specialty hospitals; and even micromanaging the amount of epo a kidney dialysis patient should take. But government can lend a productive hand in the creation of a successful consumer-driven health care system, if its involvement is limited to appropriate redistribution, regulatory, and oversight functions.

Government plays three crucial roles in any consumer-driven system: it oversees the solvency and integrity of participants; it provides transparency; and it subsidizes the purchase of important items for the needy.

When it comes to health care, the government should

- Prosecute fraudulent providers, enrollees, and insurers and assure the financial solvency of insurers (as discussed in Chapter 10).
- Use our tax money to subsidize those who cannot afford health insurance (Chapter 7).
- Require the dissemination of audited data about the performance of providers (Chapter 10).

The Role of Nonprofits in a Consumer-Driven Health Care System

What is the role of nonprofit organizations in consumer-driven health care? Traditionally, organizational theorists have advanced three reasons for the existence of the nonprofit form of organization. The first alleges that nonprofits are efficient in providing public goods relative to governments. Although government can step in and correct our collective failings by providing public goods on our behalf, it is less likely to know what we want than a nonprofit that relies on our donations for its revenues. The second theory is that nonprofits are more altruistic than businesses. And the third is that nonprofits are agents that protect the people who cannot adequately protect themselves. Nonprofits are better agents than businesses because they are more concerned with quality and less focused on their bottom lines.

All three theories fail to provide a definitive argument for the unique value of nonprofits. When it comes to public goods, for example, a business could provide the same environmental pollution controls as a nonprofit. Further, because businesses are typically more transparent than nonprofits, we can judge whether they are earning excessive profits and/or paying their executives excessive amounts when they carry out these public good functions.[11] The presumption of altruism in nonprofits is simply a presumption: the behavior of some of the nonprofit hospitals discussed earlier in this book could hardly be classified as altruistic.[12] Last, there is no conclusive evidence of higher quality for nonprofit activities relative to for-profit ones. Business executives can and do diminish quality in order to maximize profit, but nonprofit executives may diminish quality too, to enhance their salaries and to increase the size of their organization. If businesses go too far, new entrants will win market share by offering better quality or prices. But when it comes to non-profits in health care, this competitive dynamic does not work as well.[13] As we have seen, for example, the nonprofit hospitals are adept in exploiting the "nonprofit" title to suppress the competition that could threaten them.

The best protection for consumers comes not from the non-profit form, but from the combination of transparency and regulation that penalizes fraudulent behavior that will be discussed in Chapter 10.

How Entrepreneurial Businesses Can Do Good and Do Well in Health Care

As you will see in the course of this chapter, there is considerable opportunity for businesses to make money and provide vital services to people in need of care or striving to preserve their good health, efficiently and effectively. I will show the nature of these opportunities and describe some of the brave entrepreneurs who, despite all obstacles, have made inroads into our present insular system and have created important new health care products and services.

Providing Health Insurance

Ironically, our country is the richest in the world, yet more than 40 million people lack health insurance. Its high price—up to $10,000 to $15,000 per family—is a major barrier. There is plenty of opportunity to provide innovative, low-priced insurance products for people who simply cannot afford the ridiculous price tag of the current offerings.

Low-Price Health Insurance

Definity Health, a venture-capital-backed business, designed a new policy that offered insurance only for catastrophically expensive health care, usually coupled with tax-supported health savings or reimbursement accounts whose funds can be used to pay for uninsured medical needs and 100 percent of preventive care. The policy was up to 40 percent cheaper than traditional ones. The results? Only a few years after the policies were first offered, by Definity and others, more than 9 million Americans had enrolled. As for Definity, it did well, while it did good—the firm was purchased a few years after its founding by UnitedHealth Group for approximately $340 million in 2004.[14]

Health Insurance Markets

The company eHealthInsurance Services, Inc., a for-profit marketplace, is the nation's leading online source of health insurance for individuals, families, and small businesses. It offers more than 5,000 health plans underwritten by more than 140 leading health insurance companies. It has accomplished important social goals: in 2005, 25 percent of its customers earned less than $35,000,[15] and more than 40 percent of those who bought a high-deductible policy were previously uninsured.[16] Like Definity, the firm did well while it did good. When it went public in 2006, it achieved a market valuation of more than half a billion dollars.

Improving Access to Services

You're Sick, We're Quick

Overworked, two-career, sandwich-generation Americans find it difficult to access health care for minor, but debilitating, health care problems, such as allergies and strep throat. Scheduling a doctor's visit often requires weeks of waiting, and hospital emergency rooms triage these patients to the lowest level of urgency, with hours spent in line.

The costs of these inconvenient services—from $100 for the physician up to thousands for the emergency room—are disproportionate to the need. Last, clogging up emergency rooms with allergy victims is akin to using Daytona 500 garage facilities to service a Toyota.

MinuteClinic, a Minneapolis-based private firm, helped to solve these problems with a chain of walk-in clinics in convenient locations, such as drug and department stores, office buildings, and college campuses. Nurse practitioners treat ailments in 10 to 15 minutes, usually with no appointments needed, at a typical price of $59. (They call customers on their cell phones if there is a wait.) The clinics are open 12 hours on weekdays and 6 hours on weekends. Software generates a patient record that is automatically sent to the patient's physician.[17] Their customer orientation is implemented by a CEO with extensive experience with customer-oriented firms, such as Procter & Gamble. Because these clinics exist, doctors and emergency rooms are able to focus on those who can most benefit from their services.

This firm too has done well. Founded in 2000, by 2005, it operated 73 centers in nine states, and it had plans to open 200 more in 2006.[18] In 2006, it was sold to CVS, a major drugstore chain.[19]

Concierge Medicine for Middle- and Low-Income People

Washington State's Dr. Garrison Bliss and his software entrepreneur partner, Norman Wu, provide middle- and lower-income patients with concierge physician services 24 hours a day, seven days a week to meet their patients' primary care needs, including common X rays and lab tests. Cost? Only about $60 per patient per month, no insurance required or accepted, with no patient copays, deductibles, or coinsurance. In 2002, a two-person household spent more on vehicle insurance.[20]

Customers receive same-day or next-day office visits for urgent care, same-month physical exams, plus 24/7 phone and e-mail access to a physician, in clinics open 12 hours a day, seven days a week. Staffing ratios permit physicians and their nurse practitioners to spend the time required to fully address their patients' medical needs—30 minutes for a typical appointment.

For the uninsured, the affordable and predictable cost combined with the continuity of care from one's own physician will provide a welcome alternative to frequenting emergency rooms or avoiding proper medical care altogether.[21] Those who want and can afford greater coverage can combine the concierge primary care services with a high-deductible health plan for full specialist and hospital coverage, achieving a typical savings of 30 to 40 percent over the cost of traditional low-deductible health insurance, including out-of-pocket expenses.

Redeploying Profits to Help the Poor Gain Access to Health Care

India's Narayana Hrudayalaya (NH) Heart Hospitals use their profits to subsidize care for the poor. To assist this mission, NH has implemented an operational strategy that enables it to carry out a large volume of surgeries daily, almost eight times the Indian national average. It reaches out to the poor in rural areas with the largest telemedicine network in India and a mobile cardiac diagnostic lab.[22]

India's Aravind Eye Hospital, which employs similar strategies, ensures equity by using the same medical personnel to staff its Free Hospital and the regular one. Affirming its do-good, do-well nature, its founder noted, "[In government hospitals] patients feel obliged to tip the support staff to get even routine things done. Worse still, poor villagers feel totally intimidated. We want to make all sorts of people feel at ease, and this can only come if the clinical . . . and . . . support staff view the entire exercise as a spiritual experience."[23]

Improving the Quality and Controlling the Costs of Health Care Delivery

Business innovations can simultaneously improve quality and control costs.

Focused Health Care Factories

Focused health care factories can provide victims of most chronic diseases and disabilities with convenient, effective access to the team of health care providers they need. For-profit, partially physician-owned specialty surgical hospitals that focus on one field, such as MedCath in cardiovascular surgery, are one example: they typically provide quality of care that is equal to or better than the general, everything-for-everybody hospitals.[24] Further, the competition they create helps to lower the costs of their competitors by motivating them to become more efficient.[25]

Global Health Services

Businesses in Dubai, India, Thailand, and Singapore are positioning themselves as lower-cost, high-quality sources of health care ser-vices.[26] Market estimates for India's revenues from international patients range from $2 billion to $12 billion by 2012; Singapore has set a $3 billion target;[27] and a third of the million patients in Thailand's Bumrungrad Hospital come from outside the country.[28]

These globalized services offer three benefits. First, they enable developing countries to minimize the massive capital investments health care facilities require. For example, despite Bangladesh's poverty, it is one of the top 10 sources of foreign patients for Singapore, and its patients receive customized services at Bumrungrad.[29] Second, globalized services reduce the waiting times and the capacity pressures in single-payer countries. In the United Kingdom, for example, more than 800,000 patients were waiting for hospital admissions, and 41,000 had waited for more than six months.[30] Last, they are typically cheaper than similar services in developed countries. Thailand's costs, for example, are a tenth of those in the United States.[31]

The globalized competitors achieve cost savings not only because of the lower cost of living in the host countries, but also because they have different, and likely more efficient, organizations for delivery.

One Indian hospital company, Fortis Healthcare, for example, is setting up a hub-and-spoke organization, with each multispecialty hospital linked to a network of superspecialty hospitals.[32]

In most of the world, the absence of health care services and insurance represents another major opportunity for businesses to do good and do well. For example, India, projected to become the world's third-largest economy in about two decades, spent only $14 billion on health care delivery and $250 million on health insurance in 2004, while China's per capita health care spending is only three times India's.[33] And, in countries where public-sector national health insurance programs exist, such as the United Kingdom and Canada, opportunity lies in the lack of effective and efficient systems of delivery.

Barriers to Entrepreneurial Business Involvement in Health Care

Yet significant barriers remain to fulfilling these opportunities because of many prevailing laws barring or limiting for-profit health care. Policy makers are gravely suspicious of for-profit health care.

Barring Health Care Business

In some countries, leaders believe that the profits returned to shareholders should, instead, be spent on caring for the sick. As a result, Canada and some U.S. states do not allow businesses to own health care facilities.[34] But the consequences are grave because businesses can deliver more efficient, better health care services. For example, Toronto, Canada's Shouldice Hospital, world famous for its excellent, inexpensive treatment of hernias, was not permitted to expand. (Because Shouldice Hospital existed before Canada's national health care system went into effect, it was allowed to retain its for-profit ownership structure.) Canadians, as we have seen, must sometimes queue up for lengthy periods to obtain health care services. If they could have obtained them at Shouldice, they would have received excellent, lower-cost care.

Increasingly, "rogue" for-profit enterprises are filling the void left by the government-controlled health care system. To underscore their acceptance, the president of the "rogue" Cambie Surgery Centre, in Vancouver, was the 2007–2008 president of the Canadian Medical Association.[35] What a shame that these important, well-accepted health care organizations cannot operate within the law.

Barring Physician Ownership of Health Care Facilities

In 2003, the U.S. Congress stopped payments to entrepreneurial physician-owned specialty hospitals for Medicare and Medicaid patients who were referred by physicians with a financial interest in the facility. As discussed in Chapter 5, critics complained that specialty hospitals could reap the benefits of profitable services without having to cross-subsidize unprofitable services; that they "cherry-picked" patients who were less severely ill; and that physician-owners might over-refer patients to increase their profits.[36]

The Congressional cure of eliminating entrepreneurial businesses is horrendous. The right solution is a pricing mechanism that establishes prices that are neither excessively generous nor excessively stringent. Only the *market* can achieve such correct prices. It is not that the insurance and government bureaucrats who currently set prices are incompetent or venal, but rather that they are incapable of simulating market prices.[37] As a result, they make costly errors and distort investment; for example, a 2003 analysis showed that overly generous prices for procedures in hospital-based outpatient departments cost $1 billion more than the prices for the same procedures in free-standing surgery centers.[38]

Although the overuse that characterizes physician-owned imaging laboratories and physical therapy facilities appears genuine and persuasive, it is primarily caused by a system in which a third party, rather than the user, pays.[39] Users who pay are more sensitive to the value for the money than third parties. One analysis revealed a 16 percent decrease in volume for a 10 percent price increase when consumers paid for a bundle of medical services.[40] Patients were also sensitive to quality measures: providers who appeared to skimp on quality lost patients.[41] Similarly, one high-deductible insurer's analysis of the impact on costs and quality found cost increases reduced by 30 to 50 percent compared to managed care, while diabetic and asthmatic patients experienced reduced flare-ups, likely because of their increased compliance with medications.[42]

A consumer-driven insurance system in which users select from a wide array of products at different prices means we consumers will be more price sensitive. For example, in the consumer-driven Swiss health care system, one of the most popular insurance options is a high-deductible policy in which enrollees are frequently sent copies of their bills for the insured services they received. Consumer oversight is likely a major reason that the excellent Swiss health care system consumes 11 percent of GDP versus 17 percent for the United States.[43]

In a consumer-driven health care system, complaints against physician ownership would be obviated because cross-subsidization would be eliminated as each bundle is priced to be profitable on its own, and is risk adjusted, thus eliminating profits earned solely by selecting patients who are relatively healthy. Excellent information and consumer involvement would also minimize over-referral.

Barring Physician-Owned Institutions from Insurance Reimbursement

Notes Dr. Bruce Wilson, CEO of the now-defunct Heart Hospital of Milwaukee:

As in virtually all cities with heart hospitals, Milwaukee's general hospitals removed my partners from their emergency room on-call lists, and in some cases instructed emergency room doctors to call other cardiologists, even if the patient was ours. Those with a financial interest in the Heart Hospital were told they would never again receive referrals from doctors with whom we once had close personal and professional relationships. Pressure was exerted on large insurance companies to exclude coverage for our hospital. Although hospital administrators denied all this, it's true.[44]

Requiring Innovative Physicians to Register as Insurers

Public policy may require that physicians with concierge medical practices register as insurance companies. This onerous requirement would obligate these small practices to complete insurance company filings, replete with unique insurance accounting standards, and to maintain sizable reserves. The eight small concierge practices in one state were compelled to incur the unusual and sizable expense of hiring an expensive lobbyist to protect themselves against such requirements.[45]

Contracting with a Single Payer

Many innovative health services are reluctant to contract with a single-payer monopolist that can easily change the rules. For example, the U.S.-based surgical hospital chain National Surgical Hospitals Inc., decided not to respond to the U.K. government's request for proposals for new diagnostic and treatment centers. Although the contract was for a five-year period and there was substantial pent-up demand in the resource-constrained U.K. health care system, the firm's CEO worried about "the potential of government budget pressures or a change in government policy imposing unacceptably low reimbursement."[46]

Distorting Prices of Medical Technology

Erroneous pricing also affects innovation in medical devices. Notes one physician:

> *[At one time], one of the most expensive line items in the Medicare program was cataract surgery. The perceived "excess" was addressed in several ways, including capping of reimbursements for the intraocular lenses used in the procedure. The new lenses were more versatile, more durable, and easier to work with (thus shortening the procedure time); [but because] Medicare set a flat fee per lens, lower than the cost of the innovative lens, there was a virtual shutdown of innovation within the industry overnight.*

[Similarly, at the time when] the expenditures by Medicare for cardiac pacemakers for those with potentially lethal irregularities of their heart rhythms became targeted as "out of control," new and innovative versions of these pacemakers were regularly being introduced. However, after these devices became price-fixed by Medicare, innovation stopped. A 1999 continuing medical education lecture on pacemaker management noted that the devices were all but unchanged from the early 1990s.[47]

Let the Flowers Bloom

Health care business innovators could provide many other improvements if they were not hamstrung by governmental regulations. Medicare pricing policies that, for example, pay for fragments of care rather than care by an integrated team, and legal prohibitions that limit the involvement of the physicians (who know the most about the delivery of health care) as owners stop innovation before it can even begin.

Ironically, for all its many regulations, government does not provide the important ones. The role of government is not to micromanage business. Governments are not entrepreneurs. They cannot create better, cheaper ways of accomplishing important goals. Rather, the role of government is to prevent fraud and abuse, help the needy, and provide transparency. Because of the absence of consumer control and transparency, businesses and the U.S. Congress can enter into unhealthy relationships that are not in the patients' best interests, as we've seen in the overuse of epo.

Jack Morgan might still be alive today if he had been under the care of a physician-owned organization that featured an integrated team of providers in a focused factory for kidney care. A transparent, consumer-controlled system that obviates governmental meddling in the process of delivering health care would have encouraged the involvement of such competent, creative entrepreneurs and helped to keep Jack Morgan alive.

CHAPTER 10

THE STICKS
Let Information Flow

Standing in the brightly lit supermarket aisle, I examined the box of raisin bran cereal I was thinking of buying. In an instant, I knew its price, nutritional qualities, calories, and expiration date. All this information was printed right on the package. The information is there because the government requires its publication. Yet if I needed a mastectomy for breast cancer, I would know nothing about the results achieved by a surgeon when he or she operates on people like me for this disease or by the hospitals in which he or she performs the surgery. I would not even know their prices.

What does not get measured does not get managed.

Because we do not measure the quality and prices of our health care providers, Jack Morgan died: it is highly unlikely that he would have chosen the HMO had he known the outcomes of its treatment of kidney transplant patients. One little statistic can make the difference between life and death: how long the HMO's patients—those who are as sick as Jack was—wait for their kidney transplants.

Sunshine is the best disinfectant.

In this chapter I discuss how to let the sun shine in on our health care system through the creation of a new government agency that forces transparency.

The Impact of Information on Markets

Information makes ignorant people smart.

I confess: I have only the dimmest notion of how a car functions.

After all, a car is a high-tech device, studded with microchips. My notions of the mechanical compression and ignition of gasoline that lead to an explosion whose energy ultimately rotates the wheels of a car are as dated as my first car, the 1957 Dodge that I purchased in 1966. It got seven miles to the gallon, rivaled a stretch limo in length, and belched pollutants.

I do not think that I am alone in my ignorance. When I see someone in an automobile showroom peering under the hood of a car, I think to myself, "What the heck are you looking at?" Nevertheless, I can readily find the kind of car I want at a price I am willing to pay. My quality choices have increased substantially since 1966, while the cost of a car has decreased as a proportion of income:[1] as a result, 48 percent of the poor own cars, and 14 percent own more than one.[2]

How is it that an ignoramus like me can easily find cars that are better and cheaper?

And, as only one person in a vast sea, why am I not pillaged in the automobile market?

The answers to these questions rest on an understanding of how markets work—how weak, solo participants, like me, are offered better and cheaper products. Two ingredients are crucial.

One is information. It enables me to be an intelligent car shopper, despite my ignorance.

I peruse the rating literature for a car that embodies the attributes I value: safety, reliability, environmental friendliness, and price. Objective, trustworthy information about these attributes is easily available to me. When I studied *Consumer Reports* for cars with these attributes, two brands satisfied my requirements: Volvo and Buick. I skipped the earnest reviews of how the engines work, fuel efficiency, comfort, handling, styling, and so on. Safety, environmental quality, reliability, and price—these are what interest me.

I opted for the Buick. Although it was not quite as reliable as the Volvo, it was cheaper.

But many who shared my views of the qualities desired in a car opted for the Volvo. It grew from an obscure Swedish brand to sales of 456,000 cars in 2004.[3] When Volvo's rivals saw that a meaningful number of customers were interested in safety and reliability, they introduced these qualities into their cars. In the quest for safety, Ford, for example, acquired Volvo, and other automobile manufacturers improved their reliability.[4] By 2005, U.S. cars exceeded European ones in reliability, and the Japanese cars had only a small edge.[5] Quite a change from 1980, when U.S. cars were three times as unreliable as Japanese ones and twice as unreliable as European vehicles.[6]

So information made me smart and caused car manufacturers to respond with the qualities that I wanted; but what stops the car manufacturers from refusing to cut their prices? After all, I am only one person.

The critical second ingredient for an effective market is a small group of marginal, tough-minded buyers. At a high price, there are only a few buyers who are more or less price insensitive. The good news for businesses is that these customers are willing to pay a very high price. The bad news is that there are only a few of them. To attract more customers, suppliers reduce their prices. The increased volume of customers more than compensates for the reduction in price. Suppliers continue to cut prices until they hit a brick wall: the last picky, tough-minded customers who clear the market. The price these tough-nosed buyers are willing to pay is roughly equal to the marginal cost of making the product. The rest of us benefit from the assertiveness of the last-to-buy crowd. And it is a relatively small group. A McKinsey study showed, for example, that only 100 investors "significantly affect the share prices of most large companies."[7]

These hard-nosed buyers are highly adept in finding, interpreting, and using information. They are the show-me crowd, the marginal consumers bloodlessly depicted on the bottom of the Economics 101 downward-sloping demand curve. This relatively small group of demanding consumers rewards suppliers who reduce price and improve quality.

The car market illustrates their impact. Currently, automobile prices are the lowest in two decades. In 1991, for example, the average family required 30 weeks of income for the purchase of a new vehicle; but by 2005, a new vehicle required only 26.2 weeks of their income—a 14 percent decline.[8] Simultaneously, automobile quality is at an all-time high.[9] The range of choices is better too, as the quality differences between the best and worst manufacturers have declined.[10]

Health Care Consumers of Information

As in the automobile market, smart, informed consumers—consumers who have access to good information and the freedom to choose health care plans and providers, optimized in classic Economics 101 fashion will make our health care system better and cheaper—For example, the satisfaction and cost data collected by the Buyers Health Care Action Group (BHCAG), the Twin Cities' employer coalition described in Chapter 7, encouraged patients to leave high-cost/low-satisfaction plans for lower-priced/higher-satisfaction plans, thereby prompting physicians to offer more bang for the buck. The program led to a nearly 20 percent drop in high-cost/low-satisfaction plans and a 50 percent increase in low-cost/high-satisfaction plans.[11]

Even in the absence of consumer control, the gathering and dissemination of information exerts powerful effects on suppliers.[12] In accounting, this phenomenon is known as the *audit effect*:[13] firms improve their management in anticipation of an accounting audit. In health care, many of the reviews of the impact of published performance data on physicians, hospitals, and insurers have concluded that they resulted in improved outcomes and/or processes.[14] One study of obstetrics performance found that hospitals whose results were disclosed publicly had significantly greater improvement than those with private reports.[15]

Yet health care policy analysts argue that a consumer-driven health care system cannot work because average consumers will be stymied by the process of selecting among differentiated health insurance products.[16] These analysts may fail to appreciate the impact of those tough-minded buyers on a market. Nevertheless, their argument does raise a question: does a marginal group of tough-nosed, market-clearing consumers exist in health care?

To explore this, let's take a minute to focus on characteristics of American consumers. Current generations are much better educated: In 2004, 27.7 percent of the population had attained a college education or more, and 85.2 percent were high school graduates.[17] In 1960, in contrast, fewer than half the people were high school graduates, and only 7 percent had a college education.[18]

Higher levels of educational attainment increase not only income and ability but also self-confidence (referred to as "self-efficacy" in the health policy literature[19]). For example, churchgoers increasingly stand rather than kneel, likely expressing their notion that a service provides an opportunity for a personal encounter with God rather than for reverential worship. About 80 percent of the pews ordered from the country's largest manufacturer now come without kneelers.[20]

Affluent Web surfers embody this self-efficacy—they spend more time than others searching for information on the Net before making a purchase and are much more likely to buy, once they have found a good value for the money.[21] Those who focus only on their affluence miss the point: affluent or not, they eat the same bread, buy the same appliances, and wear the same jeans. The same Toyota is sold in poor inner-city areas and affluent suburbs. The activism of the affluent Web surfers improves these products for everybody.

Consumers surf the Web for health care information. A 2005 report found that 95 million people used the Internet for health information,[22] 6 million of them daily.[23] Some even study medical information, such as the millions of people who spent an average of 20 minutes at the government's National Institutes of Health Web site, studded with arcane medical journal articles.[24] A few even express their activism directly by mastering medical skills, such as CPR and the use of external defibrillators.[25]

The assertiveness and self-confidence that typify marginal consumers are evident in these health care Internet users. They agree more than average U.S. adults with the following statements: "I like to investigate all options, rather than just ask for a doctor's advice" and "People should take primary responsibility and not rely so much on doctors."[26] Their pragmatism is apparent too. They do not search idly. More than 70 percent want online evaluations of physicians,[27] and when they obtain the information, they use it.[28] Consumers are willing to change hospitals in response to information about their quality.[29] Nor is consumer assertiveness limited to the United States. For example, 70 percent of Canadian doctors note that their patients are briefed by Internet information.[30]

Thus, although average buyers of health care are not experts, individual consumers can reshape the health care system. As with the automobile markets, the markets that make up the health care system will be guided not by average consumers, but by the marginal customers who drive the toughest bargain. What they need is information.

The Role of Government in Creating Transparency

The role of government in providing transparency is surprisingly controversial. In the view of Nobel economics laureate George Stigler, the truth will out in markets as competitors expose each others' weaknesses or market analysts unearth it.[31] Stigler's analyses have asserted that government regulation of information disclosure is not essential to the efficiency of markets.[32] Although his claims and similar research have been widely tested,[33] the empirical research examining the necessity of government action to ensure an efficient market has not yet settled the question.

Rather, the debate must fundamentally be resolved on a theoretical basis: information disclosure is a public good—that is, one in which the government must be involved—in the sense that it enables free riders—those who do not pay for the benefits they receive. Because disclosers cannot charge all users of the information for the benefits they derive, they lack incentives for full disclosure.[34] As a result, the quantity of publicly available information may be undersupplied or issued selectively, favoring some recipients and excluding others.[35] For this reason, the quantity and quality of the information currently available in health care through voluntary measures is deficient.

The Failure of Voluntary Transparency

Voluntary transparency does not work. Consider the case of the voluntary Greater Cleveland Health Quality Choice Coalition, a group of local area businesses who joined forces to collect hospital performance data. The effort was widely lauded. For example, one hospital claimed that the significant decrease in its rate of caesarean sections was "purely driven by the Cleveland Coalition."[36] An evaluation concluded that reductions in risk-adjusted mortality rates and lengths of stay were linked to the performance reports.[37]

Nevertheless, the effort collapsed when the famous Cleveland Clinic left the group, allegedly because it did not like the performance ratings process. Notes a local doctor, "What the Clinic really didn't like is that they weren't shown to be the best at everything."[38] And the employer group that sponsored the effort did not actively use its results. The only hospital to achieve great results expected that the data would yield many new patients as employers referred their enrollees there, but the predicted surge never materialized. Noted one employer, lamely, "We weren't that aggressive."[39] As we saw earlier in this book, the bureaucratic and paternalistic human resources staff relies on limited choice and managed care as agents of change. They do not believe in the power of information to transform health care.

Voluntary, hospital- and insurance-led mechanisms don't work well either. A *Modern Healthcare* editorial about the Joint Commission on Accreditation of Healthcare Organizations (JCAHO), the national hospital-accreditation group, whose governance the providers dominate, noted: "JCAHO [has] . . . repeatedly failed at initiatives designed to judge hospitals and other healthcare providers based on their performance—how well they take care of sick people. The projects always are announced with much fanfare and heady names such as 'Agenda for Change.' And they're invariably scrapped, watered down or delayed."[40] An academic evaluation found no correlation between JCAHO scores and outcome measures, such as mortality and complications, for the hospitals it studied.[41] Similarly, health insurance buyers may question the value of the health insurance industry–led accreditations because virtually every health plan has it.[42] Doctors also opt out of voluntary reporting efforts. A study of a voluntary error reporting system found that only 2 percent of the nearly 100,000 responses were filed by physicians.[43]

The Impact of the U.S. Securities and Exchange Commission (SEC) on Financial Transparency

But when the federal government required disclosure, we got it! The story of how the U.S. SEC's requirement for transparency transformed the money markets is told below.

Virtually every interest group that has been required to measure its outcomes claims its work is so diffuse that its impact cannot be measured. Such claims delayed the measurement of the performance of businesses until the mid-1930s. The stunning absence of information at that time is analogous to the situation in today's health care system: in 1923, only 25 percent of the firms traded on the New York Stock Exchange provided shareholder reports.[44] Investors were flying blind then, just like today's health care consumers.

The absence was all the more surprising because accounting, the measurement tool for business performance, has existed since the middle of the fifteenth century, when double-entry bookkeeping was first codified.[45] But business executives' claims that accounting could not accurately measure company performance and that the cost of measurement exceeded its benefits prevented widespread disclosure of information about the economic performance of the firms they led.[46]

In the 1930s, U.S. President Franklin Delano Roosevelt (FDR) promulgated the laws that created the SEC. Bucking powerful business opposition, state government involvement, and his own advisors' counsel that he promote laws to grade the firms in the security markets, FDR instead created the SEC to compel audited disclosure of the performance of publicly traded firms, using generally accepted accounting principles (GAAP).[47]

The SEC is a genuine private-public partnership. The governmental SEC requires disclosure, but the auditors and the organizations charged with creating and implementing the audit rules (including the promulgators of GAAP) are housed in private organizations such as the Financial Accounting Standards Board (FASB).

Governmental regulation of securities is nothing new. As early as 1285, King Edward I required licensing of London brokers.[48] But FDR's SEC differed from traditional regulation that relied on authorities to evaluate the worthiness of a security. He opted for sunlight. As he noted: "The Federal Government cannot and should not take any action that might be construed as approving or guaranteeing that . . . securities are sound. . . . " Rather, his SEC was a "truth" agency, established to ensure full disclosure of all material facts. In Roosevelt's words, "It puts the burden of telling the truth on the seller."[49] To put teeth in its mission, the SEC was given the power to enforce "truth in securities" and to regulate the trading of securities in markets through brokers and exchanges.

Like all human endeavors, the SEC is not without faults. The corporate accounting and governance problems of public U.S. businesses in the 1990s were exacerbated by lax SEC enforcement.[50] Nevertheless, the transparency created by the SEC enabled the broad participation of average Americans in the securities markets and the markets' efficiency.[51] (*Efficiency* in this context is the degree to which information is so broadly disseminated throughout a market that no participants can benefit from having access to special information available only to them.) Financial reporting reduces the investor's risk, narrows the differences between sophisticated and less sophisticated investors, and reduces the firm's cost of capital. Currently, the U.S. SEC serves as a worldwide model: for example, foreign firms that switch to U.S. transparency practices and standards benefit financially.[52] For this reason, Japan is considering adoption of the SEC model to curb the substantial transparency failures of its capital markets.[53]

All measuring tools improve with use. Accounting was not nearly as accurate a measure of economic performance in 1934 as it is today. No doubt, accounting will improve in the future. In 1687, Newton first measured gravity. By 2000, physicists could measure the minute energy of a tau neutrino buried deep within an atom.[54]

In 1953, Crick and Watson first measured the structure of DNA. By 2007, biologists could manipulate the structure of individual genes.[55] Today's health information measures will also be refined with practice and time.

Private-Sector Sources of Financial Information

Much of the information that lies at the heart of the efficiency of the financial markets comes not from the SEC but from three private-sector groups: the businesses themselves, the FASB, and the accounting profession. The interaction among these groups promotes fuller consideration of diverse points of view. Unlike a government agency, these organizations do not sing out of one hymnal. And their private sector nature requires the political and financial backing of their supporters for continued existence, unlike government organizations, which can continue to exist with little regard for their impact on their constituency. Indeed, the predecessors to the FASB collapsed when their GAAP pronouncements could not find broad-based support.

To be "certified," the independent accountants who audit the financial statements must pass examinations and fulfill stringent educational and practice requirements. Many work in one of the four large U.S. accounting firms that audit the companies that account for nearly 99 percent of our stock market's capitalization.[56] Accounting firms may be held legally liable for negligence, fraud, and breach of contract. One firm, for example, paid the SEC $50 million in penalties to compensate investors in the Adelphia scandal.[57] Arthur Andersen, once among the largest public accounting firms, collapsed in the wake of the Enron debacle.[58] Accountants have even been found criminally liable.[59] In 2005, for example, the former chief financial officers and controllers of the large public firms WorldCom, Enron, Adelphia, and HealthSouth were serving prison terms for fraud.[60]

In abdicating much of its authority to set accounting standards to the private sector, the SEC recognized the following advantages: (1) Practicing accountants were closer to the firms and thus could more accurately identify emerging issues; (2) private-sector involvement encouraged greater compliance than government mandates; and (3) the SEC could more readily audit the work of the private-sector information disclosers than its own, thus resolving a conflict of interest.[61]

But the accounting abuses that emerged in the early twenty-first century caused a shift in this stance. Many blamed the structure of the accounting firms for these debacles, citing the conflict of interest created by their simultaneously offering lucrative consulting and low-profit auditing services to clients. Past SEC attempts to bar accountants from offering consulting contracts had been stymied by the Congress.[62] This time around, the SEC relied on its internal rule-making authority to reclaim some of its powers. It introduced rules to prompt faster, more complete disclosure and to create a new entity to oversee the accounting professionals.[63] Similarly, the rule-making Financial Accounting Standards Board has been chastened by the loopholes that its complex rules enabled and has promised to simplify and streamline them in the future.[64]

A Health Care SEC

U.S. securities markets feature the characteristics that health care consumers want: (1) prices are fair in the sense that they reflect all publicly available information, and (2) buyers use this information to reward effective organizations and penalize ineffective ones. Thus, in the financial markets, positive disclosure of results lowers the firms' cost of capital.[65]

If these characteristics were present in health care, they would divert resources from health providers that offer a bad value for the money to those that offer a good one. Poor-value-for-the-money providers would shrink or improve. Good-value-for-the-money providers would flourish.

Current health care consumers have little information about the quality of their providers. Indeed, they have better information on raisin bran cereals—they need only read the label—than they have on the surgeon who will operate on their breast or prostate cancer tumors. Publication and widespread dissemination of data about the quality of individual providers, as measured by generally accepted health care outcome principles and audited by certified, independent appraisers of such information, will help ameliorate this problem. Eventually, independent analysts will use this information to compile readily accessible ratings of providers, similar to Morningstar's excellent system for classifying and rating mutual funds.

The key to achieving these desirable characteristics in health care is legislation for a health care SEC that replicates these essential elements of the SEC model:

1. *Private-sector analysis* The evaluation process is primarily conducted by private-sector analysts, who disseminate their frequently divergent ratings. To encourage similar private-sector health care analysts, the new agency should require public dissemination of all outcomes for providers, including clinical measures of quality, and related transaction costs.

2. *Focus on outcomes, not processes* The SEC and FASB focus on measuring the financial performance of organizations. FDR firmly rejected dictating business processes or rating businesses as appropriate roles for the SEC.

3. *An independent agency with a singular focus* The SEC is an independent agency charged solely with overseeing the integrity of securities and the exchanges on which they are traded. Because of these clear goals and organizational characteristics, the SEC's mission is not muddied, and it can be held clearly accountable for its performance.

4. *Penalties* The SEC requires firms that trade their securities in interstate markets and all such market makers to register with the agency. A corresponding health care agency would oversee the integrity and require public disclosure of information for entities that provide health insurance and services. Like the SEC, it would be armed with powerful penalties for undercapitalized and unethical market participants, including imprisonment, civil money penalties, and the disgorgement of illegal profits.[66]

5. *Private-sector disclosure and auditing* The SEC relies heavily on private-sector organizations that contain no governmental representation. The new health care agency should similarly delegate the power to derive the principles used to measure health care performance to an independent, private, nonprofit organization that, like the FASB, represents a broad nongovernmental constituency. The agency would require auditing of the information by independent professionals, who would render an opinion on the information and bear legal liability for failure to disclose fairly and fully.

The SEC is essentially a profit center, generating a substantial surplus from its filing and penalty fees that offsets its billion-dollar budget.[67] A health care version of the SEC could be similarly self-financed, offsetting its expenses with filing fees and fines collected from its constituency.

How Not to Make Health Care Transparency Happen

Unfortunately, many well-intended proposals undermine one or more of these essential SEC characteristics.

Private-Sector Analysis

All too often, these proposals require that the health care regulators evaluate and micromanage health insurers and the markets in which they operate.[68] But these suggestions place inappropriate responsibility on the regulator. One organization should not simultaneously assure the release of accurate data and analyze the data. After a while, the organization might be sorely tempted to skew the data so that the analysis is proven correct. As an example of the kind of pressure that a government agency can exert on analysis, 15 percent of the Federal Drug Administration's scientists have said they were inappropriately asked to exclude or alter information in their conclusions.[69]

In the financial markets, neither the SEC nor the FASB assesses the quality of the output produced by corporations. Instead, they ensure the provision of reliable, useful information. Private-sector intermediaries, including firms such as Morningstar, Merrill Lynch, and Standard & Poor's, can then analyze the information and present it to consumers.

Other proposals include the government as a participant in private, nonprofit FASB-like entities such as the National Quality Forum.[70] This kind of organizational structure places government on both sides of the table, allowing it to act as both regulator and standard setter. It thus compromises the checks and balances that exist between the private-sector FASB and the governmental SEC.

Measuring Outcomes, Not Process

The SEC focuses on measures of financial *outcomes*—such as profitability, liquidity, and solvency. It does not dictate *process*—how businesses should achieve these results.

The pay-for-performance (P4P) movement is a worrisome example of the confusion between the two kinds of measures.[71] A focus on measuring process may deter innovative improvements in quality. For example, one expert concluded that "in diabetes the emphasis on measuring preventative processes of care, rather than assessing outcome measures such as blood pressure and the markers of sugar in the blood of diabetics, may have the unintended consequence of diverting resources and attention from [the] clinically more productive tasks."[72]

An Independent Agency with Singular Focus

Some proposals would compromise the focus and independence that characterize the SEC's organizational structure. They recommend, for example, that an SEC-like agency be housed under the Department of Health and Human Services (HHS),[73] which oversees the government payments for Medicare and Medicaid, among other activities. This organizational setting could compromise the mission. Because HHS accounts for a large fraction of U.S. health care payments, a health care SEC housed under its wings could be focused on serving the interests of payers, rather than consumers.

Further, the clear accountability of a free-standing agency would be lost in this setting. President George W. Bush's first SEC commissioner was forced to step down because of the SEC's failures in ensuring transparency in the financial markets. Because the SEC was a separate agency, he was clearly responsible for its failing; but who in HHS was held responsible for similar failings with implementation of its drug plan?[74] Although 5 percent of all Medicare recipients who called its drug plan help line were disconnected and nearly a third found the advice difficult to use, inappropriate, or erroneous, no one was held responsible for these failings.[75]

Opposition to Transparency about Health Care Prices and Quality

We live in an information age, surrounded by ubiquitous newspapers, televisions, telephones, computers, radios, magazines, and books, available worldwide, round-the-clock. They address three of our senses—sound, vision, and, for the vision- and hearing-impaired, touch. In 2004, the 8 million people who said they had created a blog were visited by 14 million viewers.[76] The ubiquity of information responds to people's desires: when there is no demand, there is no supply.

The best sources combine information and accessibility: Morningstar's and *Zagat*'s restaurant guides' pithy reviews, J.D. Power's powerful brand name, and *Consumer Reports*' accurate, comprehensive ratings typify these qualities. But those who do not like these sources can find many others: If investors judge Morningstar excessively terse, the SEC's EDGAR system contains much more information about publicly traded corporations.[77] If they prefer professional restaurant reviewers to *Zagat*'s amateurs, they can turn to the *Boston Globe*'s "Food" section or its equivalent in their own hometown paper. If they question J.D. Power's objectivity or feel that *Consumer Reports* is biased against American cars, they can turn to the federal government's data about cars and airlines, such as those provided by the National Highway Traffic Safety Administration and the Federal Aviation Administration,[78] or *Car and Driver* magazine and *Consumers Digest*. The point is that there is a wealth of information available, and interested consumers can drill down into it as little or as much as they need.

The providers of information help themselves too. In 2006, Google's founders became billionaires because they helped people achieve greater productivity by answering their questions easily and efficiently. Michael Bloomberg also gained billionaire status because he provided information that helped people to invest in financial instruments with confidence.[79]

Many complain about the absence of similar consumer-driven health care quality information.[80] The wired generation is especially demanding—80 percent of respondents have noted that the absence of quality information was the most negative aspect of e-health plans.[81] When information is available, health care consumers have stated that they would use it.[82] Prescient entrepreneurs and wannabe billionaires are already providing them with some of the information they want. The market value of the WebMD consumer health care portal, for example, doubled in four months after its September 2005 IPO.[83]

But many powerful opponents, including the academics and providers discussed above, constrain its development.

Health Care Providers' Opposition to Information

Providers who like the theory of consumer-based choice and information may dislike the reality—the requirement that they be accountable for their performance. More than two-thirds of surveyed physicians have said that the general public should not have access "to information on clinical outcomes."[84]

To urge their cause, some may claim that performance is intrinsically unmeasurable. But if the performance of medicine cannot be measured, there is no basis for teaching, research, or clinical practice in the field. Others may claim that only they can correctly interpret the data. In this claim, they misunderstand the role of marginal consumers in making markets work.

Yet other providers note the cost and difficulty of obtaining reliable data about the performance of providers who see few patients with a particular medical condition. For example, one *Journal of the American Medical Association* article explained that the cost of collecting the data no doubt exceeds its benefits.[85] The cost? As much as $0.59 to $2.17 per member per month. And the benefits? The article does not address the question, perhaps because the benefits easily exceed the data collection costs. For example, if quality data improve the costs of treating a diabetic by as little as 1 percent, the data collection costs will be repaid fiftyfold in less than one year.[86]

The same report also notes that many data cannot be reliably measured for most doctors because they treat so few of the sick. For example, "a physician would need to have more than 100 patients with diabetes . . . for a profile to have a reliability of 0.8 or better, while more than 90 percent of all primary care physicians at the HMO [he studied] had fewer than 60 patients with diabetes."[87] A hospital-based study similarly concluded that "the operations for which surgical mortality has been advocated as a quality indicator are not performed frequently enough to judge hospital quality."[88]

But the purpose of performance measurement is to protect the patient, not the physician or the hospital. Physicians who see many diabetics are more likely to develop the expertise needed to care for this complex, challenging disease. If quality data were published, the low-volume physicians and hospitals that cannot generate statistically reliable data would likely lose their patients to those who are achieving excellent outcomes, in part because they see so many diabetics.

The Quality of Health Care Information

A serious but correctable objection is voiced by those who point out that physicians and hospitals should not be held responsible for things they do not control.[89] It is a correctable objection because there are industries that have a long history with management control systems, which are used to evaluate managers. These systems are designed to focus on those outcomes that managers control.[90] Their experiences could be adapted to health care.

Others worry about the quality of the information. First, much of the language for measuring health care quality has yet to be defined. Second, the risk adjusters that would make it possible to compare the performance of high-risk specialists to those who treat less-severely-ill patients are not yet fully developed.[91] Third, the raw data are flawed. For example, the federal government's data bank of the adverse actions taken against physicians and dentists has repeatedly been cited for severe flaws, including errors and substantial under-reporting of problems.[92]

These are substantial concerns. In the absence of solutions, the information will be seriously distorted. For example, a study that compared the rates of caesarean sections in hospitals, with and without adjustment for the fact that some hospitals might just have more patients prone to caesareans, found that adjustment caused the performance of a fourth of the hospitals in the study to change dramatically; among other changes, 10 percent of those originally classified as especially high or low users of these surgeries were reclassified as normal and some that were classified as normal were reclassified as having greater or lesser rates of surgery than the average.[93] Physicians may also be dissuaded from caring for very sick patients if outcome measures do not correctly reflect the severity of illness. With imperfect adjustments, physicians will look much better if they care for only those patients who are more likely to recover from their illnesses.

Measurement issues like these are typically resolved with time and experience. The continual evolution in measures of performance of investment management—such as generally accepted accounting principles and *beta*, the measure of risk of different investments—provides an example. Beta has been continually refined since it was first suggested in 1952. Similarly, the system used by Morningstar to rate the investment performance of mutual funds evolved over time. For example, it was changed to allow for the difficulty of generating earnings in different types of investments. It now permits mutual funds operating in poorly performing sectors, say, technology, to earn high ratings if they performed substantially better than their peers, a form of risk adjustment.[94]

As the refinement of the measures of financial performance continued, investors had ever-better data with which to evaluate their mutual funds and stocks. Patients who put their health on the line deserve no less. The best way to improve the quality of these data is not to suppress them, but rather, to open them to the public.

How Health Care Information Would Have Kept Jack Morgan Alive

Only a few words can make the difference between life and death in health care—a couple of words that compared how long Jack's HMO kept its patients waiting for a kidney transplant versus other insurers for patients with similar levels of illness in the same region. This information would have quickly identified his HMO's problems in managing its kidney transplant service. It is highly unlikely that Jack would have remained with the HMO if these data were regularly published and widely disseminated. These few words would have kept Jack Morgan alive.

Would Jack have read the information? Like the millions of Americans who access selected Internet sites, watch narrow niche TV like the Food Network, and read special-topic magazines and newspapers, Jack was an eager user of information that he found helpful. We know, for example, that to improve as a chef, he even taught himself French. To excel in his occupation, Jack continued to seek information on new cooking techniques, ingredients, and models of restaurant management. But he lacked the information about the quality of his health care provider that would have kept him alive.

To avoid Jack's fate, U.S. health care consumers must have the information that will enable them to shop intelligently for providers and treatment. They need and want it, and they have shown they will use it when it's available.[95] By requiring the disclosure of audited financial information and its dissemination, the U.S. government's SEC has succeeded in providing such information to investors: our financial markets are lauded for their transparency and efficiency. The SEC's essential organizational characteristics—independence, focus on outcomes, reliance on private-sector analysts and auditors—should be replicated in a new government agency that will give newly empowered health care consumers the information they need.

CHAPTER 11

A BOLD NEW CONSUMER-DRIVEN HEALTH CARE SYSTEM
The Laws and Their Legislators

We have incrementalized our way, one law at a time, into the health care system that killed Jack Morgan. U.S. health care costs too much, and it does too little for too few. Let's toss out the old laws that empowered all the third parties who helped to kill Jack Morgan—the employers, hospitals, insurers, Congress, and academics. We need bold new laws that empower us and the entrepreneurial medical care providers who provide our health care so we can make the system work the way it should.

For political, policy, and corporate leaders, for families and children, for all of us who need and who practice health care, we are only a few major actions away from a consumer-driven system in the United States and from seeing similar benefits in Canada and Europe. In the United States, these actions will involve our federal and state governments, but most of all they will involve all of us as individuals using our influence to convince our governments to heal our $2 trillion health care problem.

The Goals of a Bold Consumer-Driven Health Care System

To cure our health care problem, we need innovators and laws that sweep away the obstacles. Incremental changes to our laws without a clear vision of what we are trying to attain got us into this mess; for example, Richard Nixon's ad hoc stabs at health care public policy entangled us with managed care and congressional management of the care for kidney disease. Incremental changes to our laws will not solve the problem. We need vision and boldness, not politics as usual.

A consumer-driven health care system can keep the Jack Morgans hale and healthy without breaking the back of our economy or the spirit of our doctors. When you control the money in the health care system, the institutions that helped to kill Jack Morgan will either change their behavior or find themselves replaced by new, entrepreneurial, consumer-driven ones.

Consumer-driven **insurers** will design consumer-friendly insurance policies that give you the benefits, coverage, and doctors you want at a price you are willing to pay. If you want managed care, OK; but if you want another kind of policy, you will have access to that too.

Consumer-friendly **hospitals** will take part in integrated teams that give you everything you need for your disease or disability. They will abandon their quest to dominate the health care delivery system.

Consumer-friendly **employers** will direct their HR staff to give you back the part of your salary that they used to buy your health insurance, and then they will help you choose from the many new varieties of policies that become available.

The **U.S. Congress** will pass laws that enable you to buy your health insurance with tax-free income, help to create information about the quality and prices of medical care providers, and transfer money to the poor so they can shop for health insurance like all other Americans. Senators and representatives will stop practicing medicine and setting prices. They will get out of the way, and let the doctors do the doctoring and us do the shopping.

Last, the **academics** will research how to make this consumer-driven market work better, just like the Nobel Prize–winning economists who help to uncover inefficiencies in the financial markets and devise ways to correct them.

Bold Consumer-Driven Health Care: The Role of the Federal Government

Sadly, on the federal government level, representatives from the Republicans and Democrats have quaffed deeply from the Beltway Kool-Aid well. Neither believes in the power of innovators and consumers to reshape markets. Neither is in the small-is-beautiful camp. Both believe that more oversight of health care by the government and the academics is the solution. Both believe that big-is-beautiful.

The big-is-beautiful group is typically termed "liberal," and thus Democratic; but Thomas Jefferson, founder of the Democratic Party, is likely turning over in his grave at this use of the term. To Jefferson, the champion of small businesses and the nemesis of big government, "liberty" meant maintaining a range of choices. Liberty could flourish only when we could govern ourselves: "Were we directed from Washington when to sow and when to reap, we shall soon want bread."[1] Clearly, Jefferson is much more aligned with the small-is-gorgeous camp that believes in entrepreneurial, consumer-driven markets and the possibilities of productivity than he is with current Democrats. Barry Goldwater, the founder of the conservative wing of the Republican Party, is similarly rolling around in his grave, dismayed by the big-government deficit spending and limitation of choice that are now standard Republican fare.

To appreciate the similarity of both parties' big-is-beautiful ideas, consider the Democrats' versus Republicans' views of Medicare. The Democrats want the federal government to negotiate drug prices on our behalf, while the Republicans want to set up a new government agency that would evaluate the value for the money of each drug and tell us which ones we can use.[2] We had a good view of how the federal government deals with drugs when we reviewed the Congress's love affair with epo, the drug used for fighting anemia in victims of kidney disease. Do we really want the feds telling us which drugs we can buy and or negotiating the price for us? Federal control of drug pricing will distort and curtail the critically important innovations in biotechnology that could help the millions of victims of genetic diseases.

Similarly, when it comes to health insurance, while the Republicans rely more than the Democrats on private-sector initiatives, they are hardly small-is-beautiful stalwarts. Yes, they promise greater choices of insurance options in Medicare, but the Republican idea of choice boils down to either traditional Medicare or Medicare managed care plans. The many Republican fans of managed care intend to lure seniors with a $60 billion subsidy. Their idea of a competitive health care market harkens back to Richard Nixon. Like him, they stack the decks for managed care by using federal coffers to subsidize it. And the George W. Bush administrators of Medicare who stringently micromanage the prices and processes of health care providers in their pay-for-conformance initiatives, put innovators in a straitjacket or drive them to desert the health care sector.

Last, while the Republicans trumpet the need for an information-based consumer-driven health care system, their idea of information is hardly consumer driven. They want it to emanate from the federal government. Under Republican control, from 2000 to 2006, the federal government not only specified what should be measured but also the protocols that health care providers must follow. These monopolistic powers were cloaked in the pseudoscientific mantle of "evidence-based medicine." The title implied that the guidelines were shaped by intelligent saints, devoid of a shred of self-interest or vanity, guided only by "evidence." Try that one on the many medical innovators who have been derided or ignored by the establishment for the last 50 years because their ideas have run counter to medical orthodoxy, like Joe Murray, who, for many years, received little federal research support because his ideas about transplantation ran afoul of those whose entire careers had been staked on different ways of dealing with kidney disease.

With the unraveling of the human genome, we can begin to conquer diseases and not merely palliate them. Consumer-driven competition among brilliant independent scientists and doctors, each with different theories about the causes and cures of illness, can better fulfill these possibilities than a monopolistic government bureaucracy dictating the process of care.

Bold Consumer-Driven Health Care: The Role of the States

At the level of the federal government, both Democrats and Republicans are so deeply committed to the big-is-beautiful vision and so indebted to so many special interests that they may prove incapable of the bold health care plan that will empower the future Jack Morgans and prevent their needless deaths at the hands of a health care system that has lost its soul. But our brilliant Founding Fathers once again will save our nation with their amazing prescience in creating a confederation of states, rather than one country: many of the consumer-driven changes in health care will likely emanate from the states.

Reflecting the diversity our Founding Fathers sought, two states have implemented considerably different systems that help the Jack Morgans stay alive. These two, Maryland and Massachusetts, have both decided to require universal health care. The devil, though, is in the details: Maryland's system is all wrong, while Massachusetts' is mostly right.

Maryland: Wrong, Wrong, Wrong

The Maryland legislature's decision to require that its big businesses spend 8 percent of payroll on health insurance has turbocharged an AFL-CIO "Fair Share Health Care" campaign to enact similar legislation in other states. As always, the word *fair* should make your hair stand on end: it is a strong signal that someone's pocket is about to be picked. In this case, it is the pockets of the American business community.[3]

Don't get me wrong. The problem the legislation addresses is serious: the lack of health insurance diminishes health status, and we all pay for the care that the uninsured receive in a round-about, ineffective way. But, however urgent the problem of the uninsured, the solution that requires businesses to spend 8 percent of payroll on health insurance is awful. Superficially, it may appear to be just: after all, requiring businesses to pay for health insurance appears to lower the burden on individuals. But it will hurt the intended beneficiaries because business payments for health insurance reduce wages. By increasing the costs of workers, the legislation also causes businesses to distort their hiring practices.

In Hawaii, for example, the requirement that businesses provide health insurance for all employees who work more than 20 hours a week substantially increased the part-time workforce from 1990 to 2000, while the number of full-timers grew by only 2.5 percent.[4] Hawaii employers' reluctance to hire weekly workers for 30 or 35 hours, the standard elsewhere, forced part-timers to hold multiple jobs.[5] Some businesses in states with an employer mandate have chosen to relocate or curtail expansions. Wal-Mart has already slowed its plans to put a large distribution center in one of Maryland's poorest counties. If the federal government were to require all businesses to pay for health insurance, some would simply go out of business, while others would find yet another reason to move their facilities abroad.

The mandate is known as the "Wal-Mart Bill" because Wal-Mart is the only larger employer that fails to meet the statutory requirement. But how long will it take for the mandate to be imposed on all but the smallest businesses? All business owners in Maryland are no doubt asking themselves that question and perhaps already putting off making new hires and examining new business locations.

Although Maryland's Fair Share Health Care Fund Act (what a name!) was overturned in an ERISA challenge, the lure to legislators of requiring employers to provide health insurance is like light to a moth.[6] It will reemerge in various guises in the future.

Mostly Right: Massachusetts

A bizarre 2006 photograph shows Senator Edward (Teddy) Kennedy (D-Massachusetts) uncomfortably smiling while standing in back of seated Republican Massachusetts Governor Mitt Romney. Not so long ago, these two were bitter rival candidates for a U.S. Senate seat. What united this odd couple? It was the bipartisan 2006 Massachusetts universal health care legislation: Kennedy got what he wanted, required universal health insurance coverage, while Romney achieved what he wanted, consumer-driven health care solutions.

Massachusetts points the way to a better solution than Maryland's employer mandate. The Massachusetts solution is consumer driven in that it primarily requires individuals, rather than businesses, to buy health insurance. It finances the poor uninsured directly with the $1 billion now used to subsidize nonprofit hospitals to deliver ostensibly "free" care for them.

The new universal health care system created by Massachusetts is not perfect. It retains excessive government meddling in the design of insurance plans and compensation for providers: individuals can purchase low-cost insurance only in a market that the Commonwealth runs and can choose from among only the plans it has designed. And because Romney left the governor's office to seek nomination as the Republican presidential candidate in 2008, he could not fully exercise his considerable administrative skills in the implementation of this law.

(Some critics also wonder about the feasibility of requiring the purchase of health insurance. Roughly the same percentage of Americans are uninsured, 17.2 percent in 2004, as lack automobile insurance, 14.6 percent. But the purchase of automobile insurance is required in all but three states, while the purchase of health insurance is voluntary.[7])

Better systems could be implemented in states that do not share the Massachusetts legislature's impulse to regulate. They would feature multiple insurance markets and plans designed by entrepreneurs, not bureaucrats. The role of the state would be limited to ensuring that the requirement for universal coverage was implemented—that is, that all citizens purchase at least a catastrophic care health insurance policy—to providing audited outcome and price data; and to ensuring the financial integrity of insurers.

Yet despite its drawbacks, a health care plan similar to the new Massachusetts system would be substantially better than our present one, in which millions are uninsured while the economy reels from the massive costs of third-party control of health care by private health insurers, the hospitals, the HR crowd, the academics, and the U.S. Congress. While the Maryland Fair Share system only entrenches the flaws of our present system, the new Massachusetts plan points the way to universal coverage, controlled costs, and greater consumer choice and satisfaction.

Ideal State Consumer-Driven Health Care Systems

If Jack lived in the Terrapin State and owned a highly competitive, low-profit-margin sort of business, he might leave the state or offer his employees only part-time work to limit the impact on his bottom line of meeting the inevitable state requirement that he spend 8 percent of his payroll on health insurance benefits. On the other hand, if Jack lived in the Bay State and owned the same sort of business, he could buy affordable health insurance from a health insurance supermarket that would offer him a variety of policies that he could buy with his pretax income. If Jack were poor, the state would subsidize him directly in his purchase of these policies.

You don't need a CPA to figure out which of these two choices is better for Jack.

The best state consumer-driven health care system would contain the following features:

1. *It would require that everybody be insured. Subsidize those consumers who cannot afford it.*
2. *It would provide the funding for the cost of universal coverage from uninsured individuals who can afford to buy it and from subsidies once given to hospitals and other health care providers. It would not tax businesses for this funding nor use federal government "reinsurance" to fund*

it either. The cost of treating the uninsured who cannot afford to pay for their care is heavily subsidized by state and local governments, especially for hospitals. But, as we have seen, hospitals do not necessarily use these subsidies to provide lower-priced services to the uninsured. Absent universal insurance, the hospitals and other health care providers will continue to demand subsidies to cover their "free care." It would make more sense to give these funds directly to the poor uninsured rather than to the hospitals that may or may not use them for these purposes.

Requiring businesses to buy health insurance will not only exacerbate the destructive role employers currently play but also distort employment patterns, as in Hawaii, and reduce wages. It is more sensible to require individuals to buy health insurance and to use some of their wages for this purchase. Individuals will buy the insurance they want at a price they are willing to pay. In contrast, employers, as we have seen, force all employees into cookie-cutter health insurance programs.

The Democrats have a different twist on the funding issue. They promise that the federal government will "repay" businesses for their catastrophic health care expenses. Although this promise is sanitized as federal "reinsurance," it represents the draconian intrusion of the federal government into the care of the sick. Once the federal government pays, the U.S. Congress will insist on managing this care. We saw how well it did this job in the case of kidney disease. When the federal government "reinsures" catastrophically expensive health care, the United States will have essentially transitioned to a single-payer health care system.

3. *It would provide for tax-free purchase of health insurance. It would not limit health insurance shoppers to a government-run supermarket as the sole means of obtaining health insurance.* The Massachusetts law cleverly uses an existing aspect of the federal tax code to enable the uninsured to buy insurance with pretax income. But there is a catch. The uninsured can buy their insurance in only one market, which is managed by the state government. Further, this market sells only those products designed by the government.

This process is like buying government-designed cars only in a government-run dealership. The states should neither design the insurance policies nor monopolize the site of sale.

4. *It would require insurance for financially catastrophic care. It would not require insurance for specific benefits, such as hospital care, doctors, and drugs. Instead, it would require health insurance that covers, for example, all medical expenses greater than $3,000 for a family earning $50,000.* Insurance for benefits has caused the fragmentation of U.S. health care. It also brings out the benefit lobbyists, who manipulate the government to maximize the amount paid to them. This process caused epo's use and revenues to grow enormously: congressional demand for increased use of epo not only cost billions of dollars but also caused some kidney disease patients grave harm. Further, payment for benefits penalizes providers who increase the patient's health. The healthier the patient, the less money is paid to the hospitals and other medical providers.

Insurance for financially catastrophic levels, in contrast, will enable innovative providers to integrate all the health care resources that the sick patient requires and to price them as a bundle. They will, for example, offer Jack Morgan a complete bundle of everything he needs for kidney care for $40,000. This price for integrated care not only improves quality and convenience for the patient but also ensures that providers are rewarded for improving the patient's health.

5. *It would provide transparency about the quality of individual providers of health care and their prices. It would not dictate the process of health care delivery.* As we have seen, the government's "performance" measures dictate the process of health care delivery to doctors and hospitals. Do we want the government to tell car manufacturers how to make cars, or do we want it to force the manufacturers to reveal their cars' safety, fuel efficiency, environmental friendliness, and price?

Who would want the government to supplant our doctor? But we do want it to help us understand just how good a doctor she is.

Consumer-Driven Health Care: The Bold Laws That Can Make It Happen

Consumer-driven health care has powerful enemies, the status quo fat cats or single-payer ideologues who spin powerful, seductive tales about its dangers.

The only ones who can make it happen are you and I.

So I am ending this book not with the literary equivalent of a flurry of drums but with a list of the five points that we should ensure are in the legislative plans that will make consumer-driven health care happen.

If we want excellent health care and insurance for all Americans at a price that citizens and taxpayers can afford, here then is the bold legislative solution, to be implemented in state legislatures and the U.S. Congress, that will create it:

1. *Everyone is required to buy his or her own insurance, using tax-sheltered income.* This step creates a consumer-driven system. To protect against bankruptcy because of medical needs, individuals are required to purchase health insurance that covers all expenses exceeding some percentage of their income and liquid assets.

   Employees get back, in salary and employer contributions, the sums that their employers currently use to pay for their health insurance and other health care needs. The employees do not pay taxes on this sum as long as they use it for health insurance and related medical needs.

2. *Government helps those who cannot afford to buy health insurance by subsidizing them.* This step enables the poor to buy health insurance just like everybody else.

3. *Providers are free to bundle care as they want to and to quote their own prices.* This step enables market-based pricing so that entrepreneurial providers can innovate freely without asking for permission to do so from insurance or government bureaucrats. This will prevent smothering new ideas with requirements for government-issued new codes, coverage, or payment schemes for every innovation. If entrepreneurs create integrated bundles of

care, for example, for the needs of a kidney disease victim in his fifties and price that bundle at, say, $65,000 a year, they will be motivated to offer preventive care and to assist the patient in managing his illness. The reason? There are actually many reasons, but one particularly good one is that when they receive a total price for the bundle of care, they can earn more profits as their patient's health improves. The ideal bundle would be a long-term payment so that the providers are motivated to take a long-term view of the patients' health.

4. *Government requires publication of data on the performance of all medical providers.* This step enables consumers to make informed decisions and protects them against providers who skimp on care, are incompetent, and/or deliver a bad value for the money.

5. *Prices are risk adjusted.* This step ensures that while sick people pay the same price for their insurance as everybody else, providers and/or insurers will receive more money for treatment of the sick. They are thus financially rewarded for attracting the sick. Because the sick account for the bulk of health care costs, we want providers to be interested in innovating cost-effective delivery systems of care for them and insurers to be interested in covering them.

To your good health and prosperity!

NOTES

For any inquiries regarding endnotes,
contact the author at rherzlinger@hbs.edu

Introduction

1. Testimony before the U.S. Congress House Committee on Ways and Means, Subcommittee on Health, Washington, D.C., July 18, 2006.
2. Ibid.
3. Lucette Lagnado, "Anatomy of a Hospital Bill," *Wall Street Journal*, September 21, 2004, p. B1.
4. Galen Institute, Congressional Staff Briefing, "Weighing the Benefits of Specialty Hospitals," Washington, D.C., July 20, 2005. Statement of Kelby Krabbenhoft, CEO, Sioux Valley.
5. Institute of Medicine (IOM), *To Err Is Human: Building a Safer Health System* (Washington, D.C.: National Academies Press, 2000), p. 1.
6. Avera Heart Hospital of South Dakota, "About Us" (www.SouthDakotaHeart.com, accessed January 14, 2007).
7. Galen Institute Congressional Staff Briefing, July 20, 2005.
8. 2004 and 2005 Internal Revenue Service (IRS) Form 990s, Sioux Valley Hospitals & Health System (Sanford Health as of February 2007), Sioux Falls, S.Dak.
9. Bradford C. Johnson, "Retail: The Wal-Mart Effect" and "What's Right with the U.S. Economy," *McKinsey Quarterly*, no. 1 (2002), pp. 40–43.

Chapter 1

1. Alain C. Enthoven and Victor R. Fuchs, "Employment-Based Health Insurance: Past, Present, and Future," *Health Affairs*, vol. 25, no. 6 (November/December 2006), pp. 1538–1547.
2. Medicare Payment Advisory Commission, *A Data Book: Healthcare Spending and the Medicare Program* (Washington, D.C.: Medicare Payment Advisory Commission, June 2006), p. 3.
3. Laura B. Benko, "McGuire's Billion-Dollar Exit: Investors Are Sad to See UnitedHealth Chief Go," *Modern Healthcare*, October 23, 2006, p. 8.
4. George Anders, "Health-Care Gold Mines: Middlemen Strike It Rich," "Rewarding Career: As Patients, Doctors Feel Pinch, Insurer's CEO Makes a Billion," "UnitedHealth Directors Strive to Please 'Brilliant' Chief," and "New Questions on Options—Selling Trout for 40 Cents a Pound," *Wall Street Journal*, April 18, 2006; and James Bandler, Charles Forelle, and Vanessa Fuhrmans, "CEO Aims to Halt Stock-Based Pay at UnitedHealth—Move Comes Amid Scrutiny of Options Timing, Gains," *Wall Street Journal*, April 19, 2006.
5. Agatha Christie, *Murder on the Orient Express* (New York: Dodd, Mead, 1985, first published in 1933).

6. Kaiser Family Foundation and Health Research and Educational Trust, *Employer Health Benefits, 2005 Annual Survey* (Menlo Park, Calif.: Henry J. Kaiser Family Foundation, 2005), p. 16.
7. "Controversy, Salaries Rise," *Modern Healthcare*, July 31, 2006; UnitedHealthcare, 2006 Proxy, p. 13.
8. Institute of Medicine (IOM), "Crossing the Quality Chasm: The IOM Health Care Initiative" (Washington, D.C.: The National Academies, iom.edu, accessed January 10, 2007).
9. Rachel M. Werner et al., "The 'Hassle Factor': What Motivates Physicians to Manipulate Reimbursement Rules?" *Archives of Internal Medicine*, vol. 162, no. 10 (May 27, 2002), pp. 1134–1139.
10. Peter J. Cunningham and Jessica H. May, *A Growing Hole in the Safety Net: Physician Charity Care Declines Again*, Tracking Report No. 13 (Washington, D.C.: Center for Studying Health System Change (CSHSC), March 2006).
11. *Revenue Reconciliation Act of 1989: Law and Explanation*, as passed by Congress on November 22, 1989 (Chicago: Commerce Clearing House, 1989); *Omnibus Budget Reconciliation Act of 1993* (Washington, D.C.: Government Printing Office, 1993); *Balanced Budget Reconciliation Act of 1995*: S.1357 to provide for reconciliation pursuant to Section 105 of the concurrent resolution on the budget for fiscal year 1996 (Washington, D.C.: Government Printing Office, 1995); and C. I. Scofield, ed., *The New Scofield Reference Bible, Authorized King James Version* (New York: Oxford University Press, 1967).
12. Allan Nevins with the collaboration of Frank Ernes Hill, *Ford: The Times, The Man, The Company* (New York: Scribner's, 1954), pp. 646–647; Price/Per Capital Income column: Robert F. Martin, *National Income in the United States, 1799–1938* (New York: National Industrial Conference Board, 1939).
13. Ha T. Tu and Paul B. Ginsburg, *Losing Ground: Physician Income, 1995–2003*, Tracking Report No. 15 (Washington, D.C.: Center for Studying Health System Change, June 2006).
14. Association of American Medical Colleges (AAMC), "Medical School Applications May Be on the Rise," December 2002, and "Medical School Enrollment Rises," November 2006 (aamc.org, accessed January 1, 2007).
15. Organ Procurement and Transplantation Network (OPTN), "Donors Recovered in the U.S. by Donor Type" and "Overall by Organ" (www.optn.org, accessed May 15, 2006).
16. Organ Procurement and Transplantation Network, "PARA Waiting Times, 1997–2000," "Donors Recovered in the U.S. by Donor Type," and "Overall by Organ" (www.optn.org, accessed May 15, 2006).

Chapter 2

1. Charles Ornstein and Tracy Weber, "Kaiser Put Kidney Patients at Risk," *Los Angeles Times*, May 3, 2006, Part A, p. 1.
2. Ibid; and U.S. Department of Health and Human Services (DHHS), Centers for Medicine & Medical Services (CMS), Statement of Deficiencies, Kaiser Foundation Hospital Renal Transplantation Center, May 12, 2006. Obtained by the author under the Freedom of Information Act.
3. Sabin Russell, "Scathing Report on Kaiser Kidney Program; Transplant Delays Assailed—Medicare Threatens to End Coverage," *San Francisco Chronicle*, June 24, 2006; and Ornstein and Weber, "The State; Kaiser Put Kidney Patients at Risk."

4. Tracy Weber and Charles Ornstein, "Kaiser Transplant Patients Express Their Fear and Fury; With Reports of Disarray Added to Their Existing Frustration, Some Don't Want the HMO Performing Their Surgeries," *Los Angeles Times*, May 6, 2006, Part A, p. 1.

5. Ornstein and Weber, "Kaiser Put Kidney Patients at Risk."

6. DHHS, Statement of Deficiencies, ID tag V114; and Russell, "Scathing Report on Kaiser Kidney Program."

7. Ibid.

8. Ibid.

9. Ibid.

10. DHHS, Statement of Deficiencies, ID tag V112, V114, and V116; and Russell.

11. DHHS, Statement of Deficiencies, ID tag V141; Ibid.; "Kaiser Permanente San Francisco Facing Transplant Troubles," Transcript, May 2 and May 8, 2006; "State Launches Probe of Kaiser Transplant Program," Transcript, May 3, 2006; "Kaiser Conducts Internal Probe into Kidney Program," Transcript, May 4, 2006; "Patient Left in Limbo by Kaiser Transplant Woes," Transcript, May 5, 2006; CBS 5 Investigates.

12. DHHS, Statement of Deficiencies, ID tag V110; Charles Ornstein and Tracy Weber, "U.S. Berates Kaiser Over Kidney Effort," *Los Angeles Times*, June 24, 2006, Part B, p. 1.

13. Ornstein and Weber, "Kaiser Put Kidney Patients at Risk." p. 1.

14. DHHS, Statement of Deficiencies, ID tag V114; and Ornstein and Weber, "Kaiser Put Kidney Patients at Risk."

15. Ibid.

16. Chris Rauber, "Kaiser Whistleblower Settles Lawsuit Over Abrupt Firing," *San Francisco Business Times*, January 12, 2007.

17. Chris Rauber, "Kaiser Whistleblower Files Lawsuit, Raises Concerns," *Sacramento Business Journal*, July 21, 2006, http://sacramento.bizjournals.com/sacramento/stories/2006/07/17/daily51.html?t=printable, accessed January 8, 2007; Charles Ornstein and Tracy Weber, "3 Sue Kaiser in Transplant Case: Lawyers Say the Action May Be the First of Many; The HMO's Arbitration Rule Could Thwart Them," *Los Angeles Times*, May 12, 2006, Part B, p. 1.

18. Ibid.

19. Talia Kennedy, "Kidney Transplant Patients Transferred to UC-Davis Medical Center," *The California Aggie*, October 4, 2006.

20. "California's Kaiser to Pay Record $2 Million Fine Over Kidney Transplant Program," *BestWire*, August 15, 2006.

21. This section is partially based on Regina E. Herzlinger, "Culture Is the Key," in *Leading Beyond the Walls*, ed. F. Hesselbein, M. Goldsmith, and I. Somerville (San Francisco: Jossey-Bass, 1999), pp. 105–121.

22. Matthew K. Wynia et al., "Do Physicians Not Offer Useful Services Because of Coverage Restrictions?" *Health Affairs*, vol. 22, no. 4 (July–August 2003), pp. 190–197.

23. Reed Abelson, "Doctors Press Oxford Health on Payments," *New York Times*, February 3, 1998, sec. D, p. 1; Lindy Washburn, "Oxford Fined a Record $275,000; State Says HMO Denied Claims," *The Record*, April 1, 2000, p. A1; Carol Eisenberg and Susan Harrigan, "Oxford's Failing Health/There's No Shortage of Diagnoses for System Decline," *Newsday*, December 9, 1997, p. A4; and Ron Winslow and Scot J. Paltrow, "Sick Business—The Resurgent Turmoil in Health Care—Ill-Managed Care: At Oxford Health, Financial 'Controls'

Were Out of Control—HMO Underestimated Costs and Overstated Revenue; Then Reality Descended—A Regulator's Ultimatum," *Wall Street Journal*, April 29, 1998, p. A1.

24. Diane Levick, "Oxford Options Pay Off: Retired Chairman Gets $73 Million," *Hartford Courant*, April 3, 2003, p. E2.

25. Stephen Brook, *God's Army: The Story of the Salvation Army* (Philadelphia: Trans-Atlantic Publications, 1999; based on the Channel 4, U.K., television series *God's Army*).

26. Werner Keller, *The Bible as History* (New York: Morrow, 1981, first published 1965).

27. Kaiser Foundation Health Plan, Inc., www.Kaiserpermanente.org and globalbb. onesource.com/brow_at_Health_Plan_Inc.

28. See, for example, "America's Best HMOs," *Newsweek*, June 24, 1996.

29. Martha Groves, "Ailing Health Care System May Get Kaiser-Style Care," *Los Angeles Times*, May 10, 1993.

30. John G. Smillie, *Can Physicians Manage the Quality and Costs of Health Care? The Story of the Permanente Medical Group* (New York: McGraw-Hill, 1991).

31. Carl T. Hall, "Huge Loss for Kaiser—Rates to Rise; $270 Million Shortfall Also Means Cost Cuts," *San Francisco Chronicle*, February 14, 1998, p. A1.

32. Robert Pear, "The Health Care Debate: Managed Care; Once in Front, H.M.O.s Lose Their Luster in Health Debate," *New York Times*, August 23, 1994.

33. Louise Kertesz, "Which Is the Real Kaiser? Is the Nation's Largest HMO a Model of Cost-Effective, Quality Care or a Greedy Medical Factory That Endangers Its Patients?" *Modern Healthcare*, August 25, 1997.

34. Chris Rauber, "Kaiser's Losses Hit $288 Million in '98," *Modern Healthcare*, February 22, 1999; Tom Abate, "Kaiser Reports It Narrowed Loss in '99," *San Francisco Chronicle*, February 29, 2000; and Laura B. Benko, "Kaiser on Track to Recovery: After Posting Losses for Two Consecutive Years, Kaiser Almost Broke Even in 1999," *Modern Healthcare*, March 6, 2000.

35. "Sierra Health Subsidiary Completes Purchase," PR Newswire, November 2, 1998.

36. Milt Freudenheim, "Kaiser H.M.O., Erring on Costs, Posts $270 Million Loss for '97," *New York Times*, February 14, 1998.

37. Kertesz, "Which Is the Real Kaiser?"

38. Ibid.

39. Smillie, *Can Physicians Manage the Quality and Costs of Health Care?*

40. Center for Studying Health Systems Change, "Physicians Are More Likely to Face Quality Incentives than Incentives That May Restrain Care," Issue Brief No. 48 (Washington, D.C.: HSC, January 2002).

41. Carl T. Hall, "$1 Billion HMO Pay Unifies Critics," *San Francisco Chronicle*, June 20, 1996, p. B1.

42. But the chorus was not universal. As early as 1986, Roger Feldman and his colleagues at the University of Minnesota warned that HMOs did not lower hospital costs or diminish hospital profits. They presciently concluded that "public policy created to induce competition must go beyond the simple stimulus of HMO growth." See R. Feldman et al., "The Competitive Impact of Health Maintenance Organizations on Hospital Finances: An Exploratory Study," *Journal of Health Politics, Policy, and Law*, vol. 10, no. 4 (winter 1986), pp. 675–697. And a 1994 report by the U.S. Office of Technology Assessment questioned the

wisdom of a national model based on the Twin Cities experience. The report concluded: "It is difficult to accurately assess whether expenditures for health care in the Twin Cities are higher or lower than in other metropolitan areas." See "A Model in Dispute," *Minneapolis Star Tribune*, July 27, 1994, p. 1A.

43. James. C. Robinson, "At the Helm of an Insurance Giant: Aetna's Richard L. Huber," *Health Affairs*, vol. 18, no.6 (November–December 1999), pp. 89–99.

44. B. Martinez, "Aetna Tries to Improve Bedside Manner in Bid to Help Bottom Line," *Wall Street Journal*, February 23, 2001, pp. A1, A9.

45. Milt Freudenheim, "Aetna's Chief Steps Down Under Pressure from Share-holders," *New York Times*, February 26, 2000, p. C1.

46. Robin Toner, "Health Care in Minnesota: Model for U.S. or Novelty?" *New York Times*, October 9, 1993, p. A1.

47. Robert H. Miller and Harold S. Luft, "HMO Plan Performance Update: An Analysis of the Literature, 1997–2001," *Health Affairs*, vol. 21, no. 4 (July–August 2002), pp. 80–81.

48. SatireWire.com, http://www.satirewire.com/news/022800/satire-hmo.shtml.

49. Paul Fronstin, "The Role of Managed Care," *Benefits Quarterly*, Second Quarter, 2001, p. 12.

50. U.S. Census Bureau, *Statistical Abstract of the United States, 1999* (Washington, D.C.: Government Printing Office, 2000), Table No. 776, p. 495.

51. Medicare Payment Advisory Commission, "Assessing Payment Adequacy and Updating Payments for Home Health Services," *Report to the Congress: Medicare Payment Policy* (Washington, D.C.: Medicare Payment Advisory Commission, March 2003), pp. 101–117.

52. Ibid.

53. Underwriting profits are earned solely from the insurance business. Many insurers also earn additional returns from investing their free cash.

54. Kristen Hallam, "Blues Report Big 1997 Operating Loss," *Business Insurance*, June 1, 1998, p. 14.

55. Congressional Budget Office (CBO), "An Analysis of the Literature on Disease Management Programs," Washington, D.C.: CBO, October 13, 2004.

56. Catherine Hoffman, Dorothy Licey, and Hai-Yen Sung, "Persons with Chronic Conditions: Their Prevalence and Costs," *Journal of the American Medical Association*, vol. 276, no. 18 (1996), pp. 1473–1479.

57. Joanne Wojcik, "HMOs Still Using Gatekeeper Model," *Business Insurance*, vol. 34 (December 11, 2000), pp. 3, 13.

58. Paul B. Ginsburg et al., "Tracking Health Care Costs: Continued Stability but at High Rates in 2005," *Health Affairs*, vol. 25, no. 6 (November–December 2006), pp. 486–495 (e-published, October 3, 2006).

59. Regina E. Herzlinger and Jeff Grahling, "Note on Financing of the U.S. Health Care Sector," HBS Case No. 304-309, Rev. August 29, 2006 (Boston: Harvard Business School Publishing, 2003).

60. Atlanta Information Services, AHIP, Kaiser Family Foundation, and eHealth-Insurance, taken from Goldman Sachs Group, "Healthcare Investment Strategy," September 20, 2006, p. 13, Exhibit 10.

61. "Three-Year Study Shows Consumer-Driven Health Plans Continue to Stimulate Positive Changes in Consumer Health Behavior," *Business Wire*, UnitedHealth Group, July 12, 2006.

62. McKinsey & Company, North American Payer Provider Practice, "Consumer-Directed Health Plan Report—Early Evidence Is Promising," June 2005.

63. American Enterprise Institute for Public Policy Research, "What Is Behind the Rapid Growth of Health Spending," Presentation, July 17, 2006, www.aei.org, accessed February 20, 2007.

64. Amy Finkelstein, "The Aggregate Effects of Health Insurance," and Amy Finkelstein and Robin McKnight, *What Did Medicare Do? (And Was It Worth It?)*, National Bureau of Economic Research (NBER) Working Papers No. 11609 and 11619, May and September 2005.

65. Finkelstein and McKnight, *What Did Medicare Do?*

Chapter 3

1. C. Guth, "Klarer Befund," pp. 16–19; and McK Wissen 19 "Krankenhaus" (December 2006), brand eins Wissen GmbH und Co. KG, Hamburg. OECD, Health Division, "Expenditures on In-Patient Care/Capita," October 10, 2006, ecosante.pr.ezpl., accessed March 7, 2007.

2. Arnold Milstein, "American Surgical Travel Is a Treatable Symptom," Testimony, U.S. Senate Special Committee on Aging, June 27, 2006; and data from the Indian Healthcare Federation, e-mail from Rajit Kamal to Professor Regina E. Herzlinger, October 27, 2006.

3. P. Ginsburg et al., "Tracking Health Care Costs," Health Affairs, October 3, 2006, W489; also Issue Brief 91 (Washington, D.C.: Center for Studying Health System Changes, December 2004).

4. Ibid.

5. Medicare Payment Advisory Commission, *Report to the Congress: Medicare Payment Policy*, (Washington, D.C.: Medicare Payment Advisory Commission, March 2006), p. 54.

6. Carlos Angrisano et al., "Accounting for the Cost of Health Care in the United States" (McKinsey & Company: McKinsey Global Institute, January 2007), p. 12.

7. Organization for Economic Co-operation & Development, *OECD Health Data 2006*, available through the *SourceOECD* database, www.oecd.org, accessed February 6, 2007.

8. Organization for Economic Co-operation & Development, *Health at a Glance: OECD Indicators 2005* (Paris: OECD Publishing, 2005), pp. 45 and 139.

9. Survey of Current Business (bea.gov); Centers for Disease Control, "Cost of Chronic Diseases," accessed March 21, 2007; American Diabetes Association, "Economic Control of Diabetes in the U. S. in 2002," *Diabetes Care*, March 2003, vol. 26 (3), pp. 917-932.

10. Robert Town et al., "The Welfare Consequences of Hospital Mergers," National Bureau of Economic Research (NBER) Working Paper 12244 (Social Science Research Network: ssrn.com).

11. www.opensecrets.org, accessed February 2, 2007.

12. "Audited Consolidated Financial Statements," University of Pittsburgh Medical Center, years ended June 30, 2006; Consejo de Latinos Unidos, hospitalpricing.com, accessed January 14, 2007.

13. McKesson Corporation, OneSource database, accessed February 8, 2007.

14. Medicare Payment Advisory Commission, *Report to the Congress: Medicare Payment Policy*. For an opposing perspective, see Charles Kahn, III, Statement of the Federation of American Hospitals, www.ftc.gov/ogc/healthcarehearing/docs/030227kahniii.pdf.

15. Christopher Rowland, "Hospital CEOs join the $1m Club," *Boston Globe*, August 31, 2006, boston.com, accessed January 15, 2007.
16. David Hyman, *Improving Healthcare: A Dose of Competition: A Report by the Federal Trade Commission and the Department of Justice* (July 2004) (Dordrecht: Springer, 2005).
17. Martin S. Gaynor, *What Do We Know About Competition and Quality in Health Care Markets?*, NBER Working Paper No. 12301, issued June 2006, available at www.nber.org.
18. American Hospital Association (AHA), *AHA Hospital Statistics 2006* (Washington, D.C.: AHA, 2006), p. 10.
19. David Hyman, *Improving Healthcare*, Chapter 4.
20. William B. Vogt and Robert Town, "How Has Hospital Consolidation Affected the Price and Quality of Hospital Cases?" The Synthesis Project, Robert Wood Johnson Foundation policysynthesis.org, pp. 6, 8. Ranjan Krishnan, "Market Restructuring and Pricing in the Hospital Industry," *Journal of Health Economics*, 20, 2001.
21. Town et al., "The Welfare Consequences of Hospital Mergers."
22. Lawton R. Burns and Mark V. Pauly, "Integrated Delivery Networks—A Detour on the Road to Integrated Health Care?" *Health Affairs*, vol. 21, no. 4, July–August 2002, pp. 128–143.
23. Paul B. Ginsburg and Cara S. Lesser, *A Decade of Tracking Health Systems Change*, Commentary No. 2 (Washington, D.C.: Center For Studying Health System Change, March 2006), p. 4; and Cara S. Lesser and Paul B. Ginsburg, "Update on the Nation's Health Care System: 1997–1999," *Health Affairs*, November–December 2000, pp. 206–216.
24. Vogt and Town, "How Has Hospital . . . "
25. David Hyman, *Improving Healthcare*, Chapter 4.
26. See, for example, Joseph P. Newhouse, "Toward a Theory of Nonprofit Institutions: An Economic Model of a Hospital," *American Economic Review*, vol. 60, no. 1, March 1970, pp. 64–74.
27. Daniel P. Kessler and Jeffrey J. Geppert, "The Effects of Competition on Variation in the Quality and Cost of Medical Care," *Journal of Economics & Management Strategy*, vol. 14. no. 3, September 2005, pp. 575–589.
28. Gaynor, *What Do We Know . . .* : Gary J. Young et al, "Community Control and Pricing Patterns of Nonprofit Hospitals," *Journal of Health Politics, Economics, and Law*, 1051, 1073 (2000).
29. Vogt and Town, "How Has Hospital . . . "
30. Regina E. Herzlinger and William Krasker, "Who Profits from Nonprofits," *Harvard Business Review*, vol. 65, no. 1, January–February, 1987, pp. 93–106.
31. Chapin White, Robert Nguyen, and Alshadye Yemanne, *Nonprofit Hospitals and the Provision of Community Benefits*, CBO Report (Washington, D.C.: Congressional Budget Office, December 2006), p. 3.
32. U.S. Senate Finance Committee, "Taking the Pulse of Charitable Care and Community Benefits at Nonprofit Hospitals," Statement of Sen. Chuck Grassley, September 13, 2006, www.finance.senate.gov.
33. White, Nguyen, *Nonprofit Hospitals and the Provision of Community Benefits*, p. 3
34. Lucette Lagnado, "Anatomy of a Hospital Bill," *Wall Street Journal*, September 21, 2004, p. 1.
35. Revenue Ruling 56-185, 1956-1 C.B. 202, 1956 IRB LEXIS 422 (1956).

36. Revenue Ruling 69-545, 1969-2 C.B. 117, 1969 IRB LEXIS 176 (1969). For a discussion of subsequent rulings, see Jack E. Karns, "Justifying the Nonprofit Hospital Tax Exemption in a Competitive Market Environment," *Widener Law Journal*, vol. 13 (2004), pp. 383–561; and a class of indigent patients denied medical treatment at various nonprofit hospitals unsuccessfully challenged the legality of the "community benefit" standard in *East Kentucky Welfare Rights Organization v. Simon*, 506 F.2d 1278 (D.C. Cir. 1974).
37. In re Evanston Northwestern Healthcare Corp., 2005 FTC LEXIS 146 (October 20, 2005).
38. Ibid., quoting Hospital Corp. of America, 807 F.2d at 1381 (7th Cir., 1986).
39. Kaiser Family Foundation, *Trends and Indicators in the Changing Health Care Marketplace, 2002*, May 2002, Exhibit 5.9, p. 56, at http:www.kff.org/insurance/3161-index..cfm, updated with 2001 data from the American Medical Association, *Patient Care Physician Survey*, 2001.
40. "Faltering Family M.D. Gets Technology Lifeline," *Wall Street Journal*, February 23, 2000, p. A1.
41. William J. Baumol and William G. Bowen, *Performing Arts: The Economic Dilemma; a Study of Problems Common to Theater, Opera, Music, and Dance* (New York: Twentieth Century Fund, 1996).
42. "What's Right with the U.S. Economy," *McKinsey Quarterly*, no. 1, 2002, pp. 40–43.
43. Sucharita Mulpuru (with Carrie A. Johnson and Brian Tesch), "2005 US eCommerce: The Year in Review, An Overview of Annual and Q-1 US Online Retail Sales" (Cambridge, Mass.: Forrester, January 20, 2006).
44. Peggy Edersheim Kalb, "Tricks of the Trade: Calling Customer Service," *Wall Street Journal*, December 20, 2006, p. D2.
45. U.S. Census Bureau, *2002 Economic Census, Selected Industry Statistics for the U.S. and States: 2002* (http://factfinder, census.gov, accessed February 21, 2007).
46. Claudia Kalb et al., "Health for Life," *Newsweek*, vol. 148, no. 14 October 16, 2006, pp. 46–73.
47. Heart hospitals had lower length-of-stay and readmission rates (R. E. Herzlinger and P. Stavros, "Medcath Corp.: A," Boston : Harvard Business School Publications, 2004). A MedPac study claiming heart hospitals had costs equal to those of a general community hospital is questionable because (1) it did not adjust costs for higher depreciation and lease expenses for heart hospitals, which are newer, and (2) it failed to use activity-based costing to measure the general hospital costs (MedPac, "Physician-Owned Specialty Hospitals Revisited," August 2006).
48. Markian Hawryluk, "Congress Eyes Boutique Hospital Backers," *American Medical News*, vol. 46, no. 18, May 12, 2003, p. 6.
49. Regina E. Herzlinger and Peter Stavros, "MedCath Corporation (A)," HBS Case No. 303-041, rev. August 2006 (Boston: Harvard Business School Publishing, 2004), p. 10.
50. Michelle Terwilleger, "Winning Patients' Hearts," *Californian*, July 16, 2001, taken from Herzlinger and Stavros, "MedCath Corporation (A)."
51. Ron Winslow, "Fed-Up Cardiologists Invest in Hospital for Heart Disease," *Wall Street Journal*, June 22, 1999, taken from Herzlinger and Stavros, "MedCath Corporation (A)."
52. Kevin Dobbs, "A Philosophical Shift Between Doctors and Administrators Transforms Cardiac Care," *Argus Leader*, March 11, 2001, taken from Herzlinger and Stavros, "MedCath Corporation (A)."

53. Ibid.; Winslow, "Fed-Up Cardiologists Invest in Hospital."
54. Kristine Henry, "Nucor Sets Pace for Steelmakers," *Hamilton Spectator*, May 13, 2002, p. D10.
55. Form 10Q, Nucor and Bethlehem Steel, U.S. Securities and Exchange Commission, Washington, D.C.: September 2003.
56. FACCT—The Foundation for Accountability and the Robert Wood Johnson Foundation, *A Portrait of the Chronically Ill in America* (Portland, Ore. and Princeton, N.J.: Robert Wood Johnson Foundation); and Steven B. Cohen and William Yu, "The Persistence in the Level of Health Expenditures Over Time: Estimates for the U.S. Population, 2002–2003," Statistical Brief 124, Agency for Healthcare Research and Quality (AHRQ), *Medical Expenditure Panel Survey*, May 2006.
57. Ralph Snyderman and R. Sanders Williams, "The New Prevention," *Modern Healthcare*, vol. 33 (2003), p. 19; and D. J. Whellan et al., "The Benefit of Implementing a Heart Failure Disease Management Program," *Archives of Internal Medicine*, vol. 161, no. 18 (October 8, 2001), pp. 2223–2228. Table 4 reports pre-enrollment costs per patient year of $16,025 vs. $2,544 of post-enrollment cost and a difference of $8,571.
58. Regina E. Herzlinger and Bruce Wilson, "MedCath Corporation (C)," HBS Case No. 305-097, Rev. May 2006 (Boston: Harvard Business School Publishing, 2005).
59. MedPac, "Physician-Owned Specialty Hospitals Revisited"; Herzlinger and Stavros, "MedCath Corp.: A."
60. MedPac, "Physician-Owned . . . ," p. vii.
61. K. B. Forbes, "Unconscionable," Consejo de Latinos Unidos, http://hospital pricing.com/unconscionable.asp, accessed October 6, 2006.
62. Abhi Raghunathan, "Lee Memorial Approves Hospital's Billing Practices," Naplesnews.com, July 30, 2004; and Andi Atwater, "Patient Group Provides Aid; Activists Say Uninsured Are Overcharged," Newpress.com, April 28, 2004.
63. Adam Bryant, "Who's Afraid of Dickie Scruggs?" *Newsweek*, December 6, 1999.
64. Harvy Lipman, "Illinois Strips Hospital of Property-Tax Exemption," *Chronicle of Philanthropy*, vol. 19, no. 1 (October 12, 2006), p. 31.
65. "Who's Afraid of Dickie Scruggs?"
66. U.S. Committee on Ways and Means, Subcommittee on Health, 109-78, "Hearing on Price Transparency," July 18, 2006, http://waysandmeans.house.gov/hearings.asp?formmode=detail&hearing=494&comm=1, accessed February 21, 2007.
67. Milstein, "American Surgical Travel Is a Treatable Symptom."
68. Cinda Becker, "The Best Care Money Can Buy?" *Modern Healthcare*, vol. 34, no. 32 (August 9, 2004), p. 26. Also Dr. Pushwaz Virk to Prof. Regina E. Herzlinger, Fall 2006.
69. For example, Bumrungrad International Hospital, www.bumrungrad.com, and Bangkok International Hospital, www.bangkokhospital.com, accessed February 2, 2007.
70. Correspondence from Dr. Pushwaz Virk to Professor Regina E. Herzlinger, October 17, 2006.
71. "Rants, Raves, and Comments on Things That Affect My Life," ShootinOff. com, accessed February 6, 2007. See, also Joe Cochrane, "Hospitals Around the World Are Drawing New Patients with Topnotch Doctors, High-Tech Equipment and Low Costs. These 10 Are Leaders in Their Fields," *Newsweek Inter-*

national, http://www.msnbc.msn.com/id/15365149/site/newsweek/from/ ET/, accessed March 3, 2007.

72. Malcolm Foster and Margie Mason, "Outsourcing Medical Treatment Gains Popularity," Associated Press, *South Florida Sun-Sentinel*, November 3, 2006, p. 16A.

73. Health Insurance Association of America (HIAA), *Source Book of Health Insurance Data 1984–85* (Washington, D.C.: HIAA, 1985), pp. 43–44, 59–60.

74. U.S. Census Bureau, *Statistical Abstract of the United States, 1995* (Washington, D.C.: Government Printing Office, 1996), p. 469, table 724.

75. National Institutes of Health, National Institute of Diabetes & Digestive & Kidney Diseases, *The National Digestive Diseases Information Clearinghouse*, http://www.pueblo.gsa.gov/cic_text/health/gallstones/gallstns.htm, accessed February 12, 2007.

76. American Hospital Association, *AHA Hospital Statistics 2007* (Chicago: American Hospital Association, 2007), pp. 6, 11.

77. U.S. Centers for Disease Control and Prevention, *National Hospital Discharge Survey 2004*, Vital Health Statistics, Series No. 13.

78. "Joint World Congress Spotlights the Newest, Brightest Developments in Cardiology Field," *BBI Newsletter*, vol. 17, no. 11 (November 1994), p. 184.

79. David M. Cutler and Robert S. Huckman, "Technological Development and Medical Productivity: The Diffusion of Angioplasty in New York State," *Journal of Health Economics*, vol. 22, no. 2 (March 2003), p. 187.

80. Daniel B. Mark et al., "Effects of Coronary Angioplasty, Coronary Bypass Surgery and Medical Therapy on Employment in Patients with Coronary Artery Disease," *Annals of Internal Medicine*, 1994, vol. 120, pp. 111–117.

81. Regina E. Herzlinger and JoEllen Slurzberg, "Note on Health Insurance Coverage, Coding, and Payment," HBS Case No. 304-005, Rev. August 2006 (Boston: Harvard Business School Publishing, 2003); and "MIS Hip Replacement Surgery: Link with Surgeon in Pioneering Work," *Sheffield Star*, September 27, 2006, www.factiva.com, accessed February 2, 2007.

Chapter 4

1. U.S. Bureau of the Census, "The 2007 Statistical Abstract," Table 706, Consumer Price Indexes, 1990 to 2005. www.census.gov/compendia/statab; and National Quality Research Center, University of Michigan, http://www. theacsi.org/index.php?option=com_content&task=view&jd=18&Itemid=33.

2. Internal Revenue Code, Section 106 (a).

3. Thomas M. Seldon and Bradley M. Gray, "Tax Subsidies for Employment-Related Insurance: Estimates for 2006," *Health Affairs*, vol. 25, no. 6 (November–December 2006), p. 1574."

4. Tarren Bragdon, e-mail to Regina E. Herzlinger, December 10, 2006, tbragdon @empirecenter.org.

5. Ibid.

6. Health Insurance Association of America, *HIAA Source Book 1999–2000* (Washington, D.C.: HIAA, 1999), p. 1.

7. "Current Population Reports" (Washington, D.C.: Government Printing Office, 2005), no. P60–22g.

8. Kaiser Family Foundation, Menlo Park, Calif., and Health Research and Educational Trust, Chicago, Ill., "Employer Health Benefits 2006," p. 4.

9. Alain C. Enthoven and Victor R. Fuchs, "Employment-Based Health Insurance: Past, Present, and Future," *Health Affairs*, vol. 25, no. 6 (November/December 2006), pp. 1538–1547.

10. Donald P. Condit, "Time to Rethink Employer Provided Insurance," *Grand Rapids Press*, February 25, 2007.

11. Thomas Gnau, "Change Is Here, More Is on the Way for General Motors, Unions," *Dayton Daily News*, January 29, 2007, p. A6; and "GM Trims Benefits Costs," *Detroit Free Press*, August 9, 2006, p. 3D.

12. Kaiser Family Foundation and Health Research and Educational Trust, "Employer Health Benefits 2006," Exhibits 6.2 and 7.6.

13. R.R. Bowker Company, *The Bowker Annual of Library and Book Trade Information* (New York: R.R. Bowker, various years); Gale Research, *Gale Directory of Publications and Broadcast Media* (Detroit, MI: Gale Research, various years); and Steven J. Carlotti, Mary Ellen Coe, and Jesko Perrey, "Making Brand Portfolios Work," *McKinsey Quarterly*, no. 4, November 2004, pp. 24–35.

14. Paul Starr, *The Social Transformation of American Medicine* (New York: Basic Books, 1982), pp. 308–309.

15. Gary Kaufman, "How to Fix HR," *Harvard Business Review*, vol. 84, no. 9 (September 1, 2006), p. 30.

16. Ann Pomeroy, "HR Skills for the Future," *HRMagazine*, vol. 51, no. 2 (February 2006), p. 16; Robert Rodriguez, "HR's New Breed," *HRMagazine*, vol. 51, no. 1 (January 2006), pp. 66–71; Sunil J. Ramlall and Michael Sheppeck, "Increasing the Relevance of the Graduate HR Curriculum," *HR Human Resource*, vol. 29, no. 2 (2006), pp. 6–11; and Rebecca A. Thacker, "Revising the HR Curriculum: An Academic/Practitioner Partnership," *Education & Training*, vol. 44, no. 1 (2002), pp. 31–40.

17. Patricia Simpson and Delphine Lenoir, "Win Some, Lose Some: Women's Status in the Field of Human Resources in the 1990s," *Women in Management Review*, vol. 18, no. 3–4 (2003), pp. 191–198; and U.S. Bureau of Labor Statistics, *Employed Persons by Detailed Occupation, Sex, Race, and Hispanic or Latino Ethnicity*, Table 11, http://www.bls.gov/cps/home/htm#annual, accessed November 15, 2006.

18. Tape at http://whitehousetapes.org/pages/listen_tapes_rmn.htm, tapermn_ e450c.

19. Kaiser Foundation Hospitals, Form 990, 2004, date filed August 8, 2005.

20. Jim Frederick, "Medco Settles False Claims Charges," *Drug Store News*, December 11, 2006.

21. "Lilly Sells Unit to Rite Aid," *Financial Times*, November 18, 1998, p. 24.

22. Frederick, "Medco Settles False Claims Charges," December 11, 2006.

23. Kaiser Family Foundation, "Employer Health Benefits 2006," Exhibit 4.1.

Chapter 5

1. J. Stewart Cameron, *A History of the Treatment of Renal Failure by Dialysis* (Oxford: Oxford University Press, 2002), pp. 311–313.

2. Eli A. Friedman, "View from Across the Atlantic: Health Care Reform Engulfs All of Us," *Nephrology Dialysis Transplantation*, vol. 11, no. 9 (1996).

3. Dialysis, www.geocities.com, accessed March 23, 2007.

4. U.S. Renal Data System, *USRDS 2006 Annual Data Report*, Chapter 11, p. 206.

5. Medicare Payment Advisory Commission (MedPAC), "Report to Congress: Issues in a Modernized Medicare Program" (Washington, D.C.: MedPAC, June 2005), p. 109.

6. National Quality Research Center, Stephen M. Ross School of Business, University of Michigan, *Scores by Industry. Life Insurance, American Customer Service Index*, http://www.theacsi.org, accessed February 22, 2007.
7. U.S. Renal Data System, *USRDS 2006 Annual Data Report*, Chapter 6, Table 6.1, p. 131.
8. Andrew Pollack, "Amgen Finds Anemia Drug Holds Risks in Cancer Use," *New York Times*, January 26, 2007, p. C3.
9. Friedman, "Health Care Reform Engulfs All of Us."
10. Craig R. Whitney, "In France, Socialized Medicine Meets Gallic Version of H.M.O.," *New York Times*, April 25, 1995, p. A5.
11. C. M. Kjellstrand, Presentation at 4th International Conference on Geriatric Nephrology and Urology, April 21, 1996, Toronto, Canada.
12. U.S. Renal Data System, Table 12.C.
13. Ibid., Fig. 12.10.
14. Ibid., Fig. 12.11.
15. Hugh C. Rayner et al., "Mortality and Hospitalization in Haemodialysis Patients in Five European Countries: Results from the Dialysis Outcomes and Practice Patterns Study (DOPPS)," *Nephrology Dialysis Transplantation*, vol. 19, no. 1 (January 2004), pp. 108–120.
16. A. Ahmad et al., "Current Chronic Kidney Disease Practice Patterns in the U.K.: A National Survey," *QJM*, vol. 99, no. 4 (April 2006), pp. 245–251.
17. Davita, Inc., Proxy filing, dated May 15, 2006; and 10-K, year ending December 31, 2006, dated March 6, 2006.
18. www.onesource.com.
19. Robert Crandall et al., "Compensating the CEO," *Directors and Boards*, vol. 31, no. 1 (Fourth Quarter 2006), p. 48; Gerald T. Garvey and Todd T. Milbourn, "Asymmetric Benchmarking in Compensation: Executives Are Rewarded for Good Luck but Not Penalized for Bad," *Journal of Financial Economics*, vol. 82, no. 1 (October 2006), p. 197; and Donna M. Carlon, Alexis A. Downs, and Stacia Wert-Gray, "Statistics as Fetishes: The Case of Financial Performance Measures and Executive Compensation," *Organizational Research Methods*, vol. 9, no. 4 (October 2006), p. 475.
20. "Davita," *Board Analyst Database*, The Corporate Library, www.boardanalyst.com, accessed January 31, 2007.
21. Amgen, Inc., Proxy filing, dated May 20, 2006; and Biography Resource Center Online, October 17, 2006.
22. Victoria Griffith, "Amgen Chief Warns on Drug Payments Policy," *Financial Times*, July 23, 2004, p. 18.
23. Kerry A. Dolan, "Amgen's Enemies; Doctors Are Rebelling Against Its Marketing Practices, Dissidents Think Medicare Is Too Generous to It and Competition Looms," *Forbes*, vol. 178, no. 9, October 30, 2006. pp. 126–128.
24. The Center for Responsive Politics, www.opensecrets.org, accessed February 22, 2007.
25. Tom Hamburger and Walter F. Roche, Jr., "Congress Closes with a Pork-filled Flourish; Dialysis Industry, Other Interests that Donated to Lawmakers Get Lavish End-of-Session Breaks," *Los Angeles Times*, December 21, 2006, Part A, p. 1.
26. Medicare Payment Advisory Commission (MedPAC), "Report to Congress: Issues in a Modernized Medicare Program," p. 109.

27. Office of Inspector General (OIG), Department of Health and Human Services, *Medicare Reimbursement for Existing End-Stage Renal Disease Drugs* (Washington, D.C.: OIG, 2004).

28. MedPAC, "Report to Congress: Issues in a Modernized Medicare Program," p. 113.

29. Dave Parks, "Patients Feel They're Mistreated: Dialysis Centers Focus on Profits, Advocates Say," *Birmingham News*, vol. 119, no. 251, November 19, 2006, p. 1A.

30. Shalleen M. Barendse, Jane Speight, and Clare Bradley, "The Renal Treatment Satisfaction Questionnaire (RTSQ): A Measure of Satisfaction with Treatment for Chronic Kidney Failure," *American Journal of Kidney Diseases*, vol. 45, no. 3 (March 2005), pp. 572–579.

31. Laura C. Plantinga et al., "Frequency of Patient-Physician Contact in Chronic Kidney Disease Care and Achievement of Clinical Performance Targets," *International Journal for Quality in Health Care*, vol. 17, no. 2 (April 2005), pp. 115–121.

32. U.S. Renal Data System, Figs. 5.21–5.26, 5.50, Fig. 1.50.

33. Ibid., Figs. 5.12 and 5.14.

34. Ibid., Section Ten, *Researcher's Guide*, Slides 5.10 and 5.11.

35. Ibid., Fig. 10.29.

36. Ibid., Fig. 5.52, Fig. 1.23.

37. Ibid., Fig. 5.28.

38. Ibid., Section Ten, *Researcher's Guide*.

39. Thomas Maeder, "The Orphan Drug Backlash," *Scientific American*, vol. 288, no. 5 (May 2003), p. 80; and Merrill Goozner, "The Making and Selling of a Star Drug, a Prescription for Profit," *Chicago Tribune*, May 24, 1999.

40. Medicare Payment Advisory Committee (MedPAC), "Outpatient Dialysis Services: Assessing Payment Adequacy and Updating Payments" (Washington, D.C.: MedPAC, 2006), p. 120.

41. MedPAC, "Report to Congress: Issues in a Modernized Medicare Program," p. 96.

42. U.S. Renal Data System, Table K.3; and MedPAC, "Report to Congress: Issues in a Modernized Medicare Program," Table 4-3, p. 96.

43. Dennis Cotter et al., "Translating Epoetin Research into Practice: The Role of Government and the Use of Scientific Evidence; Untested Research Findings That Have Been Translated Too Quickly into Policy That Encourages Large Epoetin Doses," *Health Affairs*, vol. 25, no. 5 (September–October 2006), pp. 1249–1260.

44. Cotter et al., "Translating Epoetin Research . . . ," p. 43.

45. Anatole Besarab et al., "The Effects of Normal as Compared with Low Hematocrit Values in Patients with Cardiac Disease Who Are Receiving Hemodialysis and Epoetin," *New England Journal of Medicine*, vol. 339, no. 9 (August 27, 1998), pp. 584–590.

46. Cotter et al., "Translating Epoetin Research into Practice," pp. 1249–1260.

47. The FDA posted a Public Health Advisory on epoetin alfa and darbepoetin alfa on its Web site. For additional information about the advisory, please use the following link: http://www.fda.gov/cder/drug/infopage/RHE/default.htm.

48. Robert Langreth et al., "Amgen Arrives—Company of the Year," www.forbes.com, accessed January 10, 2006.

49. David P. Hamilton, "As Other Biotechs Sink, Amgen, Genentech Soar," *Wall Street Journal*, November 18, 2002, p. A1.

50. Laurie McGinley and David P. Hamilton, "Drug Dispute Is Dragged to Capitol Hill—Amgen, Johnson & Johnson Take Battle over Anemia Drug to Legislators," *Wall Street Journal*, April 22, 2003, p. A4; and Regina E. Herzlinger and JoEllen Slurzberg, "Note on Health Insurance Coverage, Coding, and Payment," HBS Case No. 304-005, rev. August 2006 (Boston: Harvard Business School Publishing, 2003).

51. "Amgen's Fourth Quarter 2005," *Business Wire*, January 26, 2006; Langreth et al., "Amgen Arrives . . ."

52. "List of the Best-Selling Drugs in the Nation," *AP Newswires*, September 30, 2004; Maeder, "The Orphan Drug Backlash."

53. Regina E. Herzlinger, "ABC Pharmaceuticals," HBS No. 193-168, rev. August 9, 2006 (Boston: Harvard Business School Publishing, 1993); and Geeta Anand, "The Most Expensive Drugs," *Wall Street Journal*, November 16, 2005, p. A1.

54. Carl Rados, "Orphan Products: Hope for People with Rare Diseases," *FDA Consumer*, vol. 37, no. 6 (November–December 2003), pp. 10–15; and Marlene E. Haffner, "Adopting Orphan Drugs—Two Dozen Years of Treating Rare Diseases," *New England Journal of Medicine*, vol. 354, no. 5 (February 2, 2006), pp. 445–447.

55. Thomas Maeder, "The Orphan Drug Backlash."

56. Micah L. Sifry and Nancy Watzman, "Corporate Conventions: How Millions of Dollars Will Buy Influence in New York and Boston," *LA Weekly*, July 23–29, 2006, www.commondreams.org; also opensecrets.org.

57. McGinley and Hamilton, "Drug Dispute Is Dragged to Capital Hill," p. A4.

58. MedPAC, "Report to Congress: Issues in a Modernized Medicare Program," p. 88.

59. Ibid.

60. Adapted from Center for Responsive Politics, www.opensecrets.org, accessed November 2006.

61. Regina E. Herzlinger and Jeff Grahling, "Note on Financing of the U.S. Health Care Sector," HBS No. 304-039, rev. August 29, 2006 (Boston: Harvard Business School Publishing, 2003).

62. Sharon Begley and Claudia Kalb with Theodore Gideonse, "One Man's Quest to Cure Cancer [Dr. Moses Judah Folkman]," *Newsweek*, vol. 131, no. 20 (May 18, 1998).

63. Patrick J. O'Connor, "Commentary—Improving Diabetes Care by Combating Clinical Inertia," *Health Services Research*, vol. 40, no. 6, Part 1 (December 2005), p. 1854

64. Cynthia M. Boyd et al., "Clinical Practice Guidelines and Quality of Care for Older Patients with Multiple Comorbid Diseases: Implications for Pay for Performance," *Journal of the American Medical Association*, vol. 294, no. 6 (August 10, 2005), pp. 716–724; and Nancy J. O. Birkmeyer et al., "Partnering with Payers to Improve Surgical Quality: The Michigan Plan," *Surgery*, vol. 138, no. 5 (June 24, 2005), pp. 815–820.

65. www.medicare.gov/Dialysis/Include/DataSection/Questions, accessed March 24, 2007.

66. Robert S. Lockridge Jr., "The Direction of End-Stage Renal Disease Reimbursement in the United States," *Seminars in Dialysis*, vol. 17, no. 2 (March–April 2004), pp. 125–130.

67. U.S. Renal Data System, Fig. 11.16.

Chapter 6

1. "Putting America on Wheels," *Economist*, December 23, 1999, p. 82.
2. Allan Nevins with the collaboration of Frank Ernest Hill, *Ford: The Times, the Man, the Company* (New York: Scribner's, 1954), pp. 646–647; Price per capita income: Robert F. Martin, *National Income in the United States, 1799–1938* (New York: National Foundation Conference Board, 1939).
3. Harold Katz, *The Decline of Competition in the Automobile Industry, 1920–1940* (New York: Arno, 1977), p. 41.
4. Maurice Allais, "An Outline of My Main Contributions to Economic Science," *American Economic Review*, vol. 87, no. 6 (December 1997), pp. 3–12.
5. "Alain Enthoven," *Marquis Who's Who in America* (Providence, N.J.: Reed Reference, 2005); Alain C. Enthoven and Richard Kronick, "Universal Health Insurance Through Incentives Reform," *Journal of the American Medical Association*, vol. 265, no. 19 (May 15, 1991), pp. 2532–2536.
6. Robert Lilienfeld, *The Rise of Systems Theory: An Ideological Analysis* (New York: Wiley, 1978), pp. 103–104.
7. David Halberstam, *The Best and the Brightest* (Greenwich, Conn.: Fawcett Publications, 1973), p. 278.
8. Ibid.
9. Clark Murdock, "McNamara, Systems Analysis, and the Systems Analysis' Office," *Sociological Review*, vol. 22, no. 1 (February 1974), p. 93.
10. Lilienfeld, *The Rise of Systems Theory*, p. 122.
11. Charles J. Hitch and Roland N. McKean, *The Economics of Defense in the Nuclear Age* (New York: Atheneum, 1966), p. v.
12. Adam Peck, "Easier to Explain Than Execute," *Managed Healthcare*, August 1993, p. 10.
13. John Hubner, "The Abandoned Father of Health Care Reform," *New York Times Magazine*, July 18, 1993, p. 24.
14. Ibid.
15. Arnold S. Relman, "The New Medical-Industrial Complex," *New England Journal of Medicine*, vol. 303, no. 17 (October 23, 1980), pp. 963–970.
16. "Medicine as Enterprise," Editorial, *New York Times*, October 30, 1980, p. A26.
17. See, for example, Geoffrey Smith, "The Doctor's Rebuttal," *Forbes*, September 26, 1983, p. 38.
18. Pushkal P. Garg et al., "Effect of the Ownership of Dialysis Facilities on Patients' Survival and Referral for Transplantation," *New England Journal of Medicine*, vol. 341, no. 22 (November 25, 1999), p. 1653.
19. Medicare Payment Advisory Commission (MedPac), "Report to the Congress: Issues in a Modernized Medicare Program" (Washington, D.C.: MedPac, 2005).
20. Physicians' Working Group for Single-Payer Health Insurance, "Proposal of the Physicians' Working Group for Single-Payer National Health Insurance," *Journal of the American Medical Association*, vol. 290 (August 2003), pp. 798–805.
21. Regina E. Herzlinger and William S. Krasker, "Who Profits from Nonprofits," *Harvard Business Review*, January–February 1987, pp. 93–106. For critiques of their accounting in another field, see David Dranove and Michael Millenson, "Medical Bankruptcy: Myth Versus Fact," Health Affairs Web Exclusive, January–June 2006, pp. W74–83.
22. Arnold S. Relman, "Book Reviews. Consumer-Driven Health Care: Implications for Providers, Payers, and Policy-Makers," *New England Journal of Medi-*

cine, vol. 350, no. 2 (May 20, 2004), pp. 2217–2218; and Regina E. Herzlinger, ed., *Consumer-Driven Health Care: Implications for Providers, Payers, and Policymakers* (San Francisco: Jossey-Bass, 2004).

23. Richard A. Knox, "BU Dean Center of Conflict at Medical Society," *Boston Globe*, October 27, 1999.
24. Arnold S. Relman, "Money Corroding Medical Journal's Prestige," *Boston Globe*, December 12, 1999, p. D3.
25. "Does Journal's Ethical Crisis Threaten Research?" *American Health Line*, October 31, 2000.
26. See, for example, David U. Himmelstein and Stephanie J. Woolhandler, "A National Health Program for the United States. A Physicians' Proposal," *New England Journal of Medicine*, vol. 320, no. 2 (January 12, 1989), pp. 102–108.
27. R. G. Evans et al., "Controlling Health Expenditures—The Canadian Reality," *New England Journal of Medicine*, vol. 320, no. 9 (March 2, 1989), pp. 571–577.
28. Sean Gordon and Andrew Mills, "Quebec Ruling Sparks Renewed Debate Over 2-Tier System," *Toronto Star*, June 10, 2005, p. A1.
29. Christopher Mason, "Canadian Doctors Elect Advocate of Larger Private Role in Medicine," *New York Times*, August 23, 2006, p. A3.
30. James Frogue, "A High Price for Patients," Heritage Foundation, Backgrounder no. 1398, September 26, 2000, p. 14.
31. Fraser Institute, *Waiting Your Turn* (Vancouver: Fraser Institute, 2005).
32. James Brooke, "Full Hospitals Make Canadians Wait and Look South," *New York Times*, January 16, 2000, p. A3.
33. Rita Daly, "Hospital Grades Out Today," *Toronto Star*, November 1, 1998, p. A1.
34. Fraser Institute, *Waiting Your Turn: Hospital Waiting Lists in Canada, 16th Ed.*, (Vancouver: The Fraser Institute, October 2006).
35. Ibid., p. 5.
36. MRI units number per million population, 2002—Japan (highest): 35.3; OECD: 7.3; Canada: 4.3; and Mexico (lowest): 0.2. CT scanners, number per million population, 2002—Japan (highest): 92.6; OECD: 17.6; Canada: 10.3; and Mexico (lowest): 1.5. Organization for Economic Co-Operation and Development (OECD), *Health at a Glance: OECD Indicators 2005* (Paris: OECD, 2005), pp. 46–47.
37. Sheryl Ubelacker, "Outbreak in Quebec Hospital Raises National Concern," *Globe and Mail*, August 5, 2004, p. A13; and "Bacterial Infection Kills 100 Patients at Quebec Hospital in 18 Months: Study," *Canadian Press Newswire*, August 4, 2004.
38. "The Doctor's Dilemma," *The Economist*, January 22, 2000, p. 55.
39. Sarah Lyall, "In Britain's Health Service, Sick Itself, Cancer Cure Is Dismal," *New York Times*, February 10, 2000, p. A1.
40. Karen Donelan et al., "The Cost of Health System Change: Public Discontent in Five Nations," *Health Affairs*, vol. 18, no. 3 (May–June 1999), p. 214.
41. Cathy Schoen et al., "Taking the Pulse of Health Care Systems: Experiences of Patients with Health Problems in Six Countries," *Health Affairs*, Web Exclusive, 2005, pp. W5-509.
42. Michael Marmot, "Acting on the Evidence to Reduce Inequalities in Health," Perspective, *Health Affairs*, vol. 18, no. 3 (May–June 1999), p. 178.
43. William J. Mackillop et al., "Associations between Community Income and Cancer Incidence in Canada and the United States," *Cancer*, vol. 89, no. 4 (August 15, 2000), pp. 901–912.

44. David A. Alter et al., "A Survey of Provider Experiences and Perceptions of Preferential Access to Cardiovascular Care in Ontario, Canada," *Annals of Internal Medicine*, vol. 129, no. 7 (1998), pp. 567–572.
45. Lawrance D. Brown, "Management by Objection? Public Policies to Protect Choice in Health Plans," *Medical Care Research and Review*, vol. 56, supp. (March 1999), pp. 159–162.
46. Carlos Estrada et al., "Health Literacy and Numeracy," *Journal of the American Medical Association*, vol. 282, no. 6 (August 11, 1999), p. 527.
47. Robert Wood Johnson Foundation, *Community Snapshots Consumer Survey* (Princeton, N.J.: Robert Wood Johnson Foundation, 1995); Princeton Survey Research Associates, *National Survey of Americans' Views on Managed Care* (Princeton, N.J.: Princeton Survey Research Associates, 1997), p. 44.
48. Peter J. Cunningham et al., "Do Consumers Know How Their Health Plan Works?" *Health Affairs*, March/April, 2001, vol 20, no. 2, p. 178.
49. Jon R. Gabel et al., KPMG Peat Marwick, *When Employers Choose Health Plans Do NCQA Accredition and HEDIS Data Count?* (New York: Commonwealth Fund, 1998).
50. See, for example, J. H. Hibbard and J. Jewett, "Will Quality Report Cards Help Consumers?" *Health Affairs*, vol. 16, no. 3 (May–June 1997), pp. 218–228.
51. See, for example, Pacific Business Group on Health, *Report on Qualitative Research Findings: California Health Care Smart Shopper Public Education Campaign* (San Francisco: Pacific Business Group on Health, March 1998).
52. B. E. Landon et al., "Health Plan Characteristics and Consumers' Assessments of Quality," *Health Affairs*, vol. 20, no. 2 (March–April 2001), p. 274.
53. D. W. Bates and A. W. Gawande, "The Impact of the Internet on Quality Measurement," *Health Affairs*, vol. 19, no. 6 (November–December 2000), p. 106. For an expanded discussion of this topic, see also Regina E. Herzlinger and S. Bokser, "Note on Health Care Accountability and Information in the U.S. Health Care System," HBS Case No. 302-007, rev. August 2006 (Boston: Harvard Business School Publishing, 2001).
54. Bates and Gawande, "The Impact of the Internet on Quality Measurement."
55. Kaiser Family Foundation, "Trends and Implications in the Changing Health Care Marketplace, 2002," May 2002, Exhibit 5.9, p. 56, updated with 2001data from the American Medical Association, 2001 Patient Care Physician Survey.
56. K. I. Shine, "Health Care Quality and How to Achieve It," *Academic Medicine Journal of the Association of American Medical Colleges*, vol. 77, no. 1 (January 2002), pp. 91–99.
57. Paul Heiney, *The Nuts and Bolts of Life: Willem Kolff and the Invention of the Kidney Machine* (Stroud: Sutton, 2002).
58. "A Father of Invention," *Wall Street Journal*, September 28, 2002, p. 5.
59. Cynthia M. Piccolo, MedHunter.com, transplant timeline, accessed August 15, 2006.
60. Francis L. Delmonico, "Interview with Dr. Joseph Murray," *American Journal of Transplantation*, vol. 2, no. 9 (October 2002), pp. 803–808.
61. Scott Allen, "The Power of Perseverance: Dr. Joseph Murray Virtually Created a New Field of Medicine; Scientists of Today Could Learn from His Example," *Boston Globe*, December 14, 2004, p. B13.
62. Joseph Murray, "The First Successful Organ Transplants in Man," Nobel Prize acceptance speech, 1990.
63. Ibid.
64. Ibid.

Chapter 7

1. Likely, Jack Morgan would receive the amount of money men his age typically spend on health insurance. The public or private payer would risk-adjust his insurer for Jack's health status. Risk adjustment, the process of adjusting the transfer for the person's level of illness, is also discussed in Chapter 11.
2. Rebecca Voelker, "Cost of Transplant vs. Dialysis," *Journal of the American Medical Association*, vol. 281, no. 24 (June 23, 1999), p. 2277.
3. Alternatively, Jack's insurers or providers could have received more than $40,000 if Jack were sicker than the average or less if he were healthier. The pros and cons of prices that adjust for the levels of illness when given to Jack or his insurer or his provider are discussed further in this chapter and in Chapter 11.
4. Marlene Busko, "Survival Better with Short, Daily Dialysis Than with Conventional HD," *Medscape Medical News*, December 13, 2006.
5. Peter Zweifel et al., eds., *Regulation of Health: Case Studies of Sweden and Switzerland* (Boston: Kluwer Academic, 1998), Developments in Health Economics and Public Policy, No. 7; Peter Zweifel and Willard G. Manning, "Moral Hazard and Consumer Incentives in Health Care," in *Handbook of Health Economics 2000*, eds., A. J. Culyer and J. P. Newhouse (Amsterdam: North Holland Press, 2000), chap. 8; Gregory C. Pope et al., "Risk Adjustment of Medicare Capitation Payments Using the CMS–HCC Model," *Health Care Financing Review*, vol. 25, no. 4 (summer 2004), pp. 119–141; Wynand P. M. M. van de Ven et al., "Health-Adjusted Premium Subsidies in the Netherlands," *Health Affairs*, vol. 23, no. 3 (2004); Peter Zweifel and Michael Breuer, "The Case for Risk-Based Premiums in Public Health Insurance," *Health Economics, Policy and Law*, vol. 1, no. 2 (April 2006), pp. 171–188; Peter Zweifel, personal correspondence to Regina E. Herzlinger, May 24, 2006; for information on risk adjustment in Holland, www.cvz.nl, Jeroen van der Wolk, personal correspondence to Regina E. Herzlinger, May 24, 2006, and Wynand P. M. M. van de Ven, personal correspondence to Regina E. Herzlinger, May 27, 2006.
6. Greg Scandlen, "Insurance Mandates Aren't the Answer to Uninsured," *Health Care News*, March 2007, p. 12.
7. Robert Pear, "Experts See Peril in Bush Health Plan," *New York Times*, January 23, 2007.
8. "Aetna Releases Broadest Study to Date of Consumer-Directed Plans," http://www.aetna.com/news/2006/pr_20061001.htm.
9. JoAnn M. Laing, President, Information Strategies, Inc., and Don Mazzella, Publisher and Editor, *Healthcare & You*, and COO, HSAfinder.com; "CIGNA Choice Fund Study Provides New Insights on Consumer Decision-Making in Consumer-Driven Health Plans," *PRNewswire*, FirstCall, February 2, 2006; "Three-Year Study Shows Consumer-Driven Health Plans Continue to Stimulate Positive Changes in Consumer Health Behavior," *Business Wire*, United-Health Group, July 12, 2006; "Aetna Releases Broadest Study to Date of Consumer-Directed Plans," http://www.aetna.com/news/2006/pr_20061001.htm; and McKinsey & Company, North American Payer Provider Practice, "Consumer-Directed Health Plan Report—Early Evidence Is Promising," June 2005.
10. U.S. Census Bureau, *Statistical Abstract of the United States, 2001* (Washington, D.C.: Government Printing Office, 2002), Table No. 664, p. 435; also "New Health Plan Fares Poorly at 'U': Workers Pick Old Favorites over Newcomers," Minneapolis, Minn. *Star Tribune*, December 15, 2001, p. 1D.

11. See American Diabetes Association's Web site at diabetes.org.

12. Steven M. Asch et al., "Measuring Underuse of Necessary Care Among Elderly Medicare Beneficiaries Using Inpatient and Outpatient Claims," *Journal of the American Medical Association*, vol. 284, no. 18 (November 8, 2000), pp. 2325–2333.

13. Marcia A. Testa and Donald C. Simonson, "Health Economic Benefits and Quality of Life During Improved Glycemic Control in Patients with Type 2 Diabetes Mellitus: A Randomized, Controlled, Double-Blind Trial," *Journal of the American Medical Association*, vol. 280, no. 17 (November 4, 1998), pp. 1490–1496.

14. American Diabetes Association (ADA), "Economic Costs of Diabetes in the U.S. in 2002," *Diabetes Care*, vol. 26, no. 3 (March 2003), pp. 917–931.

15. American Diabetes Association, "Economic Consequences of Diabetes Mellitus in the U.S. in 1997," *Diabetes Care*, vol. 21, no. 2 (February 1998), pp. 296–309.

16. Regina E. Herzlinger, *Market-Driven Health Care: Who Wins, Who Loses in the Transformation of America's Largest Service Industry* (New York: Perseus, 2001); and Robert Wood Johnson Foundation, *A Portrait of the Chronically Ill in America, 2001* (Princeton, N.J.: Robert Wood Johnson Foundation, 2002), p. 39.

17. Benjamin B. Druss et al., "Comparing the National Economic Burden of Five Chronic Conditions," *Health Affairs*, vol. 20, no. 6 (November–December 2001), pp. 233–241.

18. "Mass Customization," *The Economist*, July 14, 2001, p. 65.

19. For more on how Dr. Cooley scaled up the Texas Heart Institute, see Denton A. Cooley and John W. Adams, Jr., "Package Pricing at the Texas Heart Institute," in Regina E. Herzlinger, ed., *Consumer-Driven Health Care: Implications for Providers, Payers, and Policymakers* (San Francisco: Jossey-Bass, 2004), Chap. 56, pp. 612–618.

20. James L. Heskett, "Shouldice Hospital Limited," HBS Case No. 683-068, rev. June 2, 2003 (Boston: Harvard Business School Publishing, 1983).

21. James C. Robinson, "Financial Capital and Intellectual Capital in Physician Practice Management," *Health Affairs*, vol. 17, no. 4 (July–August 1998), pp. 53–74.

22. Stephen M. Shortell et al., "The New World of Managed Care: Creating Organized Delivery Systems," *Health Affairs*, vol. 13, no. 5 (winter 1994), pp. 46–65.

23. See, for example, Peter P. Budetti et al., "Physician and Health System Integration," *Health Affairs*, vol. 21, no. 1 (January–February 2002), pp. 203–210.

24. Ranjay Gulati et al., "Strategic Networks," *Strategic Management Journal*, vol. 21, no. 3 (March 2000), special issue: "Strategic Networks," pp. 203–215; and Ranjay Gulati and Harbir Singh, "The Architecture of Cooperation: Managing Coordination Costs and Appropriation Concerns in Strategic Alliances," *Administrative Science Quarterly*, vol. 43, no. 4 (December 1998), pp. 781–814.

25. Kerry A. Dolan and Robyn Meredith, "Ghost Cars, Ghost Brands," *Forbes*, April 30, 2001, p. 109.

26. Ibid.; and Fred Andrews, "Dell, It Turns Out, Has a Better Idea," *New York Times*, January 26, 2000, p. C12.

27. Herzlinger, *Market-Driven Health Care*.

28. Ibid.

39. Ibid.

30. Ibid.

31. Vince Galloro and Jeff Tieman, "Hitting the Brakes: Hospital Merger-and-Acquisition Activity Declines for Third Consecutive Year," *Modern Healthcare*, January 14, 2002, p. 22.

32. Arista Marketing Associates, *2000 Survey of Integrated Delivery Systems* (Northbrook, Ill.: Arista Marketing Associates, July 15, 2000).

33. Endnote intentionally deleted.

34. Regina E. Herzlinger "Specialization and Its Discontents," *Circulation*, 109 (May 25, 2004), pp. 2376–2378.

35. Regina E. Herzlinger, "Can We Control Health Care Costs?" *Harvard Business Review*, vol. 56, no. 2 (March–April 1978), pp. 102–110.

36. Institute of Medicine (IOM), *Crossing the Quality Chasm: A New Health System for the 21st Century* (Washington, D.C.: National Academies Press, 2001), p. 174.

37. Scott Cook, chairman, Intuit, various e-mails to Regina Herzlinger, 2006 and 2007.

38. Gary McWilliams, "Big Employers Plan Electronic Health Records," *Wall Street Journal*, November 29, 2006, p. B1.

39. Personalized Medicine Coalition (PMC), *The Case for Personalized Medicine* (Washington, D.C.: PMC, November 2006), p. 3.

40. Regina E. Herzlinger, "Diagnostic Genomics," HBS Case No. 302-004, rev. December 2006 (Boston: Harvard Business School Publishing, 2001).

41. Regina E. Herzlinger and Mark P. Allyn, "Medtronic: Patient Management Initiative," HBS Case No. 302-005, rev. August 2006 (Boston: Harvard Business School Publishing, 2001).

42. C. Daniel Mullins et al., "The Impact of Pipeline Drugs on Drug Spending Growth," *Health Affairs*, vol. 20, no. 5 (September–October 2001), p. 215; see also Victor R. Fuchs and Harold C. Sox Jr., "Physicians' Views of the Relative Importance of Thirty Medical Innovations," *Health Affairs*, vol. 20, no. 5 (September–October 2001), pp. 30–32.

43. David M. Cutler and Mark McClellan, "Is Technological Change in Medicine Worth It?" *Health Affairs*, vol. 20, no. 5 (September–October 2001), pp. 11–29.

44. J. D. Kleinke, "The Price of Progress: Prescription Drugs in the Health Care Market," *Health Affairs*, vol. 20, no. 5 (September–October 2001), pp. 43–60.

45. Minah Kim, Robert J. Blendon, and John M. Benson, "How Interested Are Americans in New Medical Technologies? A Multicountry Comparison," *Health Affairs*, vol. 20, no. 5 (September–October 2001), pp. 194–201.

46. Kaiser Family Foundation, Menlo Park, Calif., and Health Research and Educational Trust, Chicago, Ill., "Employer Health Benefits 2006," p. 4.

47. Thomas Rice et al., "Workers and Their Health Plans: Free to Choose?" *Health Affairs*, vol. 21, no. 1 (January–February 2002), pp. 182–187.

48. With deep thanks to Ray Herschman and Mark Tierney for their review of this section.

49. Gail Dutton, "The Shrinking Pool of Plans," *Business & Health*, Supp: *The State of Health Care in America, 2001*, vol. 6 (July 31, 2001), p. 14.

50. Mark Penn, "Health Care Is Back," *Blueprint*, April 1, 2000, p. 70.

51. American Customer Satisfaction Index, University of Michigan, February 15, 2005; Retail Trade; Finance & Insurance; Health Care; Food Service.

52. Dr. Leo Henikoff, personal communication to Regina E. Herzlinger, 2002.

53. Professor James Fries, personal correspondence to Regina E. Herzlinger.

54. With deep thanks to Ray Herschman and Mark Tierney for their review of this section.

55. Mark Merlis et al., *Rising Out-of-Pocket Spending for Medical Care: A Growing Strain on Family Budgets* (New York: Commonwealth Fund, February 2006).

56. Gail Shearer, "Hidden from View: The Burden of Health Care Costs" (Washington, D.C.: Consumers Union, January 22, 1998), unnumbered, Table 5a; Wenke Hwang et al., "Out-of-Pocket Medical Spending for Care of Chronic Conditions," *Health Affairs*, vol. 20, no. 6 (November–December 2001), pp. 267–278; and Druss et al., "Comparing the National Economic Burden of Five Chronic Conditions."

57. Aparna Mathur, *Medical Bills and Bankruptcy Filings*, Working Paper (Washington, D.C.: American Enterprise Institute, July 19, 2006).

58. Jane Gross, "Elder-Care Costs Deplete Savings of a Generation," *New York Times*, December 30, 2006, p. 1.

59. Ron Z. Goetzel et al., "Health, Absence, Disability, and Presenteeism Cost Estimates of Certain Physical and Mental Health Conditions Affecting U.S. Employers," *Journal of Occupational and Environmental Medicine*, vol. 46, no. 4 (April 2004), pp. 398–412.

60. John L. Sinclair, "Total System Costs and the Case of the Executive's Hernia," *Benefits Quarterly*, vol. 14, no. 1 (first quarter, 1998), pp. 1, 14, 45–54.

61. Rachel M. Werner et al., "The 'Hassle Factor': What Motivates Physicians to Manipulate Reimbursement Rules?" *Archives of Internal Medicine*, vol. 162, no. 10 (May 27, 2002), pp. 1134–1139.

62. Judy Greenwald, "Taking Cost Control to Another Level: More HMOs Offering Tiered Health Plan Options," *Business Insurance*, February 11, 2002, p. T3.

63. Sally Trude et al., "Employer-Sponsored Health Insurance: Pressing Problems, Incremental Changes," *Health Affairs*, vol. 21, no. 1 (January–February 2002), pp. 66–75; and D. Stires, "The Coming Crash in Health Care," *Fortune*, October 14, 2002, pp. 205–212.

64. Steven M. Asch et al., "Who Is at Greatest Risk for Receiving Poor-Quality Health Care?" *New England Journal of Medicine*, vol. 354, no. 11 (March 16, 2006), pp. 1147–1156.

65. Scott Miller and Karen Lundegaard, "An Engineering Icon Slips—Quality Ratings for Mercedes Drop in Several Surveys," *Wall Street Journal*, February 4, 2002, p. B1.

66. Jeff Green, "Safety in Numbers," *BusinessWeek*, May 7, 2001, p. 127.

67. J. D. Power and Associates, 2005.

68. Endnote intentionally deleted.

69. Peter Brimelow, "The Economics of Panty Hose," *Forbes*, August 23, 1999, p. 70.

70. Alissa J. Rubin, "Xerox May Pay Workers to Buy Own Insurance," *Los Angeles Times*, December 4, 1999, p. A1.

71. Dutton, "The Shrinking Pool of Plans."

72. "A Conversation with Peter Lee, Quality Concerns Ensure Consumers Will Gain Clout," *Managed Care*, January 2002, p. 44.

73. Karen Damato, "Index Funds: 25 Years in Pursuit of the Average," *Wall Street Journal*, April 9, 2001, pp. R4, R9.

74. Ici.org, accessed November 29, 2006.

75. See www.vanguard.com.

76. Endnote intentionally deleted.

77. Stephen Barr, "Looking for Ways to Soften the Blow of Rising Health Insurance Costs," *Washington Post*, December 12, 2002, p. B2.
78. William J. Dennis Jr., "Wages, Health Insurance and Pension Plans: The Relationship between Employee Compensation and Small Business Owner Income," *Small Business Economics*, vol. 15 (December 2000), pp. 247–263.
79. Maggie Jackson, "For Many Generation X'ers, Grass Is Greener at Home," *New York Times*, December 11, 2001, p. C2.
80. Paul Fronstin, "Trends in Health Insurance Coverage: A Look at Early 2001 Data," *Health Affairs*, vol. 21, no. 1 (January–February 2002), p. 191, Exhibits 2, 3.
81. Cathy A. Cowan et al., "Burden of Health Care Costs: Businesses, Households, and Governments, 1987–2000," *Health Care Financing Review*, vol. 23, no. 3 (spring 2002), pp. 131–135.
82. Center on Budget and Policy Priorities (CBPP), "The Number of Uninsured Americans Continued to Rise in 2004," www.cbpp.org/8-30-05health.htm, accessed November 29, 2006.
83. U.S. Census Bureau, *Statistical Abstract of the United States, 1999* (Washington, D.C.: Government Printing Office, 2000), p. 573, Table 911.
84. Kaiser Commission on Medicaid and the Uninsured, *The Uninsured: A Primer, Key Facts about Americans without Health Insurance* (Washington, D.C.: Kaiser Family Foundation, October 2006), www.kff.org/uninsured/upload/7451-021.pdf, accessed November 29, 2006.
85. Dana E. McMurtry, vice president, health policy and analysis, WellPoint Pharmacy Management, personal communication to Regina E. Herzlinger. The $80 figure relates to employee-only contracts for subscribers aged 18 to 39 on the Basic PPO plan.
86. "New Health Plan Fares Poorly at 'U': Workers Pick Old Favorites over Newcomers," Minneapolis, Minn. *Star Tribune*, December 15, 2001, p. 1D.
87. Sarah R. Collins, Testimony before the House Ways and Means Committee , June 28, 2006.
88. Stacy Dale et al., "The Effects of Cash and Counseling on Personal Care Services and Medicaid Costs in Arkansas," *Health Affairs*, November 19, 2003, Web Exclusive, pp. W3-566–575.
89. "As Medicaid Balloons, Watchdog Force Shrinks," *New York Times*, July 19, 2005, p. A1.
90. Martin Kitchener et al., "Home and Community-Based Services: Medicaid Research and Demonstration Waivers" (San Francisco : UCSF National Center for Personal Assistance Services, November 2004).
91. Jeff Stensland, South Carolina goverment, to Regina Herzlinger, May 18, 2006.
92. cms.hhs.gov/NationalHealthExpendData.
93. Peter Cunningham and Jessica May, "Tracking Report: Medicaid Patients Increasingly Concentrated among Physicians," Washington, D.C.: Center for Studying Health System Change, No. 16, August 2006.
94. Enrollment and satisfaction data: JoAnn M. Laing, President, Information Strategies, Inc., and HSA author, and Don Mazzella, Publisher and Editor, *Healthcare & You*, and COO, personal communications; Results: McKinsey & Company "Consumer-Directed Health Plan Report" (McKinsey & Company: North American Payor Provider Practice, June 2005), Exhibit 3.
95. John Mackey, "Whole Foods Market's CD Health Plan," State Policy Network Annual Meeting, October 2004, www.worldcongress.com/news/Mackey—transcript, accessed January 12, 2005.

Chapter 8

1. Regina E. Herzlinger and Ramin Parsa-Parsi, "Consumer-Driven Health Care: Lessons from Switzerland," *Journal of the American Medical Association*, vol. 292, no. 10 (September 8, 2004).

2. Peter Zweifel, "Switzerland," *Journal of Health Politics, Policy, and Law*, vol. 25, no. 5 (2000), pp. 937–944.

3. Robert E. Moffit et al., , "Perspectives on the European Health Care Systems: Some Lessons for America," *Heritage Foundation Lectures*, no. 711 (July 9, 2001), pp. 15–16.

4. *Statistik über die Krankenversicherung 2001* (Bern, Switzerland: Bundesamt für Sozialversicherung, 2002), pp. 147, 148.

5. *Schweizerische Sozialversicherungsstatistik 2003* (Bern, Switzerland: Bundesamt für Sozialversicherung, 2003). pp. 145, 157.

6. VISANA, *Leistungsübersicht Ausgabe 2002* (Muri/Bern, Switzerland: Schweiz, Visana Versicherungen AG, 2002).

7. *Statistik der obligatorischen Krankenversicherung 2002* (Bern, Switzerland: Bundesamt für Gesundheit, 2002). p. 94.

8. *Kommunikation,* (Gümligen, Switzerland: Innova Versicherungen, June 2003). Available at http://www.innova.ch/privat/angebote/index.html. Accessed August 11, 2004.

9. *Statistik der Wahlbaren Frachisen in der Krankenverischerun,* (Bern, Switzerland: Bundesamt für Sozialversicherung; 2000), Tabelle A 4.2. p. 65.

10. Konstantin Beck et al., "Risk Adjustment in Switzerland," *Health Policy*, vol. 65, no. 1 (July 2003), pp. 63–74; and Urs Wunderlin, personal correspondence to Regina E. Herzlinger, April 18, 2006. For various approaches to risk adjustment, see Regina E. Herzlinger, *Consumer-Driven Health Care* (San Francisco: Jossey-Bass, 2004).

11. John K. Iglehart, "Revisiting the Canadian Health Care System," *New England Journal of Medicine*, vol. 342, no. 26 (June 29, 2000), pp. 2007–2012; C. D. Naylor, "Health Care in Canada: Incrementalism under Fiscal Duress," *Health Affairs*, vol. 18, no. 3 (May–June 1999); Sarah Lyall, "In Britain's Health Service, Sick Itself, Cancer Cure Is Dismal," *New York Times*, February 10, 2000, p. A1; Michael Marmot, "Acting on the Evidence to Reduce Inequalities in Health," *Health Affairs*, vol. 18, no. 3 (May–June 1999), p. 42; and R. M. Martin, "NHS Waiting Lists and Evidence of National or Local Failure: Analysis of Health Service Data," *British Medical Journal*, vol. 326, no. 7382 (January 25, 2003), p. 188.

12. Beth E. Quill and Mary Desvignes-Kendrick, "Reconsidering Health Disparities," *Public Health Reports*, vol. 116, no. 6 (November–December 2001), pp. 505–514; and Dana P. Goldman and James P. Smith. "Can Patient Self-Management Help Explain the SES Health Gradient?" *Proceedings of the National Academy of Sciences*, vol. 99, no. 16 (August 6, 2002), pp. 10929–10934.

13. Mitchell D. Wong et al., "Contribution of Major Diseases to Disparities in Mortality," *New England Journal of Medicine*, vol. 347, no. 20 (November 14, 2002), pp. 1585–1592.

14. Gerard F. Andeson et al., "It's the Prices, Stupid: Why the United States Is So Different from Other Countries," *Health Affairs*, vol. 22, no. 3 (May–June 2003), pp. 89–105.

15. *Statistik über die Krankenversicherung 2001*, p. 62.

16. "Blues," *PULSE* (Gwynedd, Pa.: Sherlock Company, June 2003), p. v.

17. *Statistik der obligatorischen Krankenversicherung 2004* (Bern, Switzerland: Bundesamt für Gesundheit (BAG), 2006), Table 1.01, p. 58.
18. Robert Cunningham and Douglas B. Sherlock, "Bounceback: Blues Thrive as Markets Cool toward HMOs," *Health Affairs*, vol. 21, no. 1 (January–February 2002), pp. 24–38; and Diana V. Shaw, "Mergers and Health Care Organizations," *Journal of Health Care Finance*, vol. 29, no. 3 (April 1, 2003), pp. 28–37.
19. *Statistik der obligatorischen Krankenversicherung 2004* (Bern, Switzerland: Bundesamt für Gesundheit (BAG), 2006) Table 5.01, pp. 140–141.
20. Ibid.
21. Peter Zweifel and Chantal Grandchamp, "Measuring the Effect of Cartelization in Medicine: An International Study," in *Measuring Market Power*, ed. Daniel J. Slottje (Oxford, U.K.: Elsevier Science B.V., 2002).
22. Lukas Steinmann and Peter Zweifel, "On the (In)efficiency of Swiss Hospitals," *Applied Economics*, vol. 35, no. 3 (January 1, 2003), pp. 361–370.
23. "Health Savings Accounts Are Not Likely to Stem Rising Health Care Spending," The Commonwealth Foundation, www.cmwf.org. See, for example, Karen Davis, "Will Consumer Directed Care Improve System Performance?" *Health Services Research*, 39 (4), pt. 2, pp. 1219-1233.
24. G. Domenighetti and L. Crivelli, *Versorgungssicherheit in der Ambulanten Medizin im Rahmen der Aufhebung des Vertragszwangs, Kurzfassung von Santésuisse*. Solothurn, Santésuisse; 2001.
25. Endnote intentionally deleted.
26. The New York Stock Exchange's 2000 average charges were 38 percent of 42 countries. (Justin Schuck, "Double Whammy," *Institutional Investor*, November 2001, p. 98. Computed as the ratio of fees and commissions to the average price of stock for the NYSE and in 42 countries, table on p. 98.)
27. Lori Lucas, "Under the Microscope: A Closer Look at the Diversification and Risk Taking Behavior of 401(k) Participants and How Plan Sponsors Can Address Key Investing Issues," *Benefits Quarterly*, vol. 16, no. 4 (Fourth Quarter 2000), pp. 24–30.
28. Jeanne Cummings, "Small Investors Now a Big Bloc," *Wall Street Journal*, September 27, 2002, p. A4; and Edward Wyatt, "Pension Change Puts the Burden on the Worker," *New York Times*, April 5, 2002, p. C2.
29. Employee Benefit Research Institute (EBRI) and Investment Company Institute, "401(k) Plan Asset Allocation, Account Balances, and Loan Activity in 1999," EBRI Issue Brief No. 230 (Washington, D.C.: Employee Benefit Research Institute, February 2001), www.ebri.org.
30. Karen Damato, "Index Funds: 25 Years in Pursuit of the Average," *Wall Street Journal*, April 9, 2001, pp. R4, R9.
31. Andrew A. Samwick and Jonathan Skinner, "How Will Defined Contribution Pension Plans Affect Retirement Income?" (National Bureau of Economic Research: Working Paper No. 6645, July 1998); Arleen Jacobius, "Nice Numbers: Amateurs Do Better Than DB Professionals in Bull Market, Study Shows," *Pensions & Investments*, January 21, 2002, pp. 3 and 77; and Andrew Samwick, private correspondence to Regina E. Herzlinger, April 7, 2002.
32. Employee Benefit Research Institute (EBRI) and Investment Company Institute, "401(k) Plan Asset Allocation, Account Balances, and Loan Activity in 2005," EBRI Issue Brief No. 296 (Washington, D.C.: Employee Benefit Research Institute, August 2006), www.ebri.org.
33. Christopher Palmeri, "Politicians Should Butt Out of Pension Funds," Commentary, *BusinessWeek*, June 11, 2001, p. 150.

34. Florian Zettelmeyer, Fiona M. Scott Morton, and Jorge Silva-Risso, *Cowboys or Cowards: Why Are Internet Car Prices Lower?* Yale School of Management Working Paper, E5-16, October 2001; and "Hotels vs. Brokers: Comparing Rates," *Consumer Reports,* July 2001, p. 13.

35. www.fidelity.com, accessed February 2, 2007.

36. Fidelity Investments, *Building Futures* (Boston: Fidelity Investments, 1999), p. 12.

37. Ibid., p. 17.

38. Ibid., p. 21.

39. Ibid., p. 27.

40. Ibid., pp. 56–57.

41. Employee Benefit Research Institute (EBRI), "401(k) Plan Asset Allocation, Account Balances, and Loan Activity in 2005," pp. 4, 14.

42. Fidelity Investments, *Building Futures,* p. 44.

43. Ibid., pp. 45 and 47.

44. Ibid., pp. 58, 60, and 63.

45. Employee Benefit Research Institute (EBRI), "401(k) Plan Asset Allocation, Account Balances, and Loan Activity in 1999."

46. "Too Much of a Good Thing?" *Institutional Investor,* February 2000, p. 121.

47. Employee Benefit Research Institute (EBRI), "401(k) Plan Asset Allocation, Account Balances, and Loan Activity in 2005," p. 11.

48. Robert Slater, *John Bogle and the Vanguard Experiment* (Chicago: Irwin, 1997), pp. 142, 146.

49. Ibid., pp. 143, 144.

50. Ibid., p. 146.

51. "What Banks Can Learn from Mutual Funds," *U.S. Banker,* March 1998, pp. 45–55.

52. Richard A. Oppel Jr., "Fund Expenses: They're Going Down, Down, Down: Conventionl Wisdom Is Belied by The Numbers," *New York Times,* Money and Business, Mutual Funds Report, July 4, 1999, pp. 11, 28; and John Bogle, personal communication to author, April 4, 2002.

53. Robert Pozen with editorial assistance by Sandra D. Crane, *The Mutual Fund Business* (Cambridge, Mass.: MIT Press, 1998), p. 416.

54. "Small Employers Adopt 401(k) Plans," *Employee Benefit Plan Review,* vol. 52, no. 9 (March 1998), pp. 40–44.

55. "A Newfangled 401(k)," *Institutional Investor,* vol. 33, no. 8 (August 1999), p. 163.

56. Employee Benefit Research Institute (EBRI), "401(k) Plan Asset Allocation, Account Balances, and Loan Activity in 2005," p. 9.

57. Regina E. Herzlinger et al., "Consumer-Driven Health Care: Medtronic's Health Insurance Options," HBS Case No. 302-006, Rev. June 2006 (Boston: Harvard Business School Publishing, 2001).

58. Atlanta Information Services, AHIP, Kaiser Family Foundation, and eHealth-Insurance, taken from Goldman Sachs Group, "Healthcare Investment Strategy," September 20, 2006, p. 13, exhibit 10.

59. Linda J. Blumberg and Len M. Nichols, "The Health Status of Workers Who Decline Employer-Sponsored Insurance," *Health Affairs,* vol. 20, no. 6 (November–December 2001), p. 185.

60. Kenneth Linde, CEO, Destiny Health, personal communication to Regina E. Herzlinger.

61. Ibid.

62. Herzlinger et al., "Consumer-Driven Health Care: Medtronic's Health Insurance Options."

63. Jon B. Christianson and Roger Feldman, "Evolution in the Buyers Health Care Action Group Purchasing Initiative," *Health Affairs*, vol. 21, no. 1 (January–February 2002), pp. 76–88.
64. Herzlinger et al., "Consumer-Driven Health Care: Medtronic's Health Insurance Options."
65. Alan Lyles et al., "Cost and Quality Trends in Direct Contracting Arrangements," *Health Affairs*, vol. 21, no. 1 (January–February 2002), pp. 89–102.
66. Herzlinger et al., "Consumer-Driven Health Care: Medtronic's Health Insurance Options."
67. Ann Robinow, former executive, Buyers Health Care Action Group (BHCAG), personal correspondence to Regina E. Herzlinger, 2002.
68. Steven Wetzell, personal communication with the author, February 2007.
69. Cummings, "Small Investors Now a Big Bloc."
70. "Fund Expenses: They're Going Down, Down, Down," *New York Times*.
71. Morningstar Mutual Funds 5000 (Chicago: Morningstar, 2000), p. 5.

Chapter 9

1. Endnote intentionally deleted.
2. George W. Wilson and Joseph M. Jadlow, "Competition, Profit Incentives, and Technical Efficiency in the Provision of Nuclear Medicine Services," *Bell Journal of Economics*, vol. 13, no. 2 (Autumn 1982), pp. 472–482; Regina E. Herzlinger and William S. Krasker, "Who Profits from Nonprofits?" *Harvard Business Review*, vol. 65, no. 2 (1987), pp. 93–106; David M. Cutler and Jill R. Horwitz, "Converting Hospitals from Not-for-Profit to For-Profit Status: Why and What Effects?" in *The Changing Hospital Industry: Comparing Not-for-Profit and For-Profit Institutions*, ed. David M. Cutler (Chicago: University of Chicago Press, 2000). Note, however, that at least one study has found that nonprofit hospitals are more efficient than for-profit hospitals: Stephen Zuckerman, Jack Hadley, and Lisa Iezzoni, "Measuring Hospital Efficiency with Frontier Cost Functions," *Journal of Health Economics*, vol. 13, no. 3 (October 1994), pp. 255–280.
3. Kevin J. Haley and Daniel M. T. Fessler, "Nobody's Watching? Subtle Cues Affect Generosity in an Anonymous Economic Game," *Evolution and Human Behavior*, vol. 26, no. 3 (2005), pp. 245–256; Melissa Bateson et al., "Cues of Being Watched Enhance Cooperation in a Real-World Setting," *Biology Letters*, vol. 2, no. 3 (September 22, 2006), pp. 412–414; and Ernst Fehr, "Human Behaviour: Don't Lose Your Reputation," *Nature*, vol. 432, no. 7016 (November 25, 2004), pp. 449–450.
4. Bettina Rockenbach and Manfred Milinski, "The Efficient Interaction of Indirect Reciprocity and Costly Punishment," *Nature*, vol. 444, no. 7120 (December 7, 2006), pp. 718–723.
5. Peter Applebome et al., "A Delicate Balance Is Undone in a Flash, and a Battered City Waits," *New York Times*, September 4, 2005, p. 25; and Evan Thomas et al., "The Lost City," *Newsweek*, September 12, 2005, p. 42.
6. K. McCauley, "Katrina Relief Lifts Wal-Mart's Image," *O'Dwyer's PR Services Report* (New York: odwyerpr.com), October 2005, p. 1.
7. Applebome et al., "A Delicate Balance Is Undone in a Flash"; and Thomas et al., "The Lost City."
8. Nicholas Confessore, "Woman Claiming to Be a Victim of Katrina Is Charged with Fraud," *New York Times*, March 23, 2006, p. B1.

9. Sandy Davis, "Charity Revamps Disaster Operation—Red Cross Takes Criticism 'to Heart,'" *Baton Rouge Advocate*, January 7, 2007.

10. Ben Worthen, "How Wal-Mart Beat Feds to New Orleans," *CIO Magazine*, November 1, 2005; and Edwin J. Feulner, "Wal-Mart's Shelf-Correcting System Is Model for Government," *Chicago Sun-Times*, February 22, 2006, p. 41.

11. Anup Malani and Eric A. Posner, "The Case for For-Profit Charities," John M. Olin Program in Law and Economics Working Paper No. 304 (2d series), The Law School, The University of Chicago, September 2006.

12. Joseph P. Newhouse, "Toward a Theory of Nonprofit Institutions: An Economic Model of a Hospital," *American Economic Review*, vol. 60, no. 1 (1970), p. 64; and Darius Lakdawalla and Tomas Philipson, "Nonprofit Production and Competition" (Cambridge, Mass.: National Bureau of Economic Research, Working Paper No. 6377, January 1998).

13. Tomas Philipson, "Asymmetric Information and the Not-for-Profit Sector: Does Its Output Sell at a Premium?" in David M. Cutler, ed., *The Changing Hospital Industry*, pp. 325–345; Anup Malani and Guy David, "Forget Quality: Do Non-profits Even Signal Their Status?" University of Virginia John M. Olin Program in Law and Economics Working Paper, 21, October 2005; and Shin-Yi Chou, "Asymmetric Information, Ownership and Quality of Care: An Empirical Analysis of Nursing Homes," *Journal of Health Economics*, vol. 21, no. 2 (March 2002), p. 293.

14. "Definity Health Acquired by UnitedHealth Group for $300m," *Health & Medicine Week*, December 27, 2004, p. 919.

15. eHealthInsurance Services, Inc. (Mountain View, Calif.: www.ehealthinsurance.com, May 2, 2006).

16. "Health Savings Accounts, January 2005–December 2005," eHealthInsurance.com, 2006, p. 5.

17. "Fast Company Magazine's 10th Anniversary Issue Puts MinuteClinic in the 'Fast 50,'" *PR Newswire*, February 28, 2006.

18. Ibid.

19. Jonathan Birchall, "CVS Buys Walk-in Medical Clinic Network," *Financial Times*, July 14, 2006, p. 24.

20. U.S. Census Bureau, *Statistical Abstract of the United States, 2005* (Washington, D.C.: Government Printing Office, 2005), p. 440, Table 661.

21. Dr. Garrison Bliss, personal communication to Regina E. Herzlinger, May 2006.

22. Tarun Khanna et al., "Narayana Hrudayalaya Heart Hospital: Cardiac Care for the Poor," HBS Case No. 505-078 (Boston: Harvard Business School Publishing, June 22, 2005).

23. V. Kasturi Rangan, "The Aravind Eye Hospital, Madurai, India: In Service for Sight," HBS Case No. 593-098 (Boston: Harvard Business School Publishing, April 1, 1993), p. 6.

24. Centers for Medicare and Medicaid Services (CMS), "Study of Physician-Owned Specialty Hospitals," U.S. Department of Health and Human Services, 2005; and Peter Cram et al., "Cardiac Revascularization in Specialty and General Hospitals," *New England Journal of Medicine*, vol. 352, no. 14 (April 7, 2005), pp. 1454–1462.

25. John E. Schneider et al., "The Effects of Specialty Hospitals on General Hospital Financial Performance, 1997–2004," Working Paper, University of Iowa, 2005.

26. McKinsey & Company, "Healthcare in India: The Road Ahead." (New Delhi: Confederation of Indian Industry and McKinsey & Company, 2002); and Dr. P. Virk, interviews with senior management of Fortis Healthcare, India, spring 2006.

27. Ministry of Trade and Industry, Economic Review Committee, Singapore, "Developing Singapore as the Compelling Hub for Healthcare Services in Asia," 2003, pp. 4–5. Available at http://app.mti.gov.sg/data/pages/507/doc/ERC_SVS_HEA_Annex1.pdf.

28. Bumrungrad International Fact Sheet, Bumrungrad Hospital Web site. Available at http://www.bumrungrad.com/htm/eng/main.asp?Filename=about/fact.htm. Accessed May 20, 2006.

29. "Foreigners Flocking to S'pore Hospitals," *Straits Times*, Singapore, March 29, 2006; and Dr. P. Virk, interview with Ms. J. L. S. Ying, assistant director, *Singapore Medicine*, March 8, 2006.

30. http://www.dh.gov.uk/PublicationsAndStatistics/PressReleases/PressReleases Notices/fs/en?CONTENT_ID=4118350&chk=Junr45 and http://www.performance.doh.gov.uk/waitingtimes/index.htm. See also "Outsourcing Your Heart," *Time*, May 29, 2006, and Alexander Shimo, "Sun, Sea, and Sand," *Macleen's*, May 21, 2006, p. 42.

31. J. Bacon-Shone et al., "Export Potential of Hong Kong's Medical Services with Special Reference to the Chinese Mainland," Social Sciences Research Centre, University of Hong Kong, 2005.

32. Dr. Pushwaz Virk, interview with Mr. H. Singh, chairman, Fortis Healthcare, India, June 16, 2006.

33. K. Sen, manager, Health, Bain & Company, India, correspondence with Regina E. Herzlinger, April 2006.

34. Clifford Krauss, "Canada's Private Clinics Surge as Public System Falters," *New York Times*, February 28, 2006.

35. Ibid.

36. Sujit Choudhry et al., "Specialty Versus Community Hospitals: What Role for the Law?" *Health Affairs*, Web Exclusive W5 (August 9, 2005), pp. 361–372; and Allan Fine, "The Specter of Specialty Hospitals, Part I," *Hospitals & Health Networks*, June 22, 2004.

37. Regina E. Herzlinger, "Specialization and Its Discontents," *Circulation*, vol. 109, no. 20 (2004), pp. 2376–2378; and "Prix-Fixe Rip-Off," *Wall Street Journal*, June 13, 2003.

38. Office of the Inspector General (OIG), Department of Health and Human Services, *Payment for Procedures in Outpatient Departments and Ambulatory Surgical Centers* (Washington, D.C.: OIG Report OEI-05-00-00340, January 2003).

39. Jennifer O'Sullivan, *Health Care: Physician Self-Referrals, Stark I and II* (Washington, D.C.: Congressional Research Service, December 6, 1996).

40. Katherine M. Harris et al., "Buyers Health Care Action Group: Consumer Perceptions of Quality Differences," in Regina E. Herzlinger, ed., *Consumer-Driven Health Care: Implications for Providers, Payers, and Policymakers* (San Francisco: Jossey-Bass, 2004), Chap. 42.

41. Ibid.

42. "UnitedHealth Group's Consumer-Directed Health Plan Reduces Costs and Actively Engages Enrollees in Health Care Decisions," *Business Wire*, June 18, 2004.

43. Regina E. Herzlinger and Ramin Parsa-Parsi, "Consumer-Driven Health Care: Lessons from Switzerland," *Journal of the American Medical Association*, vol. 292, no. 10 (September 8, 2004), pp. 1213–1220.
44. Regina E. Herzlinger, "MedCath Corporation (C)," HBS Case No. 305-097, rev. August 2006 (Boston: Harvard Business School Publishing, 2005).
45. Dr. Steven R. Flier, correspondence with Regina E. Herzlinger, May 2006.
46. Regina E. Herzlinger and Stacy Schwartz, "Hospital for Special Surgery (A)," HBS Case No. 305-076 (Boston: Harvard Business School Publishing, 2005).
47. Dr. Robert E. Hertzka, personal correspondence to Regina E. Herzlinger, June 15, 2006.

Chapter 10

1. Auto Affordability Index, http://www.Comerica.com, accessed January 17, 2006.
2. U.S. Census Bureau, *Statistical Abstract of the United States, 2006* (Washington, D.C.: Government Printing Office, 2006), p. 637, Table 962.
3. Roger K. Powers, *Ward's Automotive Yearbook* Q1, 2006 (Detroit, Mich.: Ward's Reports, 2005).
4. Kathleen Kerwin, "At Ford, the More Brands, the Merrier," *BusinessWeek*, no. 3675 (April 3, 2000), p. 58.
5. Christine Tierney, "Asian Auto Brands' Reliability Uneven: Chevy Monte Carlo, Mercury Mariner SUV Rank Among Most Dependable in *Consumer Reports* Survey," *Detroit News*, October 27, 2005, p. 1C; and Sharon Silke Carty, "Japanese Brands Show 'Nicks,'" *USA Today*, October 27, 2005, p. 5B.
6. "Twenty Years of *Consumer Reports* Surveys Show Astounding Gains," *Consumer Reports*, April 2000, p. 12.
7. Kevin P. Coyne and Jonathan W. Witter, "What Makes Your Stock Price Go Up and Down," *McKinsey Quarterly*, no. 2 (2002), pp. 29–39.
8. Auto Affordability Index, http://www.Comerica.com, May 10, 2006.
9. J.D. Power and Associates, "Initial Quality Study," 2005. http://consumer center.jdpower.com/cc /rd/cc/global/content/ratingsguide.asp, accessed January 27, 2006.
10. Ibid.
11. Ann L. Robinow, "The Buyers Health Care Action Group: Creating Incentives to Seek the Sick," in *Consumer-Driven Health Care: Providers, Payers, and Policymakers*, ed. Regina E. Herzlinger (San Francisco: Jossey-Bass, 2004), pp. 309–316.
12. Mark R. Chassin et al., "The Urgent Need to Improve Health Care Quality," *Journal of the American Medical Association*, vol. 280, no. 11 (September 16, 1998), p. 1003; Dana B. Mukamel and Alvin I. Mushlin, "Quality of Care Information Makes a Difference," *Medical Care*, vol. 36, no. 7 (July 1998), pp. 945–954; Judith H. Hibbard et al., "Hospital Performance Reports: Impact on Quality, Market Share, and Reputation," *Health Affairs*, vol. 24, no. 4 (July–August 2005), pp. 1150–1160; and Judith K. Barr et al., "Public Reporting of Hospital Patient Satisfaction: The Rhode Island Experience," *Health Care Financing Review*, vol. 23, no. 4 (summer 2002), pp. 51–70.
13. N. C. Churchill and V. Govindarajan, "Effects of Audits on the Behavior of Medical Professionals under the Bennett Amendment," *Auditing*, vol. 1 (winter 1982), pp. 69–90; and S. E. Kaplan, K. Menon, and D. D. Williams, "The Effect

of Audit Structure on the Audit Market," *Journal of Accounting and Public Policy*, vol. 9, no. 3 (fall 1990), pp. 197–201.

14. Patrick S. Romano et al., "Grading the Graders: How Hospitals in New York and California Perceive and Interpret Their Report Cards" *Medical Care*, vol. 37, no. 3 (March 1999), pp. 295–305; J. M. Bentley and D. B. Nash, "How Pennsylvania Hospitals Have Responded to Publicly Released Report on CABG," *Joint Commission Journal on Quality Improvement*, vol. 24, no. 1 (January 1998), pp. 40–49; California Institute for Health Systems Performance and the California Health Care Foundation: *Results from the Patients' Evaluation of Performance (PEO-C) Survey: What Patients Think of California Hospitals*, 2001; D. R. Longo et al., "Consumer Reports in Health Care: Do They Make a Difference in Patient Care?" *Journal of the American Medical Association*, vol. 278, no. 19 (November 19, 1997), pp. 1579–1584; Julia A. Rainwater et al., "The California Hospital Project: How Useful Is California's Report Card for Quality Improvement?" *Joint Commission Journal on Quality Improvement*, vol. 24, no. 1 (January 1998), pp. 31–39; Gary E. Rosenthal et al., "Using Hospital Performance Data in Quality Improvement: The Cleveland Health Quality Choice Experience," *Joint Commission Journal on Quality Improvement*, vol. 24, no. 7 (1998), pp. 347–359; David P. Smith et al., "Balancing Accountability and Improvement: A Case Study from Massachusetts," *Joint Commission Journal on Quality Improvement*, vol. 26, no. 5 (May 2000), pp. 299–312; "Operation That Rated Hospitals Was a Success, but the Patient Died," *Wall Street Journal*, August 23, 1999, p. A1; Catherine E. Milch et al, "Voluntary Electronic Reporting of Medical Errors and Adverse Events. An Analysis of 92,547 Reports from 26 Acute Care Hospitals," *Journal of General Internal Medicine*, vol. 21, no. 2 (February 2006), and Claire Snyder and Gerard Anderson, "Do Quality Improvement Organizations Improve the Quality of Hospital Care for Medicare Beneficiaries?" *Journal of the American Medical Association*, vol. 293, no. 23 (June 15, 2005), pp. 2900–2907.

15. Judith H. Hibbard et al., "Hospital Performance Reports: Impact on Quality, Market Share, and Reputation," *Health Affairs*, vol. 24, no. 4 (November/December 2005), pp. 1150–1160.

16. E. C. Becher and M. R. Chassin, "Improving the Quality of Health Care: Who Will Lead?" *Health Affairs*, vol. 20, no. 5 (September–October 2001), pp. 164–179; and Jeanne M. Lambrew, "'Choice' in Health Care: What Do People Really Want," Issue Brief (New York: Commonwealth Fund, September 2005). Judith H. Hibbard et al., *Decision Making in Consumer-Directed Health Plans*, Research Report 2003-05, May 2003, AARP Public Policy Institute. http:// www.aarp.org/ research/ health/privinsurance/aresearch-import-570-2003-05 .html, accessed January 30, 2006. Of course, excessive choice may not be helpful. See, for example, Barry Schwartz, *The Paradox of Choice: Why More Is Less* [New York: Ecco (HarperCollins), 2004]. But markets typically solve this problem: suppliers narrow down choices to those that generate the best consumer response.

17. U.S. Census Bureau, *Statistical Abstract of the United States, 2006* (Washington, D.C.: Government Printing Office, 2006), p. 147.

18. U.S. Census Bureau, *Statistical Abstract of the United States, 2001* (Washington, D.C.: Government Printing Office, 2002), Table 215, p. 139.

19. Judith H. Hibbard et al, "Can Patients Be Part of the Solution? Views on Their Role in Preventing Medical Errors," *Medical Care Research and Review*, vol. 62, no. 5 (October 2005), pp. 601–616.

20. Rick Hampson, "An Uprising in the Pews," *USA TODAY*, April 16, 2001, p. 1.
21. Forrester Research, "The Millionaire Online" (Cambridge, Mass.: Forrester Research, May 2000), p. 11.
22. Pew Charitable Trusts, Pew Internet and American Life Project, *Health Information Online*, May 17, 2005, p. ii.
23. Susannah Fox and Lee Rainie, *Vital Decisions: When They or Their Loved Ones Are Sick, How Internet Users Decide What Information to Trust*, www.perInternet.org/reports/pdfs, (May 22, 2002).
24. PricewaterhouseCoopers, *HealthCast 2010* (New York: PricewaterhouseCoopers, November 2000), p. 22; and Scott Reents, *Impact of the Internet on the Doctor-Patient Relationship: The Rise of the Internet Health Consumer* (New York: Cyber Dialogue, 1999), p. 4, http://www.cyberdialogue.com/pdfs/wp/wp-cch-1999-doctors.pdf.
25. Stephanie Armour, "Just Another Day at the Office: Heroes Save Co-Workers' Lives," *USA TODAY*, April 16, 2001, pp. 8 1–2b.
26. Reents, *Impact of the Internet on the Doctor-Patient Relationship*.
27. Ibid., p. 2.
28. Thomas E. Miller and Scott Reents, *The Health Care Industry in Transition: The Online Mandate to Change* (New York: Cyber Dialogue, 1998), www.cyberdialogue.com.
29. Shoshanna Sofaer et al., "What Do Consumers Want to Know about the Quality of Care in Hospitals?" *Health Services Research*, vol. 40, no. 6 (Part 2) (December 2005), pp. 2018–2036.
30. Simon Avery, "Net Not Just for Wealthy, Statscan Says; Survey Finds E-mail Most Popular Activity, Medical Information Top Search Target," *Globe and Mail* (Canada), July 9, 2004, p. A10.
31. George J. Stigler, "The Economics of Information," in *The Essence of Stigler*, Kurt R. Leube and Thomas Gale Moore, eds. (Stanford: Stanford University, Hoover Institution Press, 1986), pp. 46–66.
32. George J. Stigler, "Public Regulation of the Securities Market," *Journal of Business*, vol. 37 April 1964, reprinted in Gary John. Previts ed., *The Development of SEC Accounting* (Reading, Mass.: Addison-Wesley, 1981).
33. For similar research, see G. Benston, "Required Disclosure and the Stock Market: An Evaluation of the Securities and Exchange Act of 1934," *American Economic Review*, Mat. 63 (1973), pp. 132–155. For critiques, see, for example, Nicholas J. Gonedes, "The Capital Market, the Market for Information, and External Accounting," *Journal of Finance*, vol. 31, no. 2 (May 1976), pp. 611–630; and Edward B. Deakin, "Accounting Reports, Policy Interventions, and the Behavior of Securities Returns," *Accounting Review*, vol. 51, no. 3 (1976), pp. 590–603.
34. See, for example, Joseph E. Stiglitz et al., "The Role of the State in Financial Markets," *World Bank Research Observer* (1993), pp. 19–61; and Jill Dutt, "Unlikely Adversaries: Top Regulators in Dispute over Plan to Change Accounting Rule on Derivatives," *Washington Post*, August 24, 1997, p. H1.
35. Eventually, of course, all users could share the same information, but some would gain temporal advantage because they learned special information earlier.
36. Regina McEnery and Diane Solov, "Project's Collapse Shuts off Information on Hospital Care Quality," *Plain Dealer*, August 23, 1999, p. A1.
37. C. A. Sirio and D. Harper, "Designing the Optimal Health Assessment System: The Cleveland Quality Choice Example," *American Journal of Medical Quality Care*, vol. 11, no. 1 (spring 1996), pp. S66–S69.

38. "Operation That Rated Hospitals Was a Success, but the Patient Died," *Wall Street Journal*, August 23, 1999, p. A1.
39. Ibid.
40. D. Burda, "Dysfunctional Relationship; Despite Abuse, Hospitals Keep Coming Back for More from the Joint Commission," *Modern Healthcare*, vol. 35, no. 48 (November 28, 2005), p. 20; "Another Provider Files Antitrust Suit," *Modern Healthcare*, December 10, 2001, p. 34; and John R. Griffith et al., "Structural versus Outcomes Measures in Hospitals: A Comparison of Joint Commission and Medicare Outcomes Scores in Hospitals," *Quality Management in Health Care*, vol. 10, no. 2 (winter 2002), pp. 29–38.
41. Griffith et al., "Structural versus Outcomes Measures in Hospitals."
42. Snyder and Anderson, "Do Quality Improvement Organizations Improve the Quality of Hospital Care for Medicare Beneficiaries?"
43. Milch et al., "Voluntary Electronic Reporting of Medical Errors and Adverse Events.
44. Joel Seligman, *The Transformation of Wall Street: A History of the Securities and Exchange Commission and Modern Corporate Finance* (Boston: Houghton Mifflin, 1982), pp. 43–48.
45. Michael Chatfield, *A History of Accounting Thought* (Huntington, N.Y.: Krieger Publishing, 1977), p. 32.
46. John Carey, *The Rise of the Accounting Profession* (New York: American Institute of Certified Public Accountants, 1970), pp. 1–16.
47. Seligman, *The Transformation of Wall Street*, p. 41.
48. K. Fred Skousen, *An Introduction to the SEC* (Cincinnati: South-Western, 1991).
49. Seligman, *The Transformation of Wall Street*, pp. 54–55.
50. Mark Maremont and Deborah Solomon, "Missed Chances: Behind SEC's Failings: Caution, Tight Budget, '90s Exuberance—Its Reactive Culture Made Agency Slow off the Mark While Spitzer Raced Ahead," *Wall Street Journal*, December 24, 2003, p. A1; Paul Adams, "SEC Fund Reform: Is It Stalling? Weakening: Many Critics Say the SEC's Effort to Clean Up the Mutual Fund Industry Is Losing Steam," *Baltimore Sun*, May 11, 2004, p. 1C; Carrie Johnson, "Accountability Rules Defended: Enforcement Chief Recalls Large-Scale Frauds," *Washington Post*, March 19, 2005, p. E1; and Stephen Labaton, "S.E.C.'s Oversight of Mutual Funds Is Said to Be Lax," *New York Times*, November 16, 2003, p. 1.
51. See, for example, Seligman, *Transformation of Wall Street*, pp. 561–568.
52. David Weil et al., "The Effectiveness of Regulatory Disclosure Policies," p. 169, *Journal of Policy Analysis and Management*, vol. 25, no. 1 (2006), pp. 155–181.
53. "Moving the Market: Japan May Beef Up Market Oversight," *Wall Street Journal*, January 25, 2006, p. C3.
54. Bertram Schwarzschild, "The Tau Neutrino Has Finally Been Seen," *Physics Today*, vol. 53, no. 10 (October 2000), pp. 17–19.
55. L. Luca Cavalli-Sforza, "The Human Genome Diversity Project: Past, Present and Future," *Nature Reviews Genetics*, vol. 6, no. 4 (April 2005), pp. 333–340.
56. Kenneth L. Fisher, "The Integrity Premium," *Forbes*, vol. 176, no. 13 (December 26, 2005), p. 134.
57. Jonathan D. Glater, "Adelphia Auditor Agrees to Pay $50 Million into Investors' Fund," *New York Times*, April 27, 2005, p. 5.

58. Loren Steffy, "Sage of Ethical Accounting Foretold Andersen Demise," *Houston Chronicle*, January 14, 2005, Business, p. 1.
59. Frederick D. Greene et al., "Holding Accountants Accountable: The Liability of Accountants to Third Parties," *Employee Responsibilities and Rights Journal*, vol. 15, no. 1 (March 2003), pp. 23–29; Claire A. King, "Liability Exposures and Ethical Responsibilities for CPAs in Industry," *Ohio CPA Journal*, vol. 60, no. 4 (October 2001), pp. 15–20; and John F. Raspante and Ric Rosario, "Understanding and Minimizing CPA Liability," *CPA Journal*, vol. 71, no. 5 (May 2001), pp. 18–23.
60. Craig Schneider, "Off the Books," *CFO Magazine*, vol. 21, no. 14 (October 2005), p. 112.
61. Richard E. Baker, "Accounting Rule-Making—Still at the Crossroads," *Business Horizons*, vol. 19, no. 5 (October 1976), p. 66.
62. "SEC Chief to Impose 'Stringent' Rules on Accountants," *Buffalo News*, May 24, 2002, p. A9.
63. Roberta S. Karmel, "Realizing the Dream of William O. Douglas: The Securities and Exchange Commission Takes Charge of Corporate Governance," *Delaware Journal of Corporate Law*, vol. 30, no. 1 (2005), pp. 79–92; Anthony J. Costantini, "What's Ahead in Enforcement," *Journal of Accountancy*, vol. 198, no. 3 (September 2004), pp. 72–77; and Robert H. Colson, "Evolving Regulations and Oversight in the Public Interest: An Interview with SEC Chief Accountant Donald T. Nicolaisen," *CPA Journal*, vol. 74, no. 4 (April 2004), pp. 18–24.
64. Mike McNamee with Kerry Capell, "FASB: Rewriting the Book on Bookkeeping," *BusinessWeek*, May 20, 2002, p. 123.
65. S. P. Kothari and J. E. Short, "The Importance of Corporate Disclosure: How Market Transparency Affects the Firm's Financial Health" (Cambridge: MIT Center for Digital Business, Research Brief 2, no. 2, August 2003).
66. U.S. Securities and Exchange Commission, "About the Division of Enforcement," www.sec.gov/divisions/enforce/about.htm, accessed January 24, 2006.
67. U.S. Securities and Exchange Commission, *In Brief. Fiscal 2006. Congressional Budget Request*, February 2005, pp. 31–32, www.sec.gov/about/secfy06budgetreq.pdf, accessed January 24, 2006.
68. Lynn Etheredge, "Promarket Regulation: An SEC-FASB Model," *Health Affairs*, vol. 16, no. 6 (November–December 1997), pp. 22–25.
69. "Some FDA Scientists Claim Interference," *Reuters*, July 21, 2006.
70. T. Miller and S. Leatherman, "The National Quality Forum: A 'Me-Too' or a Breakthrough in Quality Measurement and Reporting?" *Health Affairs*, vol. 18, no. 6 (November/December 1999), pp. 233–237; John Morrissey, "Let the Safety Begin. NQF (National Quality Forum) Endorses Practices, Opens Door for Quality Standards," *Modern Healthcare*, vol. 33, no. 5 (February 3, 2003), pp. 14–15; Kenneth W. Kizer, "The National Quality Forum Enters the Game," *International Journal for Quality in Health Care*, vol. 12, no. 2 (April 2000), pp. 85–87; Kenneth W. Kizer, "The National Quality Forum Seeks to Improve Health Care," *Academic Medicine*, vol. 75, no. 4 (April 2000), pp. 320–321; and Norman Lang and Kenneth W. Kizer, "National Quality Forum, an Experiment in Democracy," *Journal of Professional Nursing*, vol. 19, no. 5 (September/October 2003), pp. 247–248.
71. Richard E. Thompson, "Is Pay for Performance Ethical?" *Physician Executive*, vol. 31, no. 6 (November–December 2005), pp. 60–62; Robert M. Pickoff, "Pay

for Performance—For Whom the Bell Tolls," *Physician Executive*, vol. 31, no. 6 (November–December 2005), pp. 12–14; Robert S. Mirsky, "Physician Buy-In Is Essential for Pay for Performance," *Physician Executive*, vol. 31, no. 6 (November–December 2005), pp. 16–19; David Ollier Weber, "The Dark Side of P4P," *Physician Executive*, vol. 31, no. 6 (November–December 2005), pp. 20–25; Allan Korn, "Professionalism Reconsidered: Physician Payment from a Health Plan Perspective," *Health Affairs*, vol. 23, no. 6 (November–December 2005), pp. 48–50; Robert Cunningham, "Professionalism Reconsidered: Physician Payment in a Small-Practice Environment," *Health Affairs*, vol. 23 no. 6 (November–December 2004), pp. 36–47; and Richard E. Thompson, "The Ethical Aspects of Gain Sharing with Physicians," *Physician Executive*, vol. 30, no. 3 (May–June 2004), pp. 20–22.

72. Patrick J. O'Connor, "Commentary—Improving Diabetes Care by Combating Clinical Inertia," *Health Services Research*, vol. 40, no. 6, Part 1 (December 2005), p. 1854.

73. Institute of Medicine (IOM), *Performance Measurement, Accelerating Improvement* (Washington, D.C.: National Academies Press, 2005).

74. Ceci Connolly, "HHS Works to Fix Drug Plan Woes; Widespread Difficulties with New Medicare Benefit Reported," *Washington Post*, January 18, 2006, p. A3; and Matthew DoBias, "Medicare Muddle; Rx Drug Benefit Confuses Both Enrollees, Providers," *Modern Healthcare*, January 2, 2006, p. 8.

75. Leslie G. Aronovitz, *Medicare: Communications to Beneficiaries on the Prescription Drug Benefit Could Be Improved: Report to Congressional Requesters*, GAO-06-654, Washington, D.C.: United States Government Accountability Office, May 2006, available at http://www.gao.gov, accessed March 5, 2007.

76. Lee Rainie, *The State of Blogging*, Pew Charitable Trusts, Pew Internet and American Life Project, January 2005, p. 3.

77. U.S. Securities and Exchange Commission (SEC), "Filings and Forms," Electronic Data Gathering, Analysis, and Retrieval System (EDGAR), www.sec.gov/edgar.shtml.

78. See, for example, safety data for cars at www.nhtsa.gov and for planes at www.faa.gov.

79. Feticity Barringer and Geraldine Fabrikant, "Coming of Age at Bloomberg L.P.," *New York Times*, March 21, 1999, p. 1.

80. Mark J. Penn, "Health Care Is Back," *Blueprint*, April 1, 2000, p. 71.

81. Bradford J. Holmes, "HMOs' eHealth Plan Threat," Techstrategy Report (Cambridge: Forrester Research, January 2001), Fig. 2.

82. S. Sofaer et al., "What Do Consumers Want to Know about the Quality of Care in Hospitals?", and Anonymous, "When Consumers Have a Choice of Hospital, Quality Record Counts, According to Survey," *Health Care Strategic Management*, vol. 22, no. 2 (February 2004), pp. 6–7.

83. Milt Freudenheim, "WebMD Wants to Go Beyond Information," *MarketPlace*, (February 23, 2006), http://www.nytimes.com/2006/02/23/business/ 23place .html?ex=1298350800&en=6935dfe, accessed February 27, 2006.

84. Michael Romano, "Performance Anxiety: Is It Too Late For Physicians to Set Their Own Rules on Pay for Performance?" *Modern Healthcare*, (May 30, 2005), p. 6.

85. Timothy P. Hofer et al., "The Unreliability of Individual Physician 'Report Cards' for Assessing the Costs and Quality of Care of a Chronic Disease," *Journal of the American Medical Association*, vol. 281, no. 22 (June 9, 1999), pp. 2098–2105.

86. Based on costs of $10,000 per diabetic and an incidence of diabetes of 7.5 percent. This leads to costs per 1,000 enrollees of $750,000 for diabetics. A 1 percent reduction, $7,500, will pay for collecting performance data from 25 doctors at a monthly cost of $2.50 per member, per month. But because the number of doctors covering 1,000 enrollees is typically 0.5, the payback is fiftyfold.
87. Hofer et al., "The Unreliability of Individual Physician 'Report Cards.'"
88. Justin B. Dimick et al., "Surgical Mortality as an Indicator of Hospital Quality: The Problem with Small Sample Size," *Journal of the American Medical Association*, vol. 292, no. 7 (August 18, 2004), pp. 847–851.
89. Eve A. Kerr et al., "Profiling the Quality of Care in Twelve Communities: Results from the CQI Study," *Health Affairs*, vol. 23, no. 3 (May–June 2004), pp. 247–256; and Michael Romano, "Performance Anxiety."
90. Natalie Frow et al., "Encouraging Strategic Behavior While Maintaining Management Control: Multi-Functional Project Teams, Budgets, and the Negotiation of Shared Accountabilities in Contemporary Enterprises," *Management Accounting Research*, vol. 16, no. 3 (September 2005), p. 269; and Matthew W. Ford and Bertie M Greer, "The Relationship between Management Control System Usage and Planned Change Achievement: An Exploratory Study," *Journal of Change Management*, vol. 5, no. 1 (March 2005), p. 29.
91. Michael A. Cucciare and William O'Donohue, "Predicting Future Healthcare Costs: How Well Does Risk-Adjustment Work?" *Journal of Health Organization and Management*, vol. 20, no. 2 (2006), p. 150; David Blumenthal et al., "The Who, What, and Why of Risk Adjustment: A Technology on the Cusp of Adoption," *Journal of Health Politics, Policy and Law*, vol. 30, no. 3 (June 2005), p. 453; and Carolyn Clancy, "Quality Improvement: Getting to How," *Health Services Research*, vol. 38, no. 2 (April 2003), p. 509.
92. Michael Romano, "System Failure; Most U.S. Hospitals Have Never Filed a Report with the Databank That Records Doctor Suspensions; Critics Say It's Time for a New Method," *Modern Healthcare*, vol. 35, no. 30 (July 25, 2005), pp. 6–8.
93. David C. Aron et al., "Impact of Risk-Adjusting Caesarean Delivery Rates When Reporting Hospital Performance," *Journal of the American Medical Association*, vol. 279, no. 24 (June 24, 1998), pp. 1968–1972.
94. "Mutual-Funds Ratings Stars Are Changing," *Wall Street Journal*, April 23, 2002, p. C1.
95. Zogby Poll, "Americans Favor Transparency in Medicare, Physician Changes," May 2, 2006, www.zogby.com.

Chapter 11

1. Burton M. Leiser, "Thomas Jefferson," in *Great Thinkers of the Western World*, ed. Ian P. McGreal (New York: HarperCollins Publishers, 1992).
2. Gail R. Wilensky, "Developing a Center for Comparative Effectiveness Information," *Health Affairs* Web Exclusive, November 7, 2006, pp. W572–W575.
3. "Short- and Long-Term Strategies to Ensure the Viability of the SHBP and the Small Group Market," Maryland Health Care Commission Report, http://mhcc.maryland.gov/health_insurance/smallgroup_viability_091505.pdf, accessed October 14, 2005.
4. Robbie Dingeman, "Medically Uninsured on Rise in Hawaii," *Honolulu Advertiser*, October 29, 2003.

5. Jordan Rau, "Hawaii Offers a Look at Mandatory Healthcare; The State's Employers Have Long Provided What Proposition 72 Calls for: Compulsory Coverage," *Los Angeles Times*, October 24, 2004.
6. National Conference of State Legislatures, www.ncsl.org/programs/health/fairsharenews.htm.
7. Greg Scandlan, "Mandatory versus Voluntary Insurance," Brief Analysis No. 569, National Center for Policy Analysis, September 6, 2006.

INDEX